Tien-Ping Ging

1984. Jan

Errora:
P. 60
P. 84
P. 126
P. 129
P. 152
P. 154
P. 159. $d'U_c \rightarrow d(U^c$

W. F. Clocksin   C. S. Mellish

Programming in Prolog

Springer-Verlag
Berlin Heidelberg New York 1981

William F. Clocksin

Department of Engineering Science, University of Oxford
Parks Road
Oxford OX1 3PJ / England

Christopher S. Mellish

Department of Artificial Intelligence, University of Edinburgh
Hope Park Square, Meadow Lane
Edinburgh EH8 9NW / Scotland

ISBN 3-540-11046-1 Springer-Verlag Berlin Heidelberg New York
ISBN 0-387-11046-1 Springer-Verlag New York Heidelberg Berlin

Library of Congress Cataloging in Publication Data. Clocksin, W. F.
(William F.), 1955- Programming in Prolog. Bibliography: p. Includes
index. 1. Prolog (Computer program language) I. Mellish, Christopher S.,
1954-. II. Title. QA76.73.P356C57. 001.64'24. 81-14459
ISBN 0-387-11046-1 (New York) AACR2

© Springer-Verlag Berlin Heidelberg 1981
Printed in Germany

Printing and bookbinding: Beltz, Offsetdruck, Hemsbach
2146/3140-54

Preface

The computer programming language Prolog is quickly gaining popularity throughout the world. Since its beginnings around 1970, Prolog has been chosen by many programmers for applications of symbolic computation, including:

- □ relational databases
- □ mathematical logic
- □ abstract problem solving
- □ understanding natural language
- □ architectural design
- □ symbolic equation solving
- □ biochemical structure analysis
- □ many areas of artificial intelligence

Until now, there has been no textbook with the aim of teaching Prolog as a practical programming language. It is perhaps a tribute to Prolog that so many people have been motivated to learn it by referring to the necessarily concise reference manuals, a few published papers, and by the orally transmitted 'folklore' of the modern computing community. However, as Prolog is beginning to be introduced to large numbers of undergraduate and postgraduate students, many of our colleagues have expressed a great need for a tutorial guide to learning Prolog. We hope this little book will go some way towards meeting this need.

Many newcomers to Prolog find that the task of writing a Prolog program is not like specifying an algorithm in the same way as in a conventional programming language. Instead, the Prolog programmer asks more what formal relationships and objects occur in his problem, and what relationships are "true" about the desired solution. So, Prolog can be viewed as a *descriptive* language as well as a *prescriptive* one. The Prolog approach is rather to describe known facts and relationships about a problem, than to prescribe the sequence of steps taken by a computer to solve the problem. When a computer is programmed in Prolog, the actual way the computer carries out the computation is specified partly by the logical declarative semantics of Prolog, partly by what new facts Prolog can 'infer' from the given ones, and only partly by explicit control information supplied by the programmer.

Prolog is a *practical* and *efficient* implementation of many aspects of 'intelligent' program execution, such as non-determinism, parallelism, and pattern-directed procedure call. Prolog provides a uniform data structure, called the term, out of which all data, as well as Prolog programs, are constructed. A Prolog program consists of a set of clauses, where each clause is either a fact about the given information or a rule about how the solution may relate to or be 'inferred' from the given facts. Thus, Prolog can be seen as a first step towards the ultimate goal of *programming in logic*. In this book we will not be concerned greatly with the wider implications of logic programming or with why Prolog is not the ultimate logic programming language. Instead, we will be concerned with showing how *useful* programs can be written using the Prolog systems that exist today.

This book can serve several purposes. The aim of this book is *not* to teach the art of programming as such. We feel that programming cannot be learned simply by reading a book or by listening to a lecturer. You've got to *do* programming to learn it. We hope that beginners without a mathematical background can learn Prolog from this book, although in this case we would recommend that the beginner is taught by a programmer who knows Prolog, as part of a course that introduces the student to programming as such. It is assumed that the beginner can obtain the use of a computer that has a Prolog system installed, and that he has been instructed in the use of a computer terminal. The experienced programmer should not require extra assistance, but he also should not dismay at our efforts to restrain mathematical affectation. We have used draft versions of this book to teach university graduates who did little mathematics as schoolchildren, and who specialised in philosophy and psychology whilst at university.

In our experience, novice programmers find that Prolog programs seem to be more comprehensible than equivalent programs in conventional languages. However, the same people tend not to appreciate the limitations that conventional languages place on their use of computing resources. On the other hand, the programmer experienced in conventional languages is better prepared to deal with abstract concepts such as variables and control flow. But, in spite of his prior experience, he may find Prolog difficult to adapt to, and he may need a lot of convincing before he considers Prolog a useful programming tool. Of course, we know of many highly experienced programmers who have taken up Prolog with much enthusiasm. However, the aim of this book is not to convert, but to teach.

Like most other programming languages, Prolog exists in a number of different implementations, each with its own semantic and syntactic peculiarities. In this book we have adopted a "core Prolog", and all of our examples conform to a standard version that corresponds to the implementations, developed mainly at Edinburgh, for four different computer systems: the DECsystem-10 running TOPS-10, the DEC PDP-11 running Unix, the DEC LSI-11 running RT-11, and the ICL 2980 running EMAS. The implementations for the DEC computers are probably the most widespead. All the examples in this book will run on all four of the implementations. In the appendices, we list some of the existing Prolog implementations, indicating how they diverge from the standard. The reader will appreciate that most of the deviations are of a purely cosmetic nature.

This book was designed to be read sequentially, although it will prove helpful to read Chapter 8 at the time the reader begins to write Prolog programs consisting of more than about ten clauses. Furthermore, it is wise to read the appropriate appendix that describes the particular implementation of Prolog. Appendices tell how to enter clauses, what debugging facilities are available, and other practical matters. It shouldn't hurt to browse through the book, but do take care not to skip over the earlier chapters.

Each chapter is divided into several sections, and we advise the reader to attempt the exercises that are at the end of many sections. The solutions to some of the exercises appear at the end of the book. Chapter 1 is a tutorial introduction that is intended to give the reader a "feel" for what is required to program in Prolog. The fundamental ideas of Prolog are introduced, and the reader is advised to study them carefully. Chapter 2 presents a more complete discussion of points that are introduced in Chapter 1. Chapter 3 deals with data structures and derives some small example programs. Chapter 4 treats the subject of backtracking in more detail, and introduces the "cut" symbol, which is used to control backtracking. Chapter 5 introduces the facilities that are available for input and output. Chapter 6 describes each built-in predicate in the standard "core" of Prolog. Chapter 7 is a potpourri of example programs collected from many sources, together with an explanation of how they are written. Chapter 8 offers some advice on debugging Prolog programs, and provides an alternative model of control flow. Chapter 9 introduces the Grammar Rule syntax, and examines the design decisions for some aspects of analysing natural language by using Grammar Rules. Chapter 10 describes the relation of Prolog to its origins in mathematical theorem proving and logic programming. Chapter 11 specifies a number of projects on which interested readers may wish to practise their programming ability.

We express our gratitude to our teachers who have influenced the way we think about programming: Rod Burstall, Peter Scott Langston, and Robin Popplestone. We thank those friends who have collaborated in the development of Prolog as a practical and useful programming tool, and who encouraged us in the preparation of this book: Alan Bundy, Lawrence Byrd, Robert Kowalski, Fernando Pereira, and David Warren. In particular, Lawrence Byrd supported the development of this book from its inception by suggesting programs, exercises, some of the projects listed in Chapter 11, and many ideas. We also thank our friends who contributed to this book by providing helpful comments and advice on earlier drafts of this book: Jon Cunningham, Richard O'Keefe, Helen Pain, Fernando Pereira, Gordon Plotkin, Robert Rae, Peter Ross, Maxwell Shorter, Aaron Sloman and David Warren. In this regard, W.F.C. especially thanks his postgraduate students of the School of Epistemics, and of the Department of Artificial Intelligence, who were compelled to be the subjects of many experiments in teaching programming. For our examples, we have been free in adapting and developing programs from the general Prolog folklore. We apologise to anyone who feels slighted or plagerised by this.

This book was prepared while the authors were employed at the Department of Artificial Intelligence, University of Edinburgh. We thank Jim Howe, Head of the Department, who provided the necessary opportunities and facilities with which to carry out this project.

W.F.C.
C.S.M.

Edinburgh, Scotland
June, 1981

Table of Contents

How a set of clauses generates a set of solutions. Using "cut" to modify the control sequence of running Prolog programs.

Facilities available for the input and output of characters and structures. Developing a program to read sentences from the user and represent the sentence as a list of words, which can be used with the Grammar Rules of Chapter 9.

Definition of the "core" built-in predicates, with sensible examples of how each one is used. By this point, the reader should be able to read reasonably complex programs, and should therefore be able to absorb the built-in predicates by seeing them in use.

Many example programs are given, covering a wide range of interests. New examples include list processing, set operations, symbolic differentiation and simplification of formulae.

By this point, the reader will be able to write reasonable programs, and so the problem of debugging will be relevant. Flow of control model, hints about common bugs, techniques of debugging.

Applications of existing techniques. Using Grammar Rules. Examining the design decisions for some aspects of analysing natural language with Grammar Rules.

Chapter 1. Tutorial Introduction

Prolog is a computer programming language that is used for solving problems that involve objects and the *relationships* between objects. In this chapter we shall show the essential elements of the language in real programs, but without becoming diverted by details, formal rules, and exceptions. At this point, we are not trying to be complete or precise. We want to bring you quickly to the point where you can write useful programs, so to do that we must concentrate on the basics: facts, questions, variables, conjunctions, and rules. Other features of Prolog, such as lists and recursion, will be treated in later chapters.

We use Prolog when we wish the computer to solve problems that can be expressed in the form of objects and their relationships. For example, when we say "John owns the book", we are declaring that a relationship, ownership, exists between one object "John" and another individual object "the book". Furthermore, the relationship has a specific order: John owns the book, but the book doesn't own John! When we ask the question "Does John own the book?", we are trying to find out about a relationship.

Some relationships don't always mention all the objects that are involved. For example, when we say "The jewel is valuable", we mean that there is a relationship, called "being valuable", which involves a jewel. We did not mention who finds the jewel valuable, or why. It all depends on what you want to say. In Prolog, when you will be programming the computer about relationships like these, the amount of detail you provide also depends on what you want the computer to accomplish.

There is one more point of philosophy to mention, then we will begin programming. We are all familiar with using rules to describe relationships between objects. For example, the rule "Two people are sisters if they are both female and have the same parents" tells us something about what it means to be sisters. It also tells us how to find out if two people are sisters: simply check to see if they are both female and have the same parents. What is important to notice about rules is that they are usually oversimplified, but they are acceptable as *definitions*. After all, one cannot expect a definition to tell us everything about something. For example, most people would agree there is much more to "being sisters" in real life than the above rule implies. However, when we are solving a particular problem, we need to concentrate on just those rules that help to solve the problem. So, we ought to consider an imaginary and simplified definition if it is sufficient for our purposes.

Computer programming in Prolog consists of:

☐ declaring some *facts* about objects and their relationships,

☐ defining *rules* about objects and their relationships, and

☐ asking *questions* about objects and their relationships.

For example, suppose we told Prolog our rule about sisters. We could then ask the question whether Mary and Jane are sisters. Prolog would search through what we told it about Mary and Jane, and come back with the answer "yes" or "no", depending on what we told it earlier. So, we can consider Prolog as a storehouse of facts and rules, and it uses the facts and rules to answer questions. Programming in Prolog consists of supplying all these facts and rules. The Prolog system enables a computer to be used as a storehouse of facts and rules, and it provides ways to make inferences from one fact to another.

Prolog is a conversational language, which means that you and the computer carry out a kind of conversation. Assume that you are seated at a computer terminal and have asked to use Prolog. The computer terminal you use has a *keyboard* and a *display*. You use the keyboard to type characters into the computer, and the computer uses the display (either a screen or paper) to type results back to you. Prolog will wait for you to type in the facts and rules that pertain to the problem you want to solve. Then, if you ask the right kind of questions, Prolog will work out the answers and show them on the display.

We will now introduce each of the fundamentals of Prolog one by one. Don't worry about not having the complete story about each feature of Prolog straight away. There will be complete summaries and more examples worked out in later chapters.

1.1 Facts

We first discuss *facts* about objects. Suppose we want to tell Prolog the fact that "John likes Mary". This fact consists of two objects, called "Mary" and "John", and a relationship, called "likes". In Prolog, we need to write facts in a standard form, like this:

```
likes(john,mary).
```

The following things are important:

- The names of all relationships and objects must begin with a lower-case letter. For example, **likes, john, mary**.

- The relationship is written *first*, and the objects are written separated by commas, and the objects are enclosed by a pair of round brackets.

- The full stop character '.' must come at the end of a fact.

When defining relationships between objects using facts, you should pay attention to what order the objects are written between the round brackets. In fact, the order is arbitrary, but we must decide on some order and be consistent about it. For example, in the above fact, we have put the 'liker' as the first of the two objects in round brackets, and we have put the object that is liked in the second slot. So, the fact **likes(john,mary)** is not the same thing as **likes(mary,john)**. The first fact says that John likes Mary, and the second fact says that Mary likes John, according to our current arbitrary convention. If we want to say that Mary likes John, then we must explicitly say so:

```
likes(mary,john).
```

Look at the following examples of facts, together with *possible* explanations in English:

Low case

```
valuable(gold).          "gold is valuable"
female(jane).            "Jane is female"
owns(john,gold).         "John owns gold"
father(john,mary).       "John is the father of Mary"
```

Each time a name is used, the name refers to a particular individual object. Because of our familiarity with English, it is fairly clear that the names **john** and **jane** refer to individuals. But, in some other facts, we have used the name **gold**, and it is not necessarily obvious what it means. When using names, we must decide on how to *interpret* the name. For example, the name **gold** could refer to an object. In this case we think of the object as some particular lump of gold that we denote by the name **gold**. And when we say in Prolog **valuable(gold)**, we would mean that this particular lump of gold, which we have named **gold**, is valuable. On the other hand, we could interpret the name **gold** to mean "the mineral gold", and when we say **valuable(gold)**, we would mean that the mineral gold is valuable. So, there is more than one way to interpret a name, and it is *you*, the programmer, who decides on the interpretation. There should be no problem as long as you interpret names consistently. By the way, in the above facts we have interpreted **gold** to be "the mineral gold", but another interpretation could have been chosen. The Prolog facts would look the same. It is important to bring out the distinctions between different interpretations early, so that we are quite certain what names mean.

Now for some terminology. The names of the objects that are enclosed within the round brackets in each fact are called the arguments. Note: computer programmers use the word 'argument' in a technical sense which bears none of the common connotations of dispute, debate, discussion, theme, or topic. The name of the relationship, which comes just before the round brackets, is called the predicate. So, **valuable** is a predicate having one argument, and **likes** is a predicate having two arguments.

The names of the objects and relationships are completely arbitrary. Instead of a rule such as **likes(john,mary),** we could just as well represent this as **a(b,c),** and remember that **a** means "likes", **b** means "John", and **c** means "Mary". However, we normally select names that help us to remember what they represent. So, we must decide in advance what our names mean, and what the order of arguments shall be. Thereafter we must remain consistent.

It does not matter to Prolog how many arguments are involved in a relationship. If we want to define a predicate called **play,** where we mention two players and a game they play with each other, we need three arguments. Here are two examples of this:

```
play(john,mary,football).
play(jane,jim,badminton).
```

It also does not matter to Prolog if we declare facts that are not true in the real world. We could write **king(john,france)** to declare that "John is the king of France" (being king is a relationship). In the real world this is obviously false, especially because France abolished the Monarchy sometime around 1792. But Prolog does not know, and does not care. Facts in Prolog simply allow you to express arbitrary relationships between objects.

In Prolog, a collection of facts is called a *database.* We will use the term "database" whenever we have collected together some facts (and later, rules) that are used to solve a particular problem.

1.2   Questions

Once we have some facts, we can ask some questions about them. In Prolog, a question looks just like a fact, except that we put a special symbol before it. The special symbol consists of a question mark and a hyphen. Consider the question:

```
?- owns(mary,book).
```

If we interpret **mary** to mean "Mary" and **book** to mean some particular book, this is like asking "Does Mary own the book?", or "Is it a fact that Mary owns the book?" We are not asking whether she owns all books, or books in general.

When a question is asked of Prolog, it will search through the database you typed in before. It looks for facts that *match* the fact in the question. Two facts *match* if their predicates are the same (spelt the same way), and if their corresponding arguments each are the same. If Prolog finds a fact that matches the question, Prolog will respond yes. If no such fact exists in the database, Prolog will respond no. The response from Prolog is printed on on the display of your computer terminal on the line just below your question. Consider the following database:

```
likes(joe,fish).
likes(joe,mary).
likes(mary,book).
likes(john,book).
```

If we typed in all those facts to the Prolog system, we could ask the following questions, and Prolog would give the answers on the line just after the question:

```
?- likes(joe,money).
no
?- likes(mary,joe).
no
?- likes(mary,book).
yes
?- king(john,france).
no
```

The answers to the first three questions should be clear to you. Prolog also answered "no" to the question of whether John was the king of France. This is because there were no facts about royal relationships in the list of four **likes** relationships above. In Prolog, the answer "no" is used to mean "not as far as I know". It is important to remember that "no" is not the same as "definitely not". For example, suppose a database about some famous Greeks contains only the following three facts:

```
human(socrates).
human(aristotle).
athenian(socrates).
```

We could ask some questions:

```
?- athenian(socrates).
yes

?- athenian(aristotle).
no

?- greek(socrates).
no
```

Although it may be true that Aristotle lived in Athens, we cannot "prove" it simply from the facts shown in the database. Furthermore, although it is shown in the database that Socrates is an Athenian, this does not "prove" he is a Greek unless more information is in the database. So, when Prolog answers "no" to a question, it means "not provable".

In the above database, both John and Mary like the same object. We know they like the same object because the same name, **book**, appears in both facts.

The facts and questions we have discussed so far are not particularly interesting. All we can do is get back the same information we put in. It would be more useful to ask questions like "What objects does Mary like?" This is what *variables* are for.

1.3 Variables

If you want to find out what things that John likes, it is tiresome to have to ask "Does John like books?", "Does John like Mary?", and so forth, with Prolog giving a yes-or-no answer each time. It is more sensible to ask Prolog to tell you something that he likes. We could phrase a question of this form as, "Does John like X?". When we ask a question, we do not know what the object is that X could *stand for*. We would like Prolog to tell us what the possibilities are. In Prolog we can not only name particular objects, but we can also use names like X to stand for objects to be determined by Prolog. Names of this second kind are called *variables*. When Prolog uses a variable, the variable can be either *instantiated* or *uninstantiated*. A variable is instantiated when there is an object that the variable stands for. A variable is uninstantiated when what the variable stands for is not yet known. Prolog can distinguish variables from names of particular objects because *any name beginning with a capital letter is taken to be a variable.*

When Prolog is asked a question containing a variable, Prolog searchs through all its facts to find an object that the variable could stand for. So when we ask "Does John like X?", Prolog searches through all of its facts to find things that John likes.

A variable, such as X, does not name a particular object in itself, but it can be used to stand for objects that we cannot name. For example, we cannot name "something that John likes" as an object, so Prolog adopts a way of saying this. Instead of asking a question like:

```
?- likes(john, "something that john likes").
```

Prolog lets us use variables, like this:

```
?- likes(john,X).
```

Variables can have longer names if we wish. This question is acceptable to Prolog:

```
?- likes(john,Somethingthatjohnlikes).
```

Why? Because a variable can be any name that begins with a capital letter.

Consider the following database of facts, followed by a question:

```
likes(john,flowers).
likes(john,mary).
likes(paul,mary).

?- likes(john,X).
```

The question asks "Is there something that John likes?". When asked the question, Prolog will respond:

```
X=flowers
```

and then wait for further instructions, which we will talk about shortly. How does this work? When Prolog is asked this question, the variable is *uninstantiated.* Prolog searches though the database, looking for a fact that *matches* the question. Now if an uninstantiated variable appears as an argument, Prolog will allow that argument to match *any* other argument in the same position in the fact. What happens here is that Prolog searches for any fact where the predicate is **likes,** and the first argument is **john.** The *second* argument in this case may be anything, because the question was asked with an uninstantiated variable as the second argument. When such a fact is found, then the variable X now stands for the second argument in the fact, whatever it may be. Prolog searches through the database in the order it was typed in (or top-to-bottom on the printed page) so the fact **likes(john,flowers)** is found first. Variable X now stands for the object **flowers.** Or, we say that X is instantiated to flowers. Prolog now *marks the place* in the database where a match is found. The place-marker is used for reasons we discuss shortly.

Once Prolog finds a fact that matches a question, it prints out the objects that the variables now stand for. In this case, the only variable was X, and it matched the object **flowers.** Now Prolog waits for further instructions, as we said above. If you type the computer terminal's RETURN key, meaning you are satisfied with just one answer, then Prolog will stop searching for more. If instead you type the semicolon (followed by RETURN), Prolog will resume its search through the database as before, *starting from where it left the place-marker.* When Prolog begins seaching from a place-marker, instead of from the beginning of the database, we say that Prolog is attempting to *re-satisfy* the question.

Suppose in response to Prolog's first answer (X=flowers) we asked it to carry on (by typing semicolon). This means we want to satisfy the question in another way; we want to find another object that X could stand for. This means that Prolog must 'forget' that X stands for **flowers**, and resume searching with X uninstantiated again. Because we are searching for an alternatve solution, the search is continued from the place-marker. The next matching fact found is **likes(john,mary)**. The variable X is now *instantiated* to **mary**, and Prolog puts a place-marker at the fact *likes(john,mary)*. Prolog will print "X=mary", and wait for further commands. If we relentlessly type another semicolon, Prolog will continue the search. In this example there is nothing more that John likes. So, Prolog will stop its search, and allow us to ask more questions or declare more facts.

What happens if, given the same facts above, we ask the question:

```
?-likes(X,mary).
```

This question asks "Is there an object that likes Mary?" By now you should see that the objects in the example that like Mary are **john** and **paul**. Again, if we wanted to see all of them, we would type ";" after Prolog types out each one of the answers:

```
?- likes(X,mary).      (our question)
X=john;                (first answer.  We type ";" in reply)
X=paul;                (second answer.  Again we type ";")
no                     (no more answers.)
```

1.4   Conjunctions

Suppose we wish to answer questions about more complicated relationships, like:

"Do John and Mary like each other?"

One way to do this would be first to ask if John likes Mary, and if Prolog tell us yes, then we ask if Mary likes John. So, this problem consists of two separate *goals* that we have to satisfy. Because a combination like this is frequently used by Prolog programmers, there is a special notation for it. Suppose we have the following database:

```
likes(mary,food).
likes(mary,wine).
likes(john,wine).
likes(john,mary).
```

We want to ask if John and Mary like each other. To do this, we ask "Does John like Mary *and* does Mary like John?" The "and" expresses that fact that we are interested in the *conjunction* of the two goals -- we want to satisfy them both one after the other. We represent this by putting a comma between the goals:

```
?- likes(john,mary), likes(mary,john).
```

and

The comma is pronounced "and", and it serves to separate any number of different goals that have to be satisfied in order to answer a question. When a sequence of goals (separated by commas) is given to Prolog, Prolog attempts to satisfy each goal in turn by searching for a matching goal in the database. All goals have to be satisfied in order for the sequence to be satisfied. Using the above list of facts, what should Prolog print out? The answer is "no". It is a fact that John likes Mary, so the first goal is true. However, the second goal is not true, since there is nowhere in the list of facts where `likes(mary,john)` occurs. Since we wanted to know if they *both* liked each other, the whole question is answered "no".

Conjunctions and the use of variables can be combined to ask quite interesting questions. Now that we know that it cannot be shown that John and Mary like each other, we ask:

"Is there anything that John and Mary both like?"

This question also consists of two goals:

☐   First, find out if there is some X that Mary likes.

☐   Then, find out if John likes whatever X is.

In Prolog the two goals would be put in a conjunction like this:

```
?- likes(mary,X), likes(john,X).
```

Prolog answers the question by attempting to satisfy the first goal. If the first goal is in the database, then Prolog will mark the place in the database, and attempt to satisfy the second goal. If the second goal is satisfied, then Prolog marks *that goal's* place in the database, and we have found a solution that satisfies both goals. It is most important to remember that each goal keeps its own place-marker. If, however, the second goal is not satisfied, then Prolog will attempt to re-satisfy the previous goal (in this case the first goal). Remember that Prolog searches the database completely for each goal. If a fact in the database happens to match, satisfying the goal, then Prolog will mark the place in the database in case it has to re-satisfy the goal at a later time. But when a goal needs to be re-satisfied, Prolog will begin the search from the goal's own place-marker, rather than from the start of the database. Our above question "is anything liked by Mary also liked by John" illustrates an example of this "backtracking" behaviour in the following way:

1. The database is searched for the first goal. As the second argument (X) is uninstantiated, it may match anything. The first such matching fact in our above database is `likes(mary,food)`. So, now X is instantiated to **food** *everywhere* in the question where X appears. Prolog marks the place in the database where it found the fact, so it can return to this point in case it needs to resatisfy the goal. Furthermore, we need to remember that X became instantiated here, so Prolog can 'forget' X if we need

to re-satisfy this goal.

2. Now, the database is searched for **likes(john,food)**. This is because the next goal is **likes(john,X)**, and X stands for **food**. As you can see, no such fact exists, so the goal fails. Now when a goal fails, we must try to re-satisfy the previous goal, so Prolog attempts to re-satisfy **likes(mary,X)**, but this time starting from the place that was marked in the database. But first we need to make X uninstantiated once more, so X may match against anything.

3. The marked place is **likes(mary,food)**, so Prolog begins searching from after that fact. Because we have not reached the end of the database yet, we have not exhausted the possibilities of what Mary likes, and the next matching fact is **likes(mary,wine)**. The variable X is now instantiated to **wine**, and Prolog marks the place in case it must re-satisfy what Mary likes.

4. As before, Prolog now tries the second goal, searching this time for **likes(john,wine)**. Prolog is not trying to re-satisfy this goal. It is entering the goal again (from the left-hand side, as it were), so it must start seaching from the beginning of the database. After not too much searching, the matching fact is found, and Prolog notifies you. Since this goal was satisfied, Prolog also marks *its* place in the database, in case you want to re-satisfy the goal. There is a place-marker in the database for each goal that Prolog is attempting to satisfy.

5. At this point, both goals have been satisfied. Variable X stands for the name **wine**. The first goal has a place-marker in the database at the fact **likes(mary,wine)**, and the second goal has a place-marker in the database at the fact **likes(john,wine)**.

As with any other question, as soon as Prolog finds one answer, it stops and waits for further instructions. If we type a semicolon, Prolog will search for more things that both John and Mary like. We know now that this amounts to re-satisfying both goals starting from the place-markers that they left behind.

To sum up, we can imagine a conjuction of goals to be arranged from left to right, separated by commas. Each goal may have a left-hand neighbour and a right-hand neighbour. Clearly, the left-most goal does not have a left-hand neighbour, and the right-most goal does not have a right-hand neighbour. When handling a conjunction of goals, Prolog attempts to satisfy each goal in turn, working from left to right. If a goal becomes satisfied (or sated perhaps?), Prolog leaves a place-marker in the database that is associated with the goal. Think of this as drawing an arrow from the goal to the place in the database where the solution is. Furthermore, any variables previously uninstantiated might now be instantiated. This happened above at Step 1. If a variable becomes instantiated, all occurrences of the variable in the question become instantiated. Prolog then attempts to satisfy the goal's right-hand neighbour, starting from the top of the database. As each goal in turn becomes satisfied, it leaves behind a place-marker in the database (draws another arrow from the goal to the matching fact), in case the goal needs to be re-satisfied at a later time. Any time a goal fails (cannot find a matching fact), Prolog goes back and attempts to re-satisfy its *left-hand* neighbour, starting from its place-marker. Furthermore, Prolog must first "uninstantiate" any variables that became instantiated at this goal. In other words, Prolog must "undo" all the variables when it resatisfies a goal. If each goal, upon being entered from its right, cannot be re-satisfied, then the failures will cause Prolog to gradually creep to the left as each goal fails. If the first goal (the left-most goal) fails, then it does not have a left-hand neighbour that it can attempt to re-satisfy. In this case, the entire conjunction fails. This behaviour, where Prolog repeatedly attempts to satisfy and resatisfy goals in a conjunction, is called *backtracking*. Backtracking is summarised in the next chapter, and is given a more complete and sophisticated treatment in Chapter 4.

When following the examples, you may find it helpful to write, below each variable in a goal, the object that has been instantiated by the success of the goal. You should also write in an arrow from the goal to its place-marker in the database. An example of this pencil-and-paper aid is shown here at several different times during the evaluation of the above example.

```
        DATABASE                                    GOALS
        --------                                    -----


   likes(mary,food).           ?- likes(mary,X), likes(john,X).
   likes(mary,wine).           ----------  ↓  -               ↓
   likes(john,wine).                      food             food
   likes(john,mary).
```

     1.   The first goal succeeds.
     2.   X is instantiated to 'food'.
     3.   Next, attempt to satisfy the second goal:

```
   likes(mary,food).           ?- likes(mary,X), likes(john,X).
   likes(mary,wine).           ----------  ↓  ------------  ↓  -
   likes(john,wine).                      food            food
   likes(john,mary).
```

     4.   The second goal fails.
     5.   Next, backtrack: forget previous value
         of X, and attempt to re-satisfy first goal.

```
   likes(mary,food).           ?- likes(mary,X), likes(john,X).
   likes(mary,wine).           ----------  ↓  -               ↓
   likes(john,wine).                      wine             wine
   likes(john,mary).
```

     6.   The first goal succeeds again.
     7.   X is instantiated to 'wine'.
     8.   Next, attempt to satisfy the second goal:

```
   likes(mary,food).           ?- likes(mary,X), likes(john,X).
   likes(mary,wine).           ----------  ↓  ------------  ↓  -
   likes(john,wine).                      wine            wine
   likes(john,mary).
```

     9.   The second goal succeeds.
    10. Prolog notifies you of success, and waits
         for a reply.

Throughout this book we will attempt to show where backtracking occurs in the examples, and what effect it has in solving the problems. Backtracking is so important that the whole of Chapter 4 is devoted to it.

Exercise 1.1: Continue the pencil-and-paper simulation of the example given above, assuming that you have just typed a semicolon ';' to initiate backtracking in order to find out if John and Mary both like anything else.

1.5 Rules

Suppose we wanted to state the fact that John likes all people. One way to do this would be to write down separate facts, like this:

```
likes(john,alfred).
likes(john,bertrand).
likes(john,charles).
likes(john,david).
    .
    .
    .
```

for every person in our database. This could become tedious, especially if there are hundreds of people in our Prolog program. Another way to say that John likes all people is to say,

"John likes any object provided it is a person."

This fact is in the form of a *rule* about what John likes, instead of listing all the people John likes. In a world where John could like every person, the rule is much more compact than a list of facts.

In Prolog, rules are used when you want to say that a fact *depends* on a group of other facts. In English, we can use the word "if" to express a rule. For example,

I use an umbrella if there is rain.
John buys the wine if it is less expensive than the beer.

Rules are also used to express definitions, for example:

"X is a bird if:
X is an animal, and
X has feathers."

or

"X is a sister of Y if:

14

X is female, and
X and Y have the same parents."

In the above English definitions, we have used variables X and Y. It is important to remember that a variable stands for the same object whenever it occurs in a rule. Otherwise we would be violating the spirit of the definition. For example, we could not show that Fred is a bird because Fido is an animal and Mary has feathers. The same principle of consistent interpretation of variables is true also for rules in Prolog.

A rule is a *general statement about objects and their relationships.* For example, not only could we say that Fred is a bird if Fred is an animal and Fred has feathers, but we could also say that Bertram is a bird if Bertram is an animal and Bertram has feathers. So, we can allow a variable to stand for a different object in each different *use* of the rule. Within a use of a rule, of course, variables are interpreted consistently as pointed out above.

Let us consider several examples, beginning with a rule using one variable and a conjunction.

"John likes anyone who likes wine"

or, in other words,

"John likes something if it likes wine"

or, with variables,

"John likes X if X likes wine."

In Prolog, a rule consists of a *head* and a *body.* The head and body are connected by the symbol ":-", which is made up of a colon and a hyphen. The ":-" is pronounced "if". The above example written in Prolog is:

Head   body

```
likes(john,X) :- likes(X,wine).
```

Notice that rules also are ended with a dot. The head of this rule is **likes(john,X)**. The head of the rule describes what fact the rule is intended to define. The body, in this case **likes(X,wine)**, describes the conjunction of goals that must be satisfied, one after the other, for the head to be true. For example, we can make John more choosy about whom he likes, simply by adding more goals onto the body, separated by commas:

```
likes(john,X) :- likes(X,wine), likes(X,food).
```

or, in words,

> *"John likes anyone who likes wine and food."*

Or, suppose John likes any female who likes wine:

```
likes(john,X) :- female(X), likes(X,wine).
```

Whenever we look at a Prolog rule, we should take notice of where the variables are. In the above rule, the variable X is used three times. Whenever X becomes instantiated to some object, all X's are instantiated *within the scope of X.* For some particular use of a rule, the *scope* of X is the whole rule, including the head, and extending to the dot "." at the end of the rule. So, in the above rule, if X happens to be instantiated to **mary,** then Prolog will try to satisfy the goals **female(mary)** and **likes(mary,wine).**

Next, as an example of a rule that uses more than one variable, consider a database consisting of facts about some of the family of Queen Victoria. We shall use the predicate **parents** having three arguments such that:

```
parents(X,Y,Z)
```

means

> *"The parents of X are Y and Z."*
> *with Y being the mother, and*
> *with Z being the father.*

We shall also use the predicates **female** and **male** in the obvious way. One part of the database might look like this:

```
male(albert).
male(edward).
female(alice).
female(victoria).
parents(edward,victoria,albert).
parents(alice,victoria,albert).
```

Now we shall use the rule about "sister of" described earlier. The rule defines the predicate **sister_of,** having two arguments so that **sister_of(X,Y)** is true if X is a sister of Y. Notice that we have used the underscore character "_" in the predicate name. Although we have not given the complete rules for how to construct names, it is permitted to include underscores in a name, and we shall summarise the rules in the next chapter. Now X is a sister of Y if:

- ☐ X is female,

- ☐ X has mother M and father F, and

- ☐ Y has the same mother and father as X does.

This can be written as the following Prolog rule.

```
sister_of(X,Y) :-
          female(X),
          parents(X,M,F),
          parents(Y,M,F).
```

We use the variable names M and F to indicate "mother" and "father" (and not "male" and "female", which is a different interpretation). Notice that we are using variables that do not appear in the head of the rule. These variables, M and F, are treated in the same way as any other variable. When Prolog uses the rule, variables M and F will initially be uninstantiated, so they will match against anything when it becomes time to satisfy the goal parent(X,M,F). However, as soon as they are instantiated, then *all* the M's and F's in this use of the rule will become instantiated. The following example should help to explain how these variables are used.

Let us ask the question:

?- sister_of(alice,edward).

When asked this question given the above database and rule for sister_of, Prolog proceeds as follows:

1. First, the question matches the head of the only sister_of rule above, so X in the rule becomes instantiated to alice and Y instantiated to edward. The place marker for the question is put against this rule. Now Prolog attempts to satisfy the three goals in the body, one by one.

2. The first goal is female(alice) because X was instantiated to alice in the previous step. This goal is true from the list of facts, so the goal succeeds. As it succeeds, Prolog marks the goal's place in the database (the third entry in the database). No new variables were instantiated, so no other note is made. Prolog now attempts to satisfy the next goal.

3. Now Prolog searches for parents(alice,M,F), where M and F will match against any arguments because they are uninstantiated. A matching fact is parents(alice,victoria,albert), so the goal succeeds. Prolog marks the goal's place in the database (sixth down from the top), and records that M became instantiated

to **victoria,** and F to **albert.** (You may write these under the goal in the rule if you like). Prolog now attempts to satisfy the next goal.

4.   Now Prolog searches for **parents(edward,victoria,albert)** because Y is known as **edward** from the question, and M and F were known to stand for **victoria** and **albert** from the previous goal. The goal succeeds, because a matching fact is found (fifth down from the top). Since it is the last goal in the conjunction, the entire goal succeeds, and the fact **sister_of(alice,edward)** is established as true. Prolog answers "yes".

Suppose we want to know if Alice is the sister of anyone. The appropriate question in Prolog is

```
?- sister_of(alice,X).
```

For this question, Prolog proceeds as follows:

1.   The question matches the head of the only **sister_of** rule. Variable X in the rule becomes instantiated to **alice.** As variable X in the question is uninstantiated, then variable Y in the rule will also be uninstantiated. However, these two variables now become "shared". As soon as one of the variables becomes instantiated to an object, the other variable becomes instantiated to the same object. At the moment, of course, they are uninstantiated.

2.   The first goal is **female(alice),** which succeeds as before.

3.   The second goal is **parents(alice,M,F),** and it matches against **parents(alice,victoria,albert).** Variables M and F are now known.

4.   As Y is not yet known, the third goal is **parents(Y,victoria,albert),** and it matches against **parents(edward,victoria,albert).** Variable Y is now known as **edward.**

5.   Since all goals succeed, the entire rule succeeds, with X known as **alice** (given in the question), and Y as **edward.** Since Y (in the rule) is "shared" with X (in the question), X (in the question) is also instantiated to **edward.** Prolog prints "X=edward".

As usual, Prolog waits for you to tell it if you want to find all the solutions to the question. As it turns out, this question has more than one solution. How Prolog finds the remaining solution[s] is set as an exercise at the end of this chapter.

As we have seen thus far, there are two ways to give Prolog information about a given predicate such as **likes**. We can provide both facts and rules. In general, a predicate will be defined by a mixture of facts and rules. These are called the *clauses* for a predicate. We shall use the word *clause* whenever we refer to either a fact or a rule.

As a further example, this time not dealing with monarchs, consider the rule:

"A person may steal something if the person is a thief and he likes the thing and the thing is valuable."

In Prolog, this is written:

```
may_steal(P,T) :- thief(P), likes(P,T), valuable(T).
```

Here we are using the predicate **may_steal**, which has two variables P and T to represent "some person P may steal thing T" This rule depends on clauses for **thief, likes,** and **valuable.** These could be represented either as facts or rules, whatever is most appropriate. For example, consider the following Prolog database, which has been made up from clauses discussed earlier. We have added some line numbers enclosed between /*...*/ brackets. This is how we write a *comment* in Prolog. Comments are ignored by Prolog, but we may add them to our programs for convenience. In the discussion that follows, we will refer to the line number comments.

Comments

```
/*1*/   thief(john).
/*2*/   likes(mary,food).
/*3*/   likes(mary,wine).
/*4*/   likes(john,X) :- likes(X,wine).
/*5*/   may_steal(X,Y) :- thief(X), likes(X,Y).
```

Notice that the definition of **likes** has three separate clauses: two facts, and a rule. To Prolog, there is no real difference. The only thing is that when a search is made throught the database to satisfy a goal, then a rule will cause further searches to be made to satisfy its own subgoals. A fact does not have subgoals, so it succeeds or fails immediately. For example, let us follow what happens when the question

"What may John steal?"

is asked. First, this question translates into Prolog as:

```
?- may_steal(john,X).
```

To answer this question, Prolog searches as follows:

1. First, Prolog searches in the database for a clause about **may_steal,** and finds one in the form of a rule at line /*5*/. Prolog marks the place in the database. Since it is a rule, its goals must be satisfied to establish whether it is true. so the X in the rule is instantiated to **john** from the question. Again we find that we have to

match two uninstantiated variables (X in the question and Y in the rule), so they will "share". Go back to the the **sister_of(X,Y)** examples if you are not sure what this means. The goals of a rule must succeed for the rule to succeed: the first goal, **thief(john)**, is now searched for.

2. The goal succeeds, since **thief(john)** is in the database (line /*1*/). Prolog marks the place in the database, and no variables have newly become instantiated. Prolog then attempts to satisfy the second goal on line /*5*/. Since X still stands for **john**, Prolog now searches for **likes(john,Y)**. Notice that Y is still instantiated at this point.

3. The goal **likes(john,Y)** matches with the head of the rule in line /*4*/. The Y in the goal "shares" with the X in the head, and both remain uninstantiated. To satisfy this rule, **likes(X,wine)** is now searched for.

4. The goal succeeds, because it matches with **likes(mary,wine)**, the fact on line /*3*/. So, X now stands for **mary**.

5. Since the goal on line /*4*/ succeeds, the whole rule succeeds. The fact **likes(john,mary)** is established from line /*4*/ because Y in line /*5*/ shares with X; it is also instantiated to **mary**.

6. Line /*5*/ now succeeds, with Y instantiated to **mary**. As Y was shared with the second argument of the original question, X in the question is now instantiated to **mary**.

The reasoning behind establishing that John may steal Mary is:

> In order to steal something, first John must be a thief. From line /*1*/, this is a fact. Next, John must like the thing. From line /*4*/, we see that John likes anything that likes wine. From line /*3*/, we see that Mary likes wine. Therefore, John likes Mary. Therefore, both conditions for stealing something can be satisfied, so John may steal Mary.

Notice that the fact on line /*2*/, that Mary likes food, is irrelevant to this particular question, because it was never needed.

In this example we have repeatedly used the variables X and Y in different clauses. For example, in the **may_steal** rule, X stands for the object that can steal something. But in the **likes** rule, X stands for the object that is liked. In order for this program to make sense, Prolog must be able to tell that X stands for two different things in different clauses. Remember that knowing the *scope* of a variable can resolve any confusion.

20

1.6 Summary and Exercises

At this point we have covered most of the basic core of Prolog. In particular, we have looked at

☐ Asserting facts about objects.
☐ Asking questions about the facts.
☐ Using variables and what their scopes are.
☐ The conjunction as a way of saying "and".
☐ Representing relationships in the form of rules.
☐ An introduction to backtracking.

With this small number of building blocks, it is possible to write useful programs for manipulating simple databases, and it would probably be a good idea if you did so by working out the exercises below.

To see how to use this book, you should read the Preface if you have not already done so. Also, when you begin to write programs for a Prolog system that is available to you, you should consult the appropriate Appendix to see what a sample programming session looks like.

After you have this much of Prolog under your control, you should carry on into the next chapter, which makes clear some of the points we did not mention in this chapter. Also, we will show how to work with numbers in Prolog. The features covered in the next few chapters are where the expressiveness and convenience of Prolog become apparent.

Exercise 1.2: When the **sister_of** rule is applied to the database of part of Queen Victoria's family discussed previously, more than one answer can be obtained. Explain how all the answers can be obtained, and what they are. *alice ↔ alice*

Exercise 1.3: This exercise has been inspired by one on Robert Kowalski's book *Logic for Problem Solving*, published by North Holland in 1979. Suppose someone has already written Prolog clauses that define the following relationships:

```
father(X,Y)      /* X is the father of Y */
mother(X,Y)      /* X is the mother of Y */
male(X)          /* X is male */
female(X)        /* X is female */
parent(X,Y)      /* X is a parent of Y */
diff(X,Y)        /* X and Y are different */
```

The problem is to write Prolog rules for the following relationships:

```
is_mother(X)     /* X is a mother */
is_father(X)     /* X is a father */
```

```
is_son(X)          /* X is a son */
sister_of(X,Y)     /* X is a sister of Y */
granpa_of(X,Y)     /* X is a grandfather of Y */
sibling(X,Y)       /* X is a sibling of Y */
```

For example, we could write a rule for **aunt**, provided we were supplied with (or wrote) rules for **female, sibling,** and **parent.**

```
aunt(X,Y) :-
        female(X),
        sibling(X,Z),
        parent(Z,Y).
```

This could also be written:

```
aunt(X,Y) :-
        sister_of(X,Z), parent(Z,Y).
```

provided that we wrote the **sister_of** rule.

Exercise 1.4: Using the **sister_of** rule defined in the text, explain why it is possible for some object to be her own sister. How would you change the rule if you did not want this property? Assume that the predicate **diff** of Exercise 1.3 is already defined.

Chapter 2. A Closer Look

In this chapter we provide a more complete discussion of the parts of Prolog that were introduced in the previous chapter. Prolog provides tools for structuring *data* as well as structuring the *order* in which attempts are made to satisfy goals. Structuring data involves knowing the syntax by which we can denote data. Structuring the order in which goals are solved involves knowing about backtracking.

2.1 Syntax

The syntax of a language describes how we are allowed to fit words together. In English, the syntax of the sentence "I see a zebra" is correct, but the syntax of "zebra see I a" is not correct. In the first chapter, we did not discuss the syntax of Prolog explicitly, but we simply showed what some parts of Prolog looked like. Here we will summarise the syntax of those parts of Prolog we have seen thus far.

Prolog programs are built from *terms.* A term is either a *constant,* a *variable,* or a *structure.* We saw each of these terms in the previous chapter, but we did not know them by these names. Each term is written as a sequence of *characters.* Characters are divided into four categories as follows:

```
A B C D E F G H I J K L M N O P Q R S T U V W X Y Z

a b c d e f g h i j k l m n o p q r s t u v w x y z

0 1 2 3 4 5 6 7 8 9

+ - * / \ ^ < > = ` ~ : . ? @ # $ &
```

The first row consists of *upper-case letters.* The second row consists of *lower-case letters.* The third row consists of *digits.* The fourth row consists of *symbols.* Each kind of term, whether it is a constant, variable, or structure, has different rules for how characters are strung together to form its name. Now we shall summarise each kind of term.

Constants

Constants are thought of a naming *specific objects* or *specific relationships*. There are two kinds of constants: *atoms*, and *integers*. Examples of atoms are the names that were given in the last chapter:

```
likes  mary  john  book  wine  owns  jewels  can_steal
```

The special symbols that Prolog uses to denote questions (?-) and rules (:-) are also atoms. There are two kinds of atoms: those made up of letters and digits, and those made up from symbols. The first kind must normally begin with a lower-case letter, as did all the ones we saw in the previous chapter. Those atoms made from symbols normally are made up from *only* symbols. Sometimes it may be necessary to have an atom beginning with a capital letter or a digit. If an atom is enclosed in single quotes ('), then the atom may have *any* characters in its name. Finally, the special underline character (_) may be inserted in the middle of an atom to improve legibility. The following are further examples of atoms:

```
a
void
=
'george-smith'
-->
george_smith
ieh2304
```

The following are not examples of atoms:

```
2304ieh
george-smith
Void
alpha
```

Integers, the other kind of constant, are used to represent numbers, so that arithmetic operations can be carried out. We have not discussed how to do arithmetic in Prolog, but this will be introduced later in this chapter. Integers are whole numbers consisting only of digits and may not contain a decimal point. In this book, only fairly small positive integers will be used, for example:

```
0  1  999  512  8192  14765  6224
```

Prolog is available on several different computers, and depending on what computer you use, you may not be able to use large numbers or negative numbers. However, in this book we will only give examples that will work on any Prolog you are likely to find. It is safe to say that you will be allowed to use any integer ranging from 0 to 16383. Depending on what computer you use, you may be allowed to use larger numbers or negative numbers, but we will not depend on them here. It is perhaps surprising that the applications for which Prolog is useful tend not to demand the ability to calculate with very large integers, fractions, or negative numbers. However, as Prolog is an extensible language, the resourceful programmer can add predicates to define such features without too much difficulty. For example, some Prolog systems provide library programs that define operations on rational numbers and numbers of arbitrary precision.

Variables

The second kind of term used in Prolog is the *variable*. Variables look like atoms, except they begin with a capital letter or an underline sign "_". A variable should be thought of as standing for some object that we may not be able to name. This corresponds to the use of a pronoun in English. In the example Prolog clauses we have seen so far, we have used variables with names like X, Y, and Z. However, the names can be as long as you like, for example:

```
Answer
Input
Gross_Pay
_3_blind_mice
```

Sometimes one needs to use a variable, but its name will never be used. For example, if we want to find out if anyone likes John, but we do not need to know just who, we can use the *anonymous variable*. The anonymous variable is a single underline character. Our example is written in Prolog as:

```
?- likes(_,john).
```

Several anonymous variables in the same clause *need not be given consistent interpretations*. This is a characteristic peculiar to the anonymous variable. It is used to save having to dream up different variable names when they will not be used elsewhere in the clause.

Structures

The third kind of term with which Prolog programs are written is the *structure*. A structure is a single object which consists of a collection of other objects, called components. The components are grouped together into a single structure for convenience in handling them.

One example of a structure in real life is an index card for a library book. The index card will contain several components: the author's name, the title of the book, the date when it was published, the location where it can be found in the library, and so forth. Some of the components can be broken down into further components. For example, the author's name consists of some initials and a surname.

Structures help to organise the data in a program because they permit a group of related information to be treated as a single object (a library card) instead of as separate entities. The way that you decompose data into components depends on what problem you want to solve, and later on we will give advice on how to do this.

Structures are also useful when there is a common kind of object, of which many may exist. Books, for example. In Chapter 1 we discussed the fact

```
owns(john,book).
```

to denote that John owns some particular book. If we later said **owns(mary,book)**, this means that Mary owns the same object that John owns, because it has the same name. There is no other way of telling objects apart, except by their name. We could say:

```
owns(john,wuthering_heights).
owns(mary,moby_dick).
```

to specify more carefully what books John and Mary own. However, in large programs, it may become confusing to have many different constants with no context to tell what they mean. Someone reading this Prolog program may not know that we meant **wuthering_heights** to be the name of the book written by the author Emily Bronte who flourished in Yorkshire, England during the 19th Century. Perhaps they will think that John has named his pet rabbit "wuthering_heights", say. Structures can help to provide this context.

A structure is written in Prolog by specifying its *functor*, and its *components*. The components are enclosed in round brackets and separated by commas. The functor is written just before the opening round bracket. Consider the following fact, that John owns the book called *Wuthering Heights*, by Emily Bronte:

```
owns(john,book(wuthering_heights,bronte)).
```

Inside the **owns** fact we have a structure by the name of **book**, which has two components, a title and an author. Since the **book** structure appears *inside* the fact as one of the fact's arguments, it is acting as an object, taking part in a relationship. If we like, we can also have another structure for the author's name, because there were three Bronte writers:

```
owns(john,book(wuthering_heights,author(emily,bronte))).
```

Structures may participate in the process of question-answering using variables. For example, we may ask if John owns any book by the Bronte sisters:

```
?- owns(john,book(X,author(Y,bronte))).
```

If this is true, **X** will then be instantiated to the title that was found, and **Y** will be instantiated

26

to the first name of the author. Or, we may not need to use the variables, so we can use anonymous ones:

    ?- owns(john,book(_,author(_,bronte))).

Remember that the anonymous variables do not "share" with each other.

We could improve the book structure by adding another argument indicating which *copy* the book was. For example, a third argument, where we would insert an integer, would provide a way of uniquely identifying a book:

    owns(john,book(ulysses,author(james,joyce),3129)).

or,

> John owns the 3,129th copy of Ulysses, by James Joyce.

If you have guessed that the syntax for structures is the same as for Prolog facts, you are correct. A predicate (used in facts and rules) is actually the functor of a structure. The arguments of a fact or rule are actually the components of a structure. There are many advantages to representing Prolog programs themselves as structures. It is not important to know why just now, but do keep in mind that all parts of Prolog, even Prolog programs themselves, are made up of constants, variables, and structures.

2.2 Characters

All of the constants that we have discussed in the previous sections were built up from strings of *characters*. Although each kind of constant (atom, integer, variable) has special rules about what characters may make up its name, it is helpful to know what all the characters are that Prolog recognises. This is because a character can be treated as an item of data in its own right. Now that we know about integers, it is appropriate to describe how characters are represented. It is most common to use "input" and "output" operations on characters; this will be discussed in Chapter 5.

Prolog recognises two kinds of characters: *printing* characters and *non-printing* characters. Printing characters cause a mark to appear on your computer terminal's display. Non-printing characters do not cause a mark to appear, but cause an action to be carried out. Such actions include printing a blank space, beginning new lines of text, and perhaps ringing a bell. The following are all the printing characters that can be used:

A B C D E F G H I J K L M N O P Q R S T U V W X Y Z

```
a b c d e f g h i j k l m n o p q r s t u v w x y z

0 1 2 3 4 5 6 7 8 9

! " # $ % & ' ( ) = - ~ ^ | \ } ] { [ _ ` @ + ; * : < > , . ? /
```

You should recognise these as a more complete set than the one given at the beginning of this chapter. Some of the characters have special meanings. For example, the round brackets are used to enclose the components of a structure. However, we shall see in later chapters that all the characters may be treated as information by Prolog programs. Characters may be printed, read from the keyboard, compared, and take part in arithmetic operations.

Characters are actually treated as small *integers* between 0 and 127. Each character has an integer associated with it, called its *ASCII code*. The term "ASCII" means "American Standard Code for Information Interchange", and it is the code which is used by many computers and computer languages in the world. The ASCII code has several advantages, as can be seen by the chart in Appendix A. The letters are arranged in alphabetical order, so comparing alphabetic order of characters means simply comparing ASCII codes using the relational operators described later in this chapter. The printing characters all have ASCII codes that are greater than 32.

Although the ASCII code may not seem useful at the moment, the next places we mention it are in Section 3.2 and 3.5.

2.3 Operators

Sometimes it is convenient to write some functors as *operators*. This is a form of syntax that makes some structures easier to read. For example, arithmetic operations are commonly written as operators. When we write the arithmetic expression "x+y*z", we call the "plus sign" and the "multiply sign" *operators*. If we had to write the arithmetic expression "x+y*z" in the normal way for structures, it would look like this:

```
+(x,*(y,z)).
```

The operators are sometimes easier to use, however, because we have grown accustomed to using them in arithmetic expressions ever since our schooldays. Also, the structure form requires that round brackets be placed around the functor's arguments, which may seem awkward at times.

First we need to know how to "read" arithmetic expressions that have operators in them. To do this, we need to know three things about each operator: its *position*, its *precedence*, and its *associativity*. In this section we will describe how to use Prolog operators with these three things in mind, but we will not go into very much detail at this point. Although many

28

different kinds of operators can be made up, we will deal only with simple operators for addition, subtraction, multiplication, and division. The reason for doing this is to make it possible to use Prolog rather like a simple pocket calculator.

The syntax of operators is somewhat freer than that of functors. First, the syntax depends on the *position* of the operator. Operators like plus (+), minus (−), multiply (*), and divide (/) are written *between* their arguments, so we call them *infix* operators. It is also possible to put operators before their arguments, as in "−x+y", where the minus sign before the x means "negative x". Operators that come *before* their arguments are called *prefix* operators. Finally, some operators may come after their argument. For example, the factorial operator, used by mathematicians, comes after the number you want to find the factorial of. In mathematical notation, the factorial of x is written "x!", where the exclamation sign is the factorial operator. Operators that are written *after* their arguments are called *postfix* operators. So, the position of an operator tells where it is written with relationship to its arguments. It turns out that the operators that we will use in the next section are all *infix* operators.

Now precedence. When we see x+y*z, we know that we multiply y by z first, then add x. This is because we were taught in school that mutiplications and divisions are done before additions and subtractions, except where brackets are used for grouping. On the other hand, the structure form

    +(x,*(y,z))

makes explicit the rule that the multiplication is done before the addition. This is because the * structure is an argument of the + structure, so if we actually wanted the computer to carry out the calculation, the * has to be carried out first in order for + to know what its arguments are. So when using operators, we need rules that tell us the order in which operations are carried out. This is what *precedence* tells us about.

The precedence of an operator is used to indicate which operation is carried out first. Each operator that is used in Prolog has a *precedence class* associated with it. The precedence class is an integer which depends on the particular version of Prolog you are using. However, it is always true that an operator with a higher precedence has a precedence class which is closer to 1. If precedence classes range from 1 to 255, then an operator in the first precedence class is carried out first, before operators belonging to the 129th (say) precedence class. In Prolog the multiplication and division operators are in a higher precedence class than addition and subtraction, so the expression "a−b/c" means "divide b by c first, then subtract the result from a", or, with round brackets, "a−(b/c)". Similarly, the expression "x+y/b−c" means "(x+(y/b))−c". In the structure forms, these two expressions would have to appear as

    −(a,/(b,c))

and

```
-(+(x,/(y,b)),c).
```

so decide for yourself which you prefer. The exact association of operators to precedence classes is not important at the moment, but it is worth remembering the relative order in which operations are carried out.

Finally, consider how different operators *associate*. How they associate comes to our attention when we have several operators of the *same* precedence. When we see the expression "8/2/2", does this mean "(8/2)/2" or "8/(2/2)"? In the first case, the answer is 2, and in the second case, 8. To be able to distinguish between these two cases, we must be able to tell whether an operator is *left associative* or *right associative*. A left associative operator must have the *same or lower* precedence operations on the left, and *lower* precedence operations on the right. For example, all the arithmetic operations (add, subtract, multiply, and divide) are left associative. This means that expressions like "8/4/4" are treated as "(8/4)/4". Also, "5+8/2/2" means "5+((8/2)/2)".

In practice, people tend to use round brackets for expressions that may be difficult to understand because of the precedence and associativity rules. In this book we will also try to make it as clear as possible by using lots of round brackets, but it is still important to know the syntax rules for operators so your understanding of operators is complete.

Remember that a structure made up of arithmetic operators is like any other structure. No arithmetic is actually carried out until commanded by the 'is' predicate described in Section 2.6.

2.4 Equality

One noteworthy predicate is *equality*, which is an infix operator written as = When an attempt is made to satisfy the goal X = Y (pronounced "X equals Y"), Prolog attempts to *match* X and Y, and the goal succeeds if it can do so. We can think of this act as *trying to make* X and Y *equal*. The equality predicate is built-in, which means that it is already defined in the Prolog system. The equality predicate works as though it were defined by the following fact:

```
X = X.
```

To see why this is, consider some clause containing some variable X, such as

```
carnivore(X) :- has_claws(X), eats(X,meat).
```

Although the variable X occurs three times, if any one of the occurrences becomes instantiated to some object, then all of the X's will instantly become instantiated to the same object. Within the use of some clause, X always *equals* X, and the equality operator also can denote this by the fact **X = X**.

Given a goal of the form **X=Y**, where X and Y are any two terms which are permitted to contain uninstantiated variables, the rules for deciding whether X and Y are equal are as follows:

☐ If X is an uninstantiated variable and if Y is any object, then X and Y are equal. As a side-effect, X will be instantiated to whatever Y is. For example, the question

```
?- rides(clergyman, bicycle) = X.
```

succeeds, and X is instantiated to **rides(clergyman,bicycle)**.

☐ Integers and atoms are always equal to themselves. For example, the following goals have the behaviour shown:

```
policeman = policeman        /* succeeds */
paper = pencil               /* fails */
1066 = 1066                  /* succeeds */
1206 = 1583                  /* fails */
```

☐ Two structures are equal if they have the same functor and number of arguments, and all the corresponding arguments are equal. For example, the following goal succeeds, and causes X to be instantiated to **bicycle**:

```
rides(clergyman,bicycle) = rides(clergyman,X)
```

Structures can be "nested" one inside another to any depth. If such nested structures are tested for equality, the test may take more time to carry out, because there is more structure to test. The following goal

```
a(b,C,d(e,F,g(h,i,J))) = a(B,c,d(E,f,g(H,i,j)))
```

would succeed, and cause B to be instantiated to b, C to c, E to e, F to f, H to h, and J to j.

What happens when we attempt to make two uninstantiated variables equal? This is just a special case of the first rule above. The goal succeeds, and the two variables *share*. If two variables share, then whenever one of them becomes instantiated to some term, the other one automatically is instantiated to the same term. So, in the following rule, the second argument will be instantiated to whatever the first argument is:

```
do_nothing(X,Y) :- X=Y.
```

Such a goal would always succeed if either argument is uninstantiated. An easier way to write such a rule is to take advantage of the fact that a variable equals itself, and write:

```
do_nothing(X,X).
```

Prolog also provides a predicate '\=' called 'not equal'. The goal X \= Y succeeds if X = Y fails, and it fails if X = Y succeeds. So, X \= Y means "X cannot be made equal to Y".

Exercise 2.1: Say whether the following goals would succeed, and which variables, if any, would be instantiated to what values:

```
pilots(A,london) = pilots(london,paris)
point(X,Y,Z) = point(X1,Y1,Z1)
letter(C) = word(letter)
noun(alpha) = alpha
'vicar' = vicar
```

2.5 Arithmetic

Many people use computers to do operations on numbers. Arithmetic operations are useful for *comparing* numbers and for *calculating* results. In this section we will see examples of each kind.

First, consider comparing numbers. Given two numbers, we can tell whether one number is *equal* to the other, or *less than* the other, or *greater than* the other. Prolog provides certain "built-in" predicates, in the form of infix operators, for comparing numbers. The predicates '=' and '\=' as discussed in Section 2.4 can be used for comparing numbers. The arguments could be variables intantiated to integers, or they could be integers written as constants. In addition, the goal A < B succeeds if A is less than B, and the goal A > B succeeds if A is greater than B. There are several other operators for comparing numbers, and we can summarise all of them here:

```
X = Y          (X and Y stand for the same number)
X \= Y         (X and Y stand for different numbers)
X < Y          (X is less than Y)
X > Y          (X is greater than Y)
X =< Y         (X is either less than or equal to Y)
X >= Y         (X is either greater than or equal to Y)
```

As these comparison operators are predicates, one might think it possible to write a Prolog fact as follows,

```
2 > 3.
```

in order to assert that 2 is actually greater than 3. A fact like this one is perfectly well-formed Prolog. However, Prolog will not allow further facts to be added to predicates that are "built in" to Prolog. This prevents you from changing the meaning of built-in predicates in unexpected ways. In Chapter 6 we shall describe all of the built-in predicates, including all those we have met thus far.

As a first example of using numbers, suppose we have a database of the reigns of the Sovereign Princes of Wales in the 9th and 10th Centuries. The predicate reigns(X,Y,Z) is true if the prince named X reigned from year Y to year Z. The list of facts in the database looks like this:

```
reigns(rhodri,844,878).
reigns(anarawd,878,916).
reigns(hywel_dda,916,950).
reigns(lago_ad_idwal,950,979).
reigns(hywel_ab_ieuaf,979,985).
reigns(cadwallon,985,986).
reigns(maredudd,986,999).
```

Now suppose we want to ask who was on the Welsh throne during a particular year. We could define a rule, which given a name and a date, would search the database, and compare the given date aginst the dates of the reign. Let us define the predicate prince(X,Y), which is true if the prince named X was on the throne during year Y:

"X was a prince during year Y if:
       X reigned between years A and B, and
       Y is between A and B, inclusive."

Now the first goal will be satisfied by using the reigns database above. The second goal is satisfied if Y is A, or B, or lies between them. You can test if Y lies between A and B by testing if Y >= A and if Y =< B. Translating all this into Prolog, we obtain:

```
prince(X,Y) :-
          reigns(X,A,B),
          Y >= A,
          Y =< B.
```

Here are some questions one might ask, with the answers that Prolog gives:

```
?- prince(cadwallon,986).
yes

?- prince(rhodri,1979).
```

```
no

?- prince(X,900).
X=anarawd
yes

?- prince(X,979).
X=lago_ab_idwal;
X=hywel_ab_ieuaf
yes
```

Notice the use of variables in the latter examples. Make sure you know how Prolog's searching mechanism allows questions like these to be answered.

Arithmetic can also be used for calculating. For example, if we know the population and ground area of a country, we can calculate the population density of the country. The population density tells us how crowded the country would be if all the people were evenly spread throughout the country. Consider the following database about the population and area of various countries in 1976. We will use the predicate **pop** to represent the relationship between a country and its population. Nowadays, the populations of countries are generally quite large numbers. Depending on what computer you use, Prolog may not be able to use such large numbers. So, we will represent population figures in millions: **pop(X,Y)** means the population of country X is about "Y million" people. The predicate **area** will denote the relationship between a country and its area (in millions of square miles):

```
pop(usa,203).
pop(india,548).
pop(china,800).
pop(brazil,108).

area(usa,3).
area(india,1).
area(china,4).
area(brazil,3).
```

Now to find the population density of a country, we must use the rule that the density is the population divided by the area. This can be represented as the predicate **density(X,Y)**, where X is a country and Y is the population density of that country. A Prolog rule for this is:

```
density(X,Y) :-
        pop(X,P),
        area(X,A),
        Y is P/A.
```

The rule is read as follows:

> "The population density of country X is Y, if:
>   The population of X is P, and
>   The area of X is A, and
>   Y is calculated by dividing P by A.

This rule uses the divide operator (/), which was introduced in the previous section. The divide operation is actually "integer division", which gives only the integer part of the quotient of the result. If you need to know the remainder as well, the **mod** operator (meaning "modulus") is used. The expression **A mod B** gives, for integers A and B, the remainder when A is divided by B.

The **is** operator is new. The **is** operator is an infix operator, which takes an unknown variable on the left, and an arithmetic expression on the right. In the above example, Y is unknown when the **is** is encountered, and it is up to the **is** to evaluate the expression, and let Y stand for the value. This means that the values of all the variables on the right of an **is** must be known.

We need to use the **is** operator in order to tell Prolog to *evaluate* the arithmetic expression. Remember that something like

        P/A

where P and A stand for integers, is just an ordinary Prolog structure like

        author(emily,bronte).

With arithmetic expressions, there is a special operation that can be applied to the structure: that of actually carrying out the bits of arithmetic and calculating the result. This is called *evaluating* the arithmetic expression. Clearly we cannot evaluate structures such as the **author** one, because **author** is not defined here as an arithmetic operation. So, we have to tell Prolog when we want it to attempt to evaluate a structure. This is what the predicate '**is**' is for.

Getting back to the population density example, it is not hard now to see that typical questions and their answers are:

        ?- density(china,X).
        X=200

        ?- density(turkey,X).
        no

In the first question, the X=200 is Prolog's answer, meaning 200 people per square mile. The second question failed, because the population of Turkey could not be found in the database.

Depending on what computer you use, various arithmetic operators can be used on the right-hand side of the **is** operator.   All Prolog systems, however, will have:

```
X + Y              (the sum of X and Y)
X - Y              (the difference of X and Y)
X * Y              (the product of X and Y)
X / Y              (the quotient of X and Y)
X mod Y            (the remainder of X divided by Y)
```

This list together with the above list of comparison operators should tell you nearly all you need for doing simple arithmetic problems.   Of course, Prolog is mainly intended for non-numerical purposes, so arithmetic facilities are not as important as in other computer languages.

clause { *facts* *rules* }

2.6   Summary of Satisfying Goals

Prolog performs a task in response to a *question* from the programmer (you).   A question provides a *conjunction* of *goals* to be *satisfied*.   Prolog uses the known *clauses* to satisfy the goals.   A fact can cause a goal to be satisfied immediately, whereas a rule can only reduce the task to that of satisfying a conjunction of *subgoals*.   However, a clause can only be used if it *matches* the goal under consideration.   If a goal cannot be satisfied, *backtracking* will be initiated.   Backtracking consists of reviewing what has been done, attempting to *re-satisfy* the goals by finding an alternative way to satisfying them.   Furthermore, if you are not content with an answer to your question, you can initiate backtracking yourself by typing a semicolon when Prolog informs you of a solution.

2.6.1   Successful satisfaction of a conjunction of goals

Prolog attempts to satisfy the goals in a conjunction, whether they appear in a rule body or in a question, in order from left to right.   This means that Prolog will not attempt to satisfy a goal until its neighbour on the left has been satisfied.   And, when it has been satisfied, Prolog will attempt to satisfy its neighbour on the right.   In the following example, we shall show the sequence of events that leads to the satisfaction of a **sister_of** predicate.   We shall not list the entire database that is used, but assume that Prolog finds certain facts and rules when it requires them.   Consider the following rule:

```
sister_of(X,Y) :- female(X), parent(X,M,F), parent(Y,M,F).
```

and the question

```
?- sister_of(mary,john).
```

Assume that Prolog uses the above rule. Now Prolog will need to satisfy the following sequence of subgoals:

```
female(mary)
parent(mary,M,F)
parent(john,M,F)
```

Let us look in detail at the second of these. Prolog will attempt to satisfy it when the first goal has been satisfied. Then, when the second goal is satisfied, Prolog will attempt to satisfy the third goal. We can illustrate this "flow of satisfaction" by means of an arrow:

Satisfying a goal involves searching the database for a *matching* clause, then marking the place in the database, and then attempting to satisfy any subgoals. Let us show the operation of marking a place in the database by the letter M. Let us also assume that Prolog finds the rule:

```
parent(C,M,F) :- mother(C,M), father(C,F).
```

Then we have:

Assuming that the **mother** and **father** goals succeed because of clauses in the database, a more complete illustration (with variable values written in) is:

This shows the general pattern of how Prolog attempts to satisfy goals in a case where the conjunction of goals succeeds. Prolog attempts to satisfy a goal when the goal's left neighbour is finished, or, if it has no left neighbour, when the appropriate rule has been chosen and marked. A goal reports its successful satisfaction to its right-hand neighbour, or, if it has no right-hand neighbour, to the goal that caused the rule to be used.

2.6.2 Consideration of goals in backtracking

When a failure is generated (because all the alternative clauses for a goal have been tried, or because you type a semicolon), the "flow of satisfaction" passes *back* along the way it has come. When it comes to an 'M' (in our illustrations), Prolog attempts to *re-satisfy* the appropriate goal by finding an alternative clause. First, it makes uninstantiated all variables that had been instantiated in the course of satisfying the goal. Then, it searches on in the database from where the placemarker was put. If it finds another matching possibility, it marks the place, and things continue as in Section 2.6.1 above. Note that work on any goals to the "right" of this (even if such goals were tackled under the previous alternative) will always start from scratch. Prolog will try to satisfy, and not to re-satisfy them. If no other matching possiblity can be found, the goal fails, and Prolog works its way back until it comes to another 'M'. In our example, if the goal **parent(john,ann,fred)** failed, Prolog would first go back to the following (notice the resetting of the variable F):

If this goal could not be re-satisfied, Prolog would go back to:

and so on. We can see from these examples the general pattern of how goals are reconsidered in backtracking. When a goal fails, it reports failure to its left neighbour. If it has no left neighbour, it reports to the goal that caused its rule to be used.

2.6.3 Matching

The rules for deciding whether a goal matches the head of a use of a clause are as follows. Note that in the use of a clause, all variables are initially uninstantiated.

- ☐ An uninstantiated variable will match any object. As a result, that object will be what the variable stands for.

- ☐ Otherwise, an integer or atom will match only itself.

- ☐ Otherwise, a structure will match another structure with the same functor and number of arguments, and all the corresponding arguments must match.

A noteworthy case in matching is one in which two uninstantiated variables are matched together. In this case, we say that these variables *share*. Two sharing variables are such that as soon as one is instantiated, so is the other (with the same value).

If you have noticed a similarity between matching and making arguments equal (Section 2.4), then you are correct. This is because the = predicate attempts to make its arguments equal by matching them.

Now we can bring together what we have discussed about operators, arithmetic, and matching. Suppose the following facts are in the database:

```
sum( 5 ).
sum( 3 ).
sum( X+Y ).
```

Consider the question

```
?- sum( 2+3 ).
```

Now, which one of the facts above will match with the question? If you think it is the first one, then you should go back and read about structures and operators. In the question the argument of the **sum** structure is a *structure* having the plus sign as its functor, and having the 2 and 3 as its components. In fact, the goal shown will match with the third fact, instantiating X to 2, and Y to 3.

On the other hand, if we actually wanted to compute a sum, we would use the **is** operator. We would write

```
?- X is 2+3.
```

or, just for fun, we could define a predicate **add** that relates two integers with their sum:

```
add( X, Y, Z ) :- Z is X+Y.
```

In this definition, X and Y must be instantiated, and Z must be uninstantiated.

Chapter 3. Using Data Structures

The *Shorter Oxford English Dictionary* defines the word "recursion" in the following way:

RECURSION. [Now rare or obs. 1616]. A backward movement, return.

This definition is cryptic and perhaps outdated. Recursion is now a very popular and powerful technique in the world of non-numerical programming. It is used in two ways. It can be used to describe structures that have other structures as components. It can also be used to describe programs that need to satisfy a copy of themselves before they themselves can succeed. Sometimes, beginners view recursion with some suspicion, because, how is it possible for some relationship to be defined in terms of itself? In Prolog, recursion is the normal and natural way of viewing data structures and programs. We hope that the theme of this chapter, recursion, will be made explicit in a comfortable and unobtrusive way.

3.1 Structures and Trees

It is usually easier to understand the form of a complicated structure if we write it as a *tree*, in which each functor is a root, and the components are branches. Each branch points to another structure, so we can have structures within structures. It is customary to write a tree diagram with the root at the top, and the branches at the bottom, like this:

```
parents(charles,elizabeth,philip)

        parents
       /  |  \
  charles |   \
          |    \
      elizabeth  \
               philip
```

```
a+b*c   (or +(a,*(b,c)))

    +
   / \
  a   *
     / \
    b   c
```

```
book(moby_dick,author(herman,melville))

        book
        /\
       /  \
 moby_dick   author
              /\
             /  \
        herman   melville
```

Notice that the last two structures have trees of the same shape, although the roots and branches are different. Before going further, you should make sure that you can write tree diagrams for each of the structures you have seen in the previous chapters.

Suppose we are given the sentence "John likes Mary", and we need to represent the syntax of the sentence. A very simple syntax for English is that a sentence consists of a noun followed by a verb phrase. Additionally, a verb phrase consists of a verb and another noun. This relationship between parts of a sentence can be described by a structure: sentence(noun,verb_phrase(verb,noun)), which has a tree like this:

```
        sentence
         /\
        /  \
    noun    verb_phrase
              /\
             /  \
          verb    noun
```

If we take our sentence ("John likes Mary"), and insert the words of the sentence into the arguments of the noun and verb functors in the structure, we obtain:

sentence(noun(john),verb_phrase(verb(likes),noun(mary)))

```
        sentence
         /\
        /  \
    noun    verb_phrase
     /         /\
    /         /  \
  john     verb    noun
            /        \
           /          \
        likes          mary
```

This shows how we can use Prolog structures to represent the syntax of a very simple English

41

sentence. In general, if we know the parts of speech of words in a sentence, it is possible
to write a Prolog structure that makes explicit the relationships between different words in
a sentence. This is an interesting topic in its own right, and later on we shall return to
the question of how we can use Prolog to make the computer "understand" some simple English
sentences.

3.2 Lists

The *list* is a very common data structure in non-numeric programming. The list is an
ordered sequence of elements that can have any length. *Ordered* means that the order of
the elements in the sequence matters. The *elements* of a list may be atoms, structures, or
any other terms, including other lists. These properties are helpful when we cannot predict
in advance how big a list should be, and what information it should contain. Furthermore,
lists can represent practically any kind of structure that one may wish to use in symbolic
computation. Lists are widely used to represent parse trees, grammars, city maps, computer
programs, and mathematical entities such as graphs, formulae, and functions. There is a
programming language called LISP, in which the only data structures available are the constant
and the list. However, in Prolog, the list is simply one particular kind of structure.

Lists can be represented as a special kind of tree. A list is either an *empty list*, having
no elements, or it is a structure that has two components: the head and tail. The end of
a list is customarily represented as a tail that is set to the empty list. The empty list is
written as [], which is an opening square bracket followed by a closing square bracket.
The head and tail of a list are components of the functor named '.', which is the dot.
Thus, the list consisting of one element 'a' is:

    .(a,[])

and its tree looks like this:

         .
        / \
       a   []

Also, the list consisting of the atoms a, b, and c could be written

    .(a,.(b,.(c,[])))

         .
        / \
       a   .
          / \
         b   .
            / \
           c   []

The dot functor happens to be defined as an operator, so it is permissible to write the above two list expressions as a.[] and a.(b.(c.[])). The second one could be written as a.b.c.[] because the dot operator is right-associative. Lists are an ordered sequence, so the list a.b is different from the list b.a.

Some people like to write the tree diagram of a list with the tree "growing" from left to right, and with the "branches" hanging down. The above list looks like this in a *vine diagram:*

```
.----.----.----[]
|    |    |
a    b    c
```

In this vine diagram, the head component of the dot functor hangs down, and the tail component grows to the right. The end of the list is clearly marked by the last tail component being the empty list. The main advantage of the vine diagram for lists is that it can be written right-to-left on a piece of paper.

The vine diagram may be suitable for writing lists on paper when we need to see the structure of a list, but such diagrams are not used for writing lists into a Prolog program. As the dot notation is often awkward for writing complicated lists, there is another syntax that can be used for writing lists in a Prolog program. This *list notation* consists of the elements of the list separated by commas, and the whole list is enclosed in square brackets. For example, the above lists can be written in the list notation as [a] and [a,b,c]. It is useful for lists to contain other lists and variables. For example, the following lists are legal in Prolog:

```
[]
[a,b,c,[d,e,f],g]
[a,V1,b,[X,Y]]
```

Variables within lists are treated the same as variables in any other structure. They can become instantiated at any time, so judicious use of variables can provide a way to put "holes" in lists that can be filled with data at a later time.

To show the structure of lists within lists, the vine diagram for the previous list is:

```
.----.----.----.----[]
|    |    |    |
a    V1   b    .----.---[]
               |    |
               X    Y
```

It is easy to see by this diagram that each horizontal "level" of the vine is a list having a certain number of elements. The top level is a list having four elements, one of which is a list. The second level, having two elements, is the fourth element of the top level list.

Lists are manipulated by splitting them up into a *head* and a *tail*. The *head* of a list is the first argument of the '.' functor that is used to construct lists. Notice that we speak of the "head" of a rule as well as the "head" of a list. These two things are different, and although they are both called "heads" by historical accident, it is easy enough to understand which "head" one is talking about at a particular time. The *tail* of a list is the second argument of the "." functor. When a list appears in the square bracket notation, the head of the list is the first element of the list. The tail of the list is a *list* that consists of every element *except* the first. The following examples show some heads and tails:

list	head	tail
[a,b,c,d]	a	[b,c,d]
[a]	a	[]
[]	(fails)	(fails)
[[the,cat],sat]	[the,cat]	[sat]
[the,cat]	the	[cat]
[the,[cat,sat]]	the	[[cat,sat]]
[the,[cat,sat],down]	the	[[cat,sat],down]
[X+Y,x+y]	X+Y	[x+y]

Notice that the empty list has neither a head nor a tail. In the last example, the "+" operator is used as a functor for the structures +(X,Y) and +(x,y).

Because a common operation with lists is to split a list into its head and tail, there is a special notation in Prolog to represent "the list with head X and tail Y". This is written [X|Y], where the symbol separating the X and Y is the vertical bar. A pattern of this form will instantiate X to the head of a list, and Y to the tail of the list, as in the following example:

```
p([1,2,3]).
p([the,cat,sat,[on,the,mat]]).

?- p([X|Y]).

X=1   Y=[2,3] ;
X=the Y=[cat,sat,[on,the,mat]]

?- p([_,_,_,[_|X]]).

X=[the,mat]
```

More examples of the list syntax, showing how various lists match, are as follows:

list1	(matches with)	list2	(instantiating variables)
[X,Y,Z]		[john,likes,fish]	X = john Y = likes Z = fish
[cat]		[X|Y]	X = cat Y = []
[X,Y|Z]		[mary,likes,wine]	X = mary Y = likes Z = [wine]
[[the,Y]|Z]		[[X,hare],[is here]]	X = the Y = hare Z = [[is,here]]
[X,Y|Z,W]	(is incorrect syntax)		
[golden|T]		[golden,norfolk]	T = [norfolk]
[vale,horse]		[horse,X]	(fails)
[white|Q]		[P|horse]	P = white Q = horse

it is not equale to [white, horse]

white horse

As the last example shows, lists do not always have to end in the empty list. The list **[white|horse]** denotes a list that has head 'white' and tail 'horse'.

There is one final use for list syntax -- representing strings. Occasionally one needs strings of characters for printing or reading text such as English sentences. If a string of characters is enclosed in double quotes, the string is represented as a list of integer codes that represent the characters. The codes are taken from what is known as the "ASCII code", which is given in the Appendix. For example, the string

"system"

is changed by Prolog into the list

[115,121,115,116,101,109].

3.3 Membership of a list

Suppose we have some list, where X stands for its head, and Y stands for its tail. Recall that we may write this list as [X|Y]. The list might contain, for example, names of those horses sired by Coriander who all won horseraces in Great Britian in the year 1927:

[curragh_tip, music_star, park_mill, portland].

Now suppose we want to find out if a given horse is in the list. The way we do this in Prolog is to find out whether the horse is the same as the head of the list: if it is, we succeed. If it is not, then we check to see if the horse is in the tail of the list. This means checking the head of the *tail* next time. And the head of *that* tail after that. If we come to the end of the list, which will be the empty list, we must fail: the horse is not in the list.

To write this in Prolog, we must first recognise that there is a relationship between an object, and a list it might appear in. This relationship, called membership, is a common enough concept in our everyday lives. We talk about people being members of clubs, and so forth. We shall write a predicate `member(X,Y)` which is true if the object that X stands for is a member of the list that Y stands for. There are two conditions to check. First, it is a fact that X will be a member of Y, if X is the same as the head of Y. In Prolog, this fact is:

```
member(X,[X|_]).
```

or

"X is a member of the list if X is the same as the head of the list"

Notice that we use the anonymous variable '_' to stand for the tail of the list. This is because we do not use the tail for anything in this particular fact. Notice that this rule also could have been written as:

```
member(X,[Y|_]) :- X = Y.
```

By this time you should understand why we can take a shortcut by using X in two places in the shorter version of the rule.

The second, and last, rule says that X is a member of a list providing it is in the tail, Y, of that list. And, what better way to find out if X is in the tail of the list, than to use **member** itself! This is the essence of recursion. In Prolog:

```
member(X,[_|Y]) :- member(X,Y).
```

or

"X is a member of the list if X is a member of the tail of the list"

Notice that we have used the anonymous variable '_', because we do not care to have any variable standing for the head of the list. The two rules together define the membership predicate, and tell Prolog how to search a list from beginning to end, looking for an item in the list. The most important point to remember, when encountering a recursively defined predicate, is to look for the *boundary conditions* and the *recursive case.* There are actually two boundary conditions for the **member** predicate. Either the object we are looking for is in the list, or it isn't in the list. The first boundary condition of **member** is recognised by the first clause, which will cause the search though the list to be stopped if the first argument of **member** matches the head of the second argument. The second boundary condition occurs when the the second argument of **member** is the empty list. How are we assured that the boundary conditions will ever be satisfied? We must look at the recursive case, the second rule of **member.** Notice that each time **member** attempts to satisfy itself, the goal is given a *shorter* list. The tail of a list is always a shorter list than the original one. Eventually, one of two things will happen: either the first **member** rule will match, or **member** will be given a list of length 0, the empty list, as its second argument. When either of these things happens, the "recurrence" of **member** goals will come to an end. The first boundary condition is recognised by a fact, which does not cause any further subgoals to be considered. The second boundary condition is not recognised by any **member** rule, so **member** will fail.

In Prolog:

```
member(X,[X|_]).
member(X,[_|Y]) :- member(X,Y).

?- member(d,[a,b,c,d,e,f,g]).
yes

?- member(2,[3,a,4,f]).
no
```

Suppose we asked the question

```
?- member(clygate,[curragh_tip,music_star,park_mill,portland]).
```

The second **member** rule would match, as clygate does not match curragh_tip. Variable Y becomes instantiated to [music_star, park_mill, portland], and the next goal is to see if clygate is a member of that. The second rule matches again, and the tail is taken again. The goal becomes **member(clygate,[park_mill,portland]).** This process recurs until we reach the goal where X is clygate and Y is [portland]. The second rule matches once more, and now Y becomes the tail of [portland], which is the empty list, and the next goal becomes **member(clygate,[]).** No rule in the database matches this, so the goal fails, and the question is false.

It is most important to remember that each time that **member** uses its second clause to attempt to satisfy **member,** Prolog treats each recurrence of the **member** goal as a different "copy". This prevents the variables in one use of a clause from being confused with variables in another use of a clause.

As the membership predicate is so useful, we shall use it in many places in the remainder of this book. The **member** predicate is also important because it is one of the smallest useful examples of a predicate that is *recursive* -- that is, the definition of **member** contains goals that can only be satisfied by **member** itself. Recursive definitions are frequently found in Prolog programs, and they are no different than any other type of definition. However, you must be careful that you do not write "circular" definitions, for example:

```
parent(X,Y) :- child(Y,X).            ] Circular
child(A,B) :- parent(B,A).
```

In this example, to satisfy **parent**, we set up **child** as a goal. However, the definition for **child** uses only **parent** as a goal. You should be able to see that asking a question about **parent** or **child** would lead to an endless loop in which Prolog would never infer anything new, and that the loop would never terminate.

One important problem to look out for in recursive definitions is that of *left recursion.* This arises when a rule causes the invocation of a goal that is essentially equivant to the original goal that caused the rule to be used. Thus if we defined:

```
person(X) :- person(Y), mother(X,Y).
person(adam).
```

and asked

```
?- person(X).,
```

Prolog would first use the rule, and generate the subgoal **person(Y)**. In trying to satisfy this, it would again pick the rule first, and generate yet another equivalent goal. And so it would go on and on, until it ran out of space. Of course, if it had a chance to backtrack, it would find the fact about Adam and start producing solutions. The trouble is, that in order to backtrack, Prolog has to have failed after trying the first possibility. In this case, the task that it finds is infinitely long, and so it never gets a chance to succeed or fail. So the moral is:

> Don't assume that, just because you have provided all the relevant facts and rules, Prolog will always find them. You must bear in mind when you write Prolog programs how Prolog searches through the database and what variables will be instantiated when one of your rules is used.

In this example, the simple solution is just to put the fact before the rule, instead of after it. In fact, as a general heuristic, it is a good idea to put facts before rules whenever possible. Sometimes putting the rules in a particular order will work if they are used to solve goals of one form but will not if goals of another form are generated. Consider the following definition of **islist(X)**, in which the predicate **islist** succeeds if X is a list ending in the empty list:

```
islist([A|B]) :- islist(B).
```

48

```
islist([]).
```

If we use these rules to answer questions like:

```
?- islist([a,b,c,d]).
?- islist([]).
?- islist(f(1,2,3)).
```

then the definition will work fine. But when we ask:

→ X will never find an instantiation

```
?- islist(X).
```

the program will loop.

A better definition of **islist** that is not susceptable to loops is provided by the following two facts:

```
islist([]).
islist([_|_]).
```

3.4 Example: Changing a Sentence into another

Let us consider a Prolog program in which we type an English sentence and Prolog replies with another sentence that is an altered version of the one we typed in. This program for "talking back" to the programmer might produce a dialogue like this:

```
You:       you are a computer
Prolog:    i am not a computer
You:       do you speak french
Prolog:    no i speak german
```

Although this dialogue may seem like a forced but sensible conversation, it is very easy to write a computer program to carry out its "part" of the dialogue simply by following these steps:

1. Accept a sentence that is typed in by the programmer.

2. If there are any "you"s in the sentence, change them to "i"s.

3. Likewise, change any "are"s to "am not"s.

4. Change "french" to "german"

5. Change "do" to "no".

When applied to carefully chosen sentences, such as those in the above dialogue, this scheme will produce a sensible altered sentence. However, it does not work on every sentence, for example:

```
You:       i do like you
Prolog:    i no like i
```

Once a simple program is written, it can be modified later to cope with sentences like this that produce awkward output.

A Prolog program to change one sentence into another can be written as follows. First, we need to recognise that there is a relationship between the original sentence and the altered sentence. So, we need to define a Prolog predicate, called **alter**, such that **alter(X,Y)** means that sentence X can be altered to give sentence Y. It is convenient for X and Y to be lists, with atoms standing for the words, so sentences can be written like this: **[this,is,a,sentence]**. Once **alter** is defined, we could ask Prolog a question of the form

```
?- alter([do,you,know,french],X).
```

and Prolog would reply

```
X=[no,i,know,german].
```

Don't be concerned yet that the input and output sentences are not tidy, and do not look like normal sentences. In later chapters we will discuss ways of typing in and printing out structures in a way that is easy to read. For the moment we will only worry about changing one list into another.

Since **alter** deals with lists, the first fact about **alter** needs to deal with what happens if the list is empty. In this case, we will say that an empty list is altered into an empty list:

```
alter([],[]).
```

Or, in words, "it is a fact that altering the empty list gives the empty list." If the reason for treating the empty list is not apparent now, it should be clearer later.

Next, we need to recognise that the main job of **alter** is to:

1. Change the head of the input list into another word, and let the head of the output list stand for that word.

2. "alter" the tail of the input list, and let the tail of the output list stand for the altered

tail.

3. If we have reached the end of the input list, then there is nothing more to go onto the output list, so we can terminate the output list with an empty list ([]).

Translated into words that are closer to Prolog:

> "altering a list with head H and tail T gives a list with head X and tail Y if:
>> changing word H gives word X, and
>> altering the list T gives the list Y".

Now we need to say what is meant by "changing" one word into another. This can be done by having a database of facts in which change(X,Y) means word X can be changed into word Y. At the end of the database we need a "catchall" fact, because if a word is not changed into another word it needs to be changed into itself. If the reason for a "catchall" is not apparent now, it should be clearer after we explain how the program works. The relevant fact is change(X,X), which means word X is changed into itself. A database to handle the changes listed above is:

```
        .
        .
        .
change(you,i).
change(are,[am,not]).
change(french,german).
change(do,no).
change(X,X).        /* this is the "catchall" */
```

Notice that we have treated the phrase "am not" as a list, so that it occupies only one argument of the fact.

Now we can translate the pseudo-Prolog text above into pure Prolog, remembering the notation [A|B] for "the list with head A and tail B". We get something like this:

```
alter([],[]).
alter([H|T],[X|Y]) :-
                change(H,X),
                alter(T,Y).
```

The first rule in this procedure checks for an empty list. The same rule also checks for the *end* of the list as well. Why? Consider this worked example:

```
?- alter([you,are,a,computer],Z).
```

This question would match with the main alter rule, making variable H stand for 'you', and variable T stand for [are,a,computer]. Next, the goal change(you,X) would succeed, setting X to stand for the word 'i'. As X is the head of the output list (in the goal of alter), the first word in the output list is 'i'. Next, the goal **alter([are,a,computer],Y)** would use the same rule. The word 'are' is changed into the list **[am,not]** by the database, and another **alter** goal is generated -- **alter([a,computer],Y)**. The fact **change(a,X)** is searched for, but as there is no **change** fact with 'a' as its first argument, the catchall fact at the bottom of the database succeeds, changing 'a' into 'a'. The **alter** rule is called for once again, with 'computer' as the head of the input list, and the *empty list* as the tail of the input list. As previously, **change(computer,X)** matches against the catchall. Finally, **alter** is called with the empty list, which matches against the very first **alter** rule. The result is the empty list, which ends the sentence (remember that a list ends with an empty tail). Finally, Prolog answers the question by responding

but it is invisible here

    Z=[i,[am,not],a,computer]

Notice that the phrase [am,not] appears in the list exactly as it was inserted.

The reasons for adding the fact **alter([],[])** and the catchall fact **change(X,X)** should now be clear. These facts are often included in a program when it is desirable to check for *boundary conditions*. It should be clear from the explanation above that boundary conditions occur when the input list becomes the empty list, and when all of the **change** facts have been searched through. In both of these boundary conditions, we wish certain actions to be performed. When the input list becomes the empty list, we wish to terminate the output list (by putting an empty list at its end). When all the **change** facts have been searched though without the given word being changed into another word, we wish to keep the word unchanged (by changing it into itself).

3.5 Example: Comparing Alphabetic Order

As we saw in Chapter 2, there are predicates provided to compare integers, to see if, say, one integer is greater than another. In applications dealing with words, such as using dictionaries, it is helpful to have a predicate to compare *words* for alphabetic order. Depending on which computer you are using, the built-in operators for comparing integers also compare the alphabetic order of atoms. However, in case the version of Prolog you are using does not, and also for tutorial reasons, we shall write a predicate that compares alphabetic order of atoms.

Consider a predicate we shall name **aless**. When **aless(X,Y)** is used as a goal, it will succeed if X and Y stand for atoms, and X is alphabetically less than Y. So, **aless(avocado, clergyman)** would succeed, and **aless(windmill, motorcar)** would fail. Also, **aless(picture,picture)** should fail. When comparing two words, we compare them letter-by-letter and, for each comparison, determine which of the following conditions is at

52

hand:

(1) We could reach the end of the first word without reaching the end of the second word. This happens when we try **aless(book, bookbinder)**. In this case, **aless** must succeed.

(2) We could find that the character in the first word was alphabetically less than the corresponding character in the second word. For example, with **aless(elephant,pencil)**, The 'e' of elephant is alphabetically less than the 'p' of pencil. In this case, **aless** succeeds.

(3) We could find that the character in the first word was alphabetically equal to the corresponding character in the second word. In this case, we need to try **aless** on the *remaining characters* in both words. For example, given **aless(lazy,leather)**, the 'l' is the same at the beginning of both arguments, so we would need to try **aless(azy,eather)**.

(4) We could find that we reach the end of the first and second words at the same time. This would happen if we tried **aless(apple,apple)**. In this case, **aless** must fail, because the two words are the same.

(5) We could run out of characters in the second word before running out of characters in the first word, such as in **aless(alphabetic,alp)**. In this case, **aless** must fail.

Once we have discovered the above conditions, it is a fairly simple task to translate them into Prolog. We shall represent words as lists of characters (small integers), so there must be a way to convert a Prolog atom into a list of characters. This is the purpose of the built-in predicate **name**. The goal **name(X,Y)** succeeds when the atom instantiated for X consists of the list of character codes (the ASCII codes) instantiated for Y. Refer to Chapter 2 for an explanation of ASCII codes. If one of the arguments is uninstantiated, then Prolog will attempt to instantiate it by creating the appropriate structure. So, we can use **name** to convert from words into the list of characters. For example, knowing that the ASCII code for 'a' is 97, 'l' is 108 and 'p' is 112, the following questions could be asked of **name**:

```
?- name(X,[97,108,112]).

X = alp

?- name(alp,X).

X = [97,108,112]
```

A first attempt at **aless** is

```
aless(X,Y) :- name(X,L), name(Y,M), alessx(L,M).
```

We have simply converted the words into lists using **name**, and used a predicate (not defined yet) for checking the lists for alphabetic order. Now we need to define **alessx**, using the set of conditions above. The first condition is true when the first argument is the empty list, and the second argument is any non-empty list:

```
alessx([],[_|_]).
```

The second condition is translated as:

```
alessx([X|_],[Y|_]) :- X < Y.
```

Remember that the arguments of <u>**alessx** are lists of numbers</u>, so it is permitted to compare them using the "<" functor. The third condition is translated as:

```
alessx([A|X],[B|Y]) :- A = B, alessx(X,Y).
```

Finally, the last two conditions are what make the predicate fail, so if we do not supply any matching facts or rules, then the searching mechanism will fail any goal for which those conditions hold.

Gathering the rules together,

```
aless(X,Y) :- name(X,L), name(Y,M), alessx(L,M).

alessx([],[_|_]).
alessx([X|_],[Y|_]) :-  X < Y.
alessx([P|Q],[R|S]) :-  P = R, alessx(Q,S).
```

Notice that the third rule could be written more conveniently as:

```
alessx([H|X],[H|Y]) :-  alessx(X,Y).
```

In the above examples, some variables are renamed simply to emphasise that the names do not matter except within the scope of the same rule.

Exercise 3.1: Work out what clause you need to add to this definition so that it succeeds when the two words are equal. This would create a predicate that checks if the first argument is alphabetically less than or equal to the second argument. Hint: look at condition (4) above, and insert a clause to handle it. *alessx([],[])*

Exercise 3.2: Why does the first rule of **alessx** have [_|_]? Why is [_] insufficient for the

Could this me nil?
Yes, when _ cannot find an instantiation.

purpose?

3.6 Example: A Parts Inventory

Suppose we work in a bicycle factory, where it is necessary to keep an inventory of bicycle parts. If we want to build a bicycle, we need to know how many parts to draw from the supplies. Each part of the bicycle may have sub-parts, for example each wheel has some spokes, a rim, and a hub. Furthermore, the hub can consist of an axle and gears. Let us consider a tree-structured database that will enable us to ask questions about how many of each part is required to build a part of a bicycle. Later, we shall see that the same data structures and programs enable us to manipulate not only parts of bicycles, but parts of sentences as well!

There are two kinds of parts that we use to build our bicycle. These are *assemblies* and *basic parts*. Each *assembly* consists of a quantity of basic parts, such as the wheel consisting of several spokes, a rim, and a hub. *Basic parts* are not made up of any smaller parts -- they simply combine with other basic parts to form assemblies.

We can represent basic parts simply as facts, as follows:

```
basicpart(rim).        basicpart(spoke).
basicpart(rearframe).  basicpart(handles).
basicpart(gears).      basicpart(bolt).
basicpart(nut).        basicpart(fork).
```

Naturally, this is not a complete list of the basic parts required for a bicycle, but it shows the general idea. Next, an assembly can be represented as the name of the assembly followed by a list of the basic parts, and the quantity of parts required. For example, the following fact represents that a "bike" is an assembly made up of two wheels and a frame:'

```
assembly(bike,[quant(wheel,2), quant(frame,1)]).
```

The quant structure is used to associate a part with how many of the parts are required. The database of assemblies required for our simplified bicycle is:

```
assembly(bike,[quant(wheel,2), quant(frame,1)]).
assembly(wheel,[quant(spoke,20), quant(rim,1), quant(hub,1)]).
assembly(frame,[quant(rearframe,1),quant(frontframe,1)]).
assembly(frontframe,[quant(fork,1),quant(handles,1)]).
assembly(hub,[quant(gears,1),quant(axle,1)]).
assembly(axle,[quant(bolt,1),quant(nut,2)]).
```

Notice that this particular set of clauses does not perfectly describe a bicycle. We have not distinguished between the front hub and the rear hub -- both have gears! The chain and pedals are missing, and there is no place for the rider to sit. Also, there is no indication of how to fit the parts together. This simply lists a few of the parts required, and the number of each.

Now we are ready to write the program that, given a part, will list all the basic parts required to construct it. If the part we want to construct is a basic part, then nothing more is required. However, if we want to construct an assembly, then we need to apply the same process to each part making up the assembly. Let us define a predicate **partsof(X,Y)**, where X is the name of a part, and Y is the list of basic parts that are required to construct X. In our first version of this program, we shall ignore how many of each kind of part are required to form assemblies. A better program will be presented in Chapter 7.

The boundary condition occurs when X is a basic part. In this case, we simply return X in a list:

```
partsof(X,[X]) :- basicpart(X).
```

The next condition is if X is an assembly. In this case, we need to find out if there is a matching **assembly** fact in the database, and if so, to use **partsof** on each member of the list of sub-parts. We shall use a predicate called **partsoflist** to handle this second task.

```
partsof(X,P) :-
            assembly(X,Subparts),
            partsoflist(Subparts,P).
```

Now **partsoflist** takes a list of **quant** structures (see the **assembly** database above), and finds the **partsof** of the first component of the **quant** structure. The second component of **quant**, the actual quantity of parts required, will be ignored for now. After calling itself to get the **partsof** for the tail of the list, **partsoflist** must glue the lists together with **append** (described below):

```
partsoflist([quant(X,N) | Tail], Total)  :-
            partsof(X,Headparts),
            partsoflist(Tail,Tailparts),
            append(Headparts,Tailparts,Total).
```

Notice that N, the number of parts required, is not used. It could be replaced by an anonymous variable.

The list processing predicate **append** is used to join two lists together to form another, new, list. For example, it is true that

```
append([a,b,c],[3,2,1],[a,b,c,3,2,1]).
```

It is defined as follows:

```
append([],L,L).
```

```
append([X|L1],L2,[X|L3]) :- append(L1,L2,L3).
```

The boundary condition is when the first list is the empty list. In this case, any list appended to the empty list is the same list. Otherwise, the following points show the principles of the second rule:

append

1. The first element of the first list (X) will always be the first element of the third list.

2. The tail of the first list (L1) will always have the second argument (L2) appended to it to form the tail (L3) of the third argument.

3. You actually have to use **append** to do the appending mentioned in point (2).

4. As we are continually taking the head from the remainder of the first argument, it will gradually be reduced to the empty list, so the boundary condition will occur.

We will refer to **append** in later examples, so it is worth getting to know it now. In later chapters we will discuss various properties of the **append** predicate.

The list which is constructed by **partsof** will not contain information about how many parts are required, and duplicate parts may appear in the list. In Chapter 7, we shall present an improved version of this program that handles these deficiencies.

There are two insights that indicate how **partsof** can be used to generate English sentences. First, sentences can be decomposed into hierarchical structures: a sentence has parts noun_phrase and verb_phrase, a noun_phrase has parts determiner and noun, and so forth. So, any simple grammar can be expressed in terms of "parts". Second, **partsoflist** always looks at the elements of its first argument from left to right, and its result is appended together in left-to-right order. These two properties of **partsof** show that we can use the same framework to generate sentences from a grammar. We can continue to use the **quant** structure, but remember its second argument does not mean anything. A typical "assembly" for a grammar might look like this:

```
assembly(sentence,[quant(noun_phrase,_), quant(verb_phrase,_)]).
assembly(noun_phrase, [quant(determiner,_), quant(noun,_)]).
assembly(determiner, [quant(the,_)]).
assembly(noun, [quant(clergyman,_)]).
assembly(noun, [quant(motorcar,_)]).
        .
        .
        .
```

And the words in the lexicon would be defined as basic parts:

```
basicpart(the).
```

```
basicpart(clergyman).
basicpart(motorcar).
    .
    .
    .
```

At this point you may wish to rewrite **partsoflist** to handle grammars. The **quant** structure could be discarded if you like. You should provide a reasonable grammar and a vocabulary. Satisfy yourself that this modified program will produce all possible grammatical sentences from the grammar and vocabulary you provide. As always, Prolog will stop at each solution, and wait for you to type a semicolon to tell it to backtrack to the next solution.

This is certainly not the last word on processing English language in this book. The whole of Chapter 9 is devoted to a more sophisticated treatment of analysing English language in Prolog.

Chapter 4. Backtracking and "Cut"

Let us summarise what we learned in Chapters 1 and 2 about what can happen to a goal:

1. An attempt can be made to *satisfy* a goal. When we satisfy a goal, we search the database from the top. Two things can happen:

    (a) A matching fact (or rule head) can be found. In this case, we say the goal has been *matched.* We mark the place in the database, and instantiate any previously uninstantiated variables that have matched. If we matched against a rule, we shall first have to attempt to satisfy the rule. If the goal succeeds, we then attempt to satisfy the next goal on the right.

    (b) No matching fact (or rule head) can be found. In this case, we say the goal has *failed.* We then attempt to *re-satisfy* the next goal on the *left.* This is what we mean by "going back" to a previous goal.

2. We can attempt to *re-satisfy* a goal. In this case, we must return to uninstantiated any variables that became instantiated when this goal was previously satisfied. This is what we mean by "undoing" all the work previously done by this goal. Next, we resume searching the database, but we begin the search from where the goal's place-marker was previously put. As before, this new "backtracked" goal may either succeed or fail, and either step (a) and (b) above would occur.

This chapter will look at backtracking in more detail. It will also look at a special mechanism that can be used in Prolog programs -- the "cut". The cut allows you to tell Prolog which previous choices it need not consider again.

4.1 Generating Multiple Solutions

The simplest way a set of facts can allow multiple solutions to a question is when there are several facts that will match against the question. For instance, if we have the following facts in which **father(X,Y)** means that the father of X is Y:

```
father(mary,george).
father(john,george).
father(sue,harry).
father(george,edward).
```

The question

```
?- father(X,Y).
```

will have several possible answers. If we prompt with a semicolon, Prolog will give us the following:

```
X=mary, Y=george;
X=john, Y=george;
X=sue, Y=harry;
X=george, Y=edward
```

It finds these answers by searching through the database to find the facts and rule about **father** in the order in which they were given. Prolog is not particularly clever about this -- it does not remember anything about what it has shown before. So if we ask

```
?- father(_,X).
```

(for which X is X a father?)

we will get:

```
X=george;
X=george;
X=harry;
X=edward
```

with **george** repeated twice because George is the father of both Mary and John. If Prolog has two ways of showing the same thing, it treats them as two different solutions.

Backtracking happens in exactly the same way if the alternatives are embedded more deeply in the processing. For example, one rule in a definition of "one of the children of X is Y" might be

```
child(X,Y) :- father(Y,X).
```

Then, the question

```
?- child(X,Y).
```

would give

```
X=george, Y=mary;
X=george, Y=john;
X=harry, Y=sue;
X=edward, Y=george
```

Because **father(Y,X)** has four solutions, so does **child(X,Y)**. Moreover, the solutions are generated in the same order. All that is different is that the order of the arguments is different, as is specified in the definition of **child**. Similarly, if we defined

```
father(X) :- father(_,X).
```

("father(X)" meaning that X is a father) then the question

```
?- father(X).
```

would evoke:

```
X=george;
X=george;
X=harry;
X=edward
```

If we mix facts and rules, the alternatives follow again in the order in which things are presented. Thus we might define:

```
person(adam).
person(X) :- mother(X,Y).
person(eve).

mother(cain,eve).
mother(abel,eve).
mother(jabal,adah).
mother(tubalcain,zillah).
```

(Adam is a person, anything is a person if it has a mother, and Eve is a person. Also, various people have various mothers). In this case, if we asked the question

```
?- person(X).
```

the answers would be:

```
X=adam;
X=cain;
X=abel;
```

```
X=jabal;
X=tubalcain;
X=eve
```

Let us look now at a more interesting case -- where there are two goals each of which has several solutions. Let us imagine we are planning a party and want to speculate about who might dance with whom. We can start writing a program as follows:

```
possible_pair(X,Y) :- boy(X), girl(Y).

boy(john).
boy(marmaduke).
boy(bertram).
boy(charles).

girl(griselda).
girl(ermintrude).
girl(brunhilde).
```

(This is not yet a perfectly balanced party!). This program says that X and Y form a possible pair if X is a boy and Y is a girl. Now let's see what possible pairs there are:

```
?- possible_pair(X,Y).

X = john, Y = griselda;
X = john, Y = ermintrude;
X = john, Y = brunhilde;
X = marmaduke, Y = griselda;
X = marmaduke, Y = ermintrude;
X = marmaduke, Y = brunhilde;
X = bertram, Y = griselda;
X = bertram, Y = ermintrude;
X = bertram, Y = brunhilde;
X = charles, Y = griselda;
X = charles, Y = ermintrude;
X = charles, Y = brunhilde
```

You should make sure that you understand why Prolog produces the solutions in this order. First of all, it satisfies the goal **boy(X)**, finding John, the first boy. Then it satisfies **girl(Y)**, finding Griselda, the first girl. At this point, we ask for another solution by causing a failure. Prolog attempts to resatisfy what it did last, which is the **girl** goal within the satisfaction of the **possible_pair** goal. It finds the alternative girl Ermintrude, and so the second solution is John and Ermintrude. Similarly, it generates John and Brunhilde as the third solution. The next time it tries to resatisfy **girl(Y)**, Prolog finds that its placemarker is at the end of the database, and so the goal fails. Now it tries to resatisfy **boy(X)**. The placemarker for this was placed at the first fact for **boy**, and so the next solution found is the second boy (Marmaduke). Now that it has resatisfied this goal, Prolog looks to see what is next -- it must now satisfy **girl(Y)** from the start again. So it finds Griselda, the first girl. The next three solutions now involve Marmaduke and the three girls. Next time we ask for an alternative, the **girl** goal cannot be resatisfied again. So another boy is found, and the search through girls starts again from scratch. And so on. Eventually, the **girl** goal fails and there are also no more solutions to the **boy** goal either. So the program can find no more pairs.

These examples are all very simple. They just involve the specification of many facts or the use of rules to access those facts. Because of this, they can only generate a finite number of possible solutions. Sometimes we might want to generate an infinite number of possibilities -- not because we want to consider them all, but because we may not know in advance how many we need. In this case, we need a definition that is *recursive*, that is, a definition that directly or indirectly appeals to itself. Consider the following definition of what it is to be an integer (where by "integer" we mean a whole number not less than 0). The goal **is_integer(N)** will succeed providing N is instantiated to an integer. If N is not instantiated at the time the goal is considered, then an **is_integer(N)** will cause an integer to be chosen, and N will be instantiated to it:

```
/* 1 */   is_integer(0).
/* 2 */   is_integer(X) :- is_integer(Y), X is Y+1.
```

If we ask the question

```
?- is_integer(X).
```

we will get as the possible answers all the integers in ascending order (0, 1, 2, 3, ...), one at a time. Each time we force backtracking to occur (perhaps by typing semicolon), **is_integer** will succeed with its argument instantiated to a new integer. So this short definition generates an infinite number of answers (actually, only as many as will fit into the computer). Why? Here is the sequence of events that leads to the first three solutions:

First solution:

```
→Goal is_integer(X)            - decided to use fact 1
  Succeeds with X=0
```

Second solution:

```
⌈ Goal is_integer(X)           - decided to use rule 2
│ X here is X in use of rule
│   →Goal is_integer(Y)        - decided to use fact 1
│     Succeeds with Y=0
│     Goal X is Y+1            - used built-in definition
│     Succeeds with X=1
⌊ Succeeds with X=1
```

Third solution:

```
⌈ Goal is_integer(X)           - decided to use rule 2
│ X here is X in use of rule
```

```
|  ⌈ Goal is_integer(Y)        - decided to use rule 2
|  | Y here is X in use of rule
|  |   →Goal is_integer(Y)     - decided to use fact 1
|  |    Succeeds with Y=0
|  |    Goal X is Y+1          - used built-in definition
|  |    Succeeds with X=1
|  ⌊ Succeeds with Y=1
|    Goal X is Y+1
|    Succeeds with X=2
⌊ Succeeds with X=2
```

and so on.   At each stage, the point marked with a '→' is where *another choice* will be made when backtracking occurs next.   So it is only the things after the '→' that change from one solution to the next.   If we miss out the variables, the choices involved can be conveniently displayed in a tree.   If we use fact 1 to solve an **is_integer** goal, no more goals are generated. However, if we use fact 2, another **is_integer** goal is created, and we then have to make the same choice for that.   According to the sequences of choices we make, different final answers are produced.

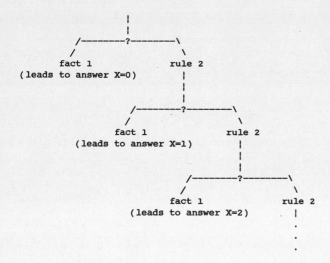

Initially, we have a choice between fact 1 and rule 2 to answer the question.   If we choose fact 1, no more choices have to be made, and we get X=0.   Otherwise we choose rule 2 and have a choice how to satisfy the goal it introduces.   If we choose fact 1, we end up with the answer X=1; otherwise we use rule 2 and must again choose how to satisfy the subgoal produced.   And so on.   At each stage, the first thing Prolog does is to pick fact 1.   Only on backtracking does it undo the last choice.   Each time it does this, it goes back to where it last chose fact 1, and instead chooses rule 2.   Once it has decided to use rule 2, a new subgoal is introduced.   Fact 1 is the first possibility for satisfying it.

Most Prolog rules will give rise to alternative solutions if they are used for goals that contain a lot of uninstantiated variables. For instance, the relation of membership of a list:

```
member(X,[X|_]).
member(X,[_|Y]) :- member(X,Y).
```

will generate alternatives. If we ask

```
?- member(a,X).
```

(notice X in the question is uninstantiated) then the successive values of X will be partially-defined lists where 'a' is the first, second, third, ... member. See if you can see why this is. A further result of allowing this definition of **member** to backtrack is that the question

```
member(a,[a,b,r,a,c,a,d,a,b,r,a]).
```

actually can succeed *five times* Clearly, there are some applications of **member** where we only need it to succeed once, if at all, and then discard the other four choices. We can tell Prolog to discard choices in this way by using the "cut".

4.2 The "Cut"

This section looks at a special mechanism that can be used in Prolog programs -- the "cut". The "cut" allows you to tell Prolog which previous choices it need not consider again when it backtracks though the chain of satisfied goals. There are two reasons why it may be important to do this:

□ your program will operate faster because it will not waste time attempting to satisfy goals that you can tell beforehand will never contribute to a solution;

□ your program may occupy less of the computer's memory space because more economical use of memory can be made if backtracking points do not have to be recorded for later examination.

In some cases, including a "cut" may mean the difference between a program that will run and a program that will not.

Syntactically, a use of "cut" in a rule looks just like the appearance of a goal which has the predicate ! and no arguments. As a goal, this succeeds immediately and cannot be resatisfied. However, it also has side-effects which alter the way backtracking works afterwards. The effect is to remove the place markers for certain goals so that they cannot be resatisfied. Let us see how this works in an example. The following is part of a program to construct a 'plan' for building a house in London. The 'plan' will be a list of structures representing the actions to be performed. There are two main possibilities -- one can get an outside builder to do the job or one can do the building oneself. In the first case, the first action to be performed is to contact the builder. The builder mentioned in the 'plan' can be either a builder who is located in London, or just any builder.

```
/* 1 */    house_build(Plan) :- outside_build(Plan).
/* 2 */    house_build(Plan) :- build(self,Plan).

/* 3 */    outside_build([contact(B)|Plan1]) :-
                builder(B), loc(B,london), !,
                build(B,Plan1).
/* 4 */    outside_build([contact(B)|Plan1]) :-
                builder(B), build(B,Plan1).

/* 5 */    builder('Rousseau & Co').
/* 6 */    builder('D Morgan').
    .
    .
    .
/* 28 */   loc('Eiffel Tower',paris).
/* 29 */   loc('Rousseau & Co',paris).
/* 30 */   loc('D Morgan',london).
    .
    .
    .
/* 50 */   build(Builder,Plan) :-
    .
    .
    .
```

(handwritten note: ← When cut succeeds this one will never be tried even because if only 3 is failed then we can try 4 by backtracking yet 3 has been fixed by cut!)

Let us see what is the effect of the cut if we ask the question ?- **house_build(X)**. Let us look at the chronological sequence of events that will have taken place shortly after the 'cut' goal is satisfied. Up to this stage, a small amount of backtracking will have taken place in the process of finding a builder who is located in London. In summary, **house_build(X)** attempts to satisfy **outside_build(Plan)** (clause 1) causing clause 3 to be investigated. The first **builder** found is Rousseau & Co., but **loc(B,london)** fails because Rousseau & Co. are located in Paris (clause 29). An attempt is made to re-satisfy **builder(B),** and it succeeds, finding D. Morgan. The **loc(B,london)** goal now succeeds, because Morgan is located in London (clause 30). The next goal is the "cut". The cut succeeds, but the effect is to "freeze" all of the decisions made since clause 3 was entered. Here is a trace of the goals satisfied so far, with the "frozen" goals indicated. For the sake of simplicity, we have not indicated all the variable values:

```
┌ Goal house_build(X)                       - decided to use rule 1
│                                +---------
│  ┌ Goal outside_build          F |- decided to use rule 3
│  │    Goal builder(B)          R |- decided to use fact 6
│  │    Succeeds                 O |
│  │    Goal loc('D Morgan',london)Z |- decided to use fact 30
│  │    Succeeds                 E |
│  │    Goal !                   N |-  built-in definition
│  │    Succeeds                   +---------
│  │    Goal build('D Morgan',Plan1)  - decided to use rule 50
```

The effect of the "cut" in the **outside_build** rule (clause 3) is to *commit the system to every decision it has made since it chose that rule.* It does this by removing the place markers from the goals between the **outside_build** goal and the cut goal. Thus, any attempt to re-satisfy these goals will fail. If backtracking subsequently takes place (because the **build** goal fails), the system will not consider alternative solutions for the goals **loc('D Morgan',london)** or **builder(B)**. Neither will it consider the second rule for **outside_build**, because the choice of the rule that the cut appears in is included in those frozen by the cut. The effect of the cut in this example is to say:

> *If, given your first choice of a builder located in London, it is not possible to create a plan for that builder to build the house, abandon the idea of getting an outside builder at all.*

In this example, the "freezing effect" of the cut went back as far as the **outside_build** goal. This is called the *parent* goal of the cut goal, because it was the goal that caused the use of the rule containing the cut. The formal definition of the effect of the cut symbol is as follows:

> *When a cut is encountered as a goal, the system thereupon becomes committed to all choices made since the parent goal was invoked. All other alternatives are discarded. Hence an attempt to resatisfy any goal between the parent goal and the cut ('I') goal will fail.*

There are several ways of describing what has happened to the choices that are affected by a cut. One can say that the choices are cut or frozen, that the system commits itself to the choices made or that the alternatives are discarded. One can also look at the cut symbol as being rather like a fence that separates goals. In this conjunction of goals,

```
foo :- a, b, c, !, d, e, f.
```

Prolog will quite happily backtrack among goals a, b, and c, *until* the success of c causes the "fence" to be crossed to the right to reach goal d. Then, backtracking can occur among d, e, and f, perhaps satisfying the entire conjunction several times. However, if d fails, causing the "fence" to be crossed to the left, then no attempt will be made to resatisfy goal c: the entire conjunction of goals will fail, and the goal **foo** will also fail.

One further note before we go on to see more examples of the cut in use. We have said that if the cut appears in some rule and the cut goal is satisfied then Prolog becomes committed to *all choices made since the parent goal was invoked.* This means that the choice of that rule, and all other choices made since then, become fixed. We will see later that it is possible to provide alternatives *within a single rule* using the built-in predicate ; ("or"). The choices introduced by this facility are affected in exactly the same way. That is, when a cut goal is satisfied, all "or" choices that have been made since the rule was chosen are fixed.

4.3 Common Uses of the Cut

We can divide the common uses of "cut" into three main areas:

☐ The first concerns places where we want to tell the Prolog system that it has found the right rule for a particular goal. Here, the cut says "if you get this far, you have picked the correct rule for this goal".

☐ The second concerns places where we want to tell the Prolog system to fail a particular goal immediately without trying for alternative solutions. Here, we use the cut in conjunction with the `fail` predicate to say "if you get to here, you should stop trying to satisfy this goal".

☐ The third concerns places where we want to terminate the generation of alternative solutions through backtracking. Here, the cut says "if you get to here, you have found the only solution to this problem, and there is no point in ever looking for alternatives".

We will now look at some examples of these three uses. You should bear in mind, however, that the cut has a *single* meaning in all these applications. The division into three main areas of use is purely for tutorial reasons, and to show what kinds of reasons you might have for putting cuts into your programs.

4.3.1 Confirming the Choice of a Rule

Very often in a Prolog program, we wish to associate several clauses with the same predicate. One clause will be appropriate if the arguments are of one form, another will be appropriate if the arguments are of another form, and so on. Often we can specify which rule should be used for a given goal by providing patterns in the rule heads that will only match goals of the right types. However, this may not always be possible. If we cannot tell in advance what forms the arguments may take, or if we cannot specify an exhaustive set of patterns, we may have to compromise. This means giving rules for some specific argument types and then giving a "catchall" rule at the end for everything else. As an example of this, consider the following program. The rules define the predicate **sum_to** such that giving Prolog the goal **sum_to(N,X)** with N having an integer value, causes X to be instantiated to the sum of the numbers from 1 to N. Thus, for instance, it produces the following:

```
?- sum_to(5,X).

X = 15;
no
```

because 1+2+3+4+5 is 15. Here is the program.

```
sum_to(1,1) :- !.
sum_to(N,Res) :-
    N1 is N-1,
    sum_to(N1,Res1),
    Res is Res1+N.
```

not complete if N ≤ 0

This is a recursive definition. The idea is that the boundary condition occurs when the first number is 1. In that case, the answer is also 1. The second clause introduces a recursive **sum_to** goal. However, the first number of the new goal is one less than the original one. The new goal that this goal will invoke will have its first argument one less again. And so on until the boundary condition is reached. Since the first arguments are always getting less, the boundary condition must be reached eventually (assuming that the original goal has a first argument not less than 1), and the program will terminate.

The interesting thing about this program is how we have handled the two cases -- when the number is 1, and when it is something else. When we defined predicates that talked about lists, it was easy to specify the two cases that would normally arise -- when the list was [] and when it was of the form [A|B]. With numbers, things are not so easy, because we cannot specify a pattern that will only match an integer not equal to 1. The solution adopted in this example is to provide a pattern for the '1' case and just to leave a variable to match against anything else. We know from the way Prolog searches through the database that it will try to match the number against 1 first and will only try the second rule if this fails. So the second rule should only be used for numbers not equal to 1. However, this is not the whole story. If Prolog ever backtracks and comes to reconsider the choice of rule when applied to the number 1, it will find that the second rule is applicable. As far as it can see, both rules provide alternatives for the goal **sum_to(1,X)**. We must tell it that on no account is the second rule ever to be tried if the number is 1. One way of doing this is to put a "cut" in the first rule (as shown). This tells Prolog that, once it has got this far in the first rule, it must never remake the decision about which rule to use for the **sum_to** goal. It will only get this far if the number is in fact 1.

Let us see what this looks like in terms of the chronology of the goals. If we call **sum_to(1,X).** in the context:

```
go :- sum_to(1,X), foo(apples).

?- go.
```

and the goal **foo(apples)** fails, then at the point of failure we will have:

```
┌ Goal go                          - decided to use 1st rule
│                                  +------------------------------->
│  ┌ Goal sum_to(1,X)         │    - decided to use 1st rule
│  │    Goal !        FROZEN │    - used built-in definition
│  │    Succeeds             │
│  │      (with X=1)         │    +------------------------------->
│  └ Goal foo(apples)              - used some other clauses
│    .......
│    FAIL!!!
```

When Prolog tries to resatisfy the goals in reverse order, it will find that two of the goals cannot be resatisfied because any choices are frozen. Hence it will correctly avoid trying alternative ways of satisfying **sum_to(1,X)**.

Exercise 4.1: What happens if the "cut" is left out here and backtracking gets round to reconsidering the **sum_to** goal? What alternative results, if any, are produced, and why?

The last example showed how "cut" can be used to make Prolog behave sensibly when we cannot distinguish between all the possible cases by specifying patterns in the heads of the rules. A more usual situation in which we cannot specify patterns to decide which rule to use arises when we want to provide extra conditions, in the form of Prolog goals, which will decide on the appropriate rule. Consider the following alternative form of the above example:

```
sum_to(N,1) :- N =< 1, !.
sum_to(N,R) :- N1 is N-1, sum_to(N1,R1), R is R1+N.
```

In this case, we say that the first rule is the one to choose if the number provided is less than or equal to one. This is slightly better than the previous formulation, because it means that the program produces an answer (rather than running on indefinitely) if the first argument is given as 0 or a negative number. If the condition is true, the result 1 can be produced immediately, and no more recursive goals are necessary. Only if the condition is not true do we want ever to try the second rule. We must tell Prolog that once it has proved N =< 1, it must never reconsider the choice about what rule to choose. This is what the cut does.

It is a general principle that uses of cut to tell Prolog when it has picked the only correct rule can be replaced by uses of **not**. This is a Prolog built-in predicate, which means that its definition is already provided when you start your Prolog session. So you can use it in your own programs without having to write down a definition each time (built-in predicates are described more fully in Chapter 6). **not** is defined in such a way that the goal **not(X)** succeeds only if X, when seen as a Prolog goal, fails. So **not(X)** means that *X is not satisfiable as a Prolog goal.* As an example of replacing cuts with uses of **not**, the two

"Not" is used to replace "!".

but less efficient.

possibilities given for the **sum_to** definition can be rewritten as:

```
sum_to(1,1).
sum_to(N,R) :- not(N=1), N1 is N-1, sum_to(N1,R1), R is N1+R1.

sum_to(N,1) :- N =< 1.
sum_to(N,R) :- not(N=<1), N1 is N-1, sum_to(N1,R1), R is N1+R1.
```

In fact, Prolog provides suitable evaluable predicates to substitute for both of these uses. For example, we can replace **not(N=1)** by **N\=1**, and **not(N=<1)** by **N>1**. In general, we will not be able to do this with all the conditions we dream up.

It is good programming style to replace cuts by the use of **not**. This is because programs containing cuts are in general harder to read than programs not containing them. If one can localise all occurrences of cut to inside the definition of **not**, then the program will be easier to understand. However, the definition of **not** involves trying to show that the goal it is given can be satisfied. Therefore, if we have a program of the general form:

```
A :- B, C.
A :- not(B), D.
```

Prolog may well end up trying to satisfy B twice. It will have to try and satisfy B when it looks at the first rule. Also, if it ever backtracks and considers the second rule, it will have to try and satisfy B again to see if **not(B)** can be satisfied. This duplication could be very inefficient if the condition B was rather complicated. This would not be the case if instead we had:

```
A :- B, !, C.
A :- D.
```

So one must sometimes weigh up the advantages of a clear program against those of a program that will run quickly. The discussion of efficiency leads us to our last example of the cut being used to fix the choice of a rule. Consider the definition of **append**:

Original

```
append([],X,X).
append([A|B],C,[A|D]) :- append(B,C,D).
```

If we are always using **append** for the case where we have two known lists and want to know what list consists of the first appended onto the front of the second, we may feel that it is inefficient that when backtracking gets to reconsider how to deal with a goal like **append([],[a,b,c,d],X)** it must try to use the second rule, even though the attempt is bound to fail. We know in this context that if the first list is [] then the first rule is the only correct one, and this information can be given to Prolog by a use of the cut. In general, Prolog implementations will be able to make better use of the available storage if they are told things like this than if they have to keep a record of apparent choices that are not really there.

not appropriate

So we could rewrite our definition as:

```
append([],X,X) :- !.
append([A|B],C,[A|D]) :- append(B,C,D).
```

Assuming our restricted use of **append**, this does not affect at all which solutions the program finds. It only increases the space and time efficiency to some extent. In exchange for this, we are liable to find that other kinds of uses of **append** will no longer work as expected, as is shown in Section 4.4.

4.3.2 The "cut-fail" Combination

In the second major application area, the cut is used in conjunction with the built-in **fail** predicate. **fail** is another built-in predicate, like **not**. It has no arguments, which means that the the success of the goal **fail** does not depend on what any variables stand for. Indeed, **fail** is defined in such a way that as a goal it always fails and causes backtracking to take place. This is just like what happens if we try to satisfy a goal for a predicate with no facts or rules. When **fail** is encountered after a cut, the normal backtracking behaviour will be altered by the effect of the cut. In fact, the particular combination "cut-fail" turns out to be quite useful in practice.

Let us consider how we might use this combination in a program to calculate how much tax somebody should pay. One thing we might want to know is whether the person is an "average taxpayer" -- in this case, the calculations might be quite simple and not have to involve considering lots of special cases. Let us define a predicate **average_taxpayer** where **average_taxpayer(X)** means that X is an average taxpayer. For instance, Fred Bloggs, who is married with 2 children and works in a bicycle factory, might be considered quite average. However, the managing director of an oil company may be earning too much, and a pensioner may be earning too little for the same kinds of tax calculations to be appropriate. We should start by considering a possible special case. It may be that special tax laws apply to somebody who is a native of another country, because he may have obligations to that country as well. Therefore, however average he may be in other respects, a foreigner will not be classed as an average taxpayer. We can start writing rules about this as follows:

```
average_taxpayer(X) :- foreigner(X), fail.
average_taxpayer(X) :- ...
```

In this extract, *which is not correct*, the first rule attempts to say "if X is a foreigner then the goal **average_taxpayer(X)** should fail". The second rule is to apply the general criterion for being an everage taxpayer for the cases when X is not a foreigner. The trouble is that if we asked the question:

```
?- average_taxpayer(widslewip).
```

about some foreigner called Widslewip the first rule would match and the **foreigner** goal would succeed. Next, the **fail** goal would initiate backtracking. In attempting to resatisfy the **average_taxpayer** goal, Prolog would find the second rule and start applying the general criterion to Widselwip. Now it is quite likely that he would pass the test, in which case the question would incorrectly be answered "yes". So our first rule has been completely ineffective in rejecting our friend as an average taxpayer. Why is this? The answer is that during backtracking Prolog tries to resatisfy *every* goal that has succeeded. So in particular it will investigate alternative ways of satisfying **average_taxpayer(widslewip)** In order to stop Prolog finding alternatives for this, we need to "cut" the choice (freeze the decision) before failing. We can do this by inserting a cut before the **fail** goal. A slightly more comprehensive definition of **average_taxpayer** incorporating this change, is given below:

```
average_taxpayer(X) :-
    foreigner(X), !, fail.
average_taxpayer(X) :-
    spouse(X,Y), gross_income(Y,Inc), Inc > 3000, !, fail.
average_taxpayer(X) :- gross_income(X,Inc), 2000 < Inc, 20000 > Inc.

gross_income(X,Y) :-
    receives_pension(X,P),
    P < 5000, !, fail.
gross_income(X,Y) :-
    gross_salary(X,Z),
    investment_income(X,W),
    Y is Z+W.

investment_income(X,Y) :- ....
```

Note the use in this program of several other "cut–fail" combinations. In the second rule for **average_taxpayer** we say that the attempt to show that someone is an average taxpayer can be abandoned if we can show that that person's spouse earns more than a certain amount. Also, in the definition of the predicate **gross_income** we say (in the first rule) that if somebody receives a pension that is below a certain amount then, whatever their other circumstances, we will consider them not to have any gross income at all.

An interesting application of the "cut–fail" combination is in the definition of the predicate **not**. Most Prolog implementations provide this already defined, but it is interesting to consider how we can provide rules for it. We require that the goal **not(P),** where P stands for another goal, succeeds if and only if the goal P fails. This is not exactly in accord with our intuitive notion of "not true" -- it is not always safe to assume that something is not true if we are unable to prove it. However, here is the definition:

```
not(P) :- call(P), !, fail.
not(P).       — when p can not be shown to be true
```

The definition of **not** involves invoking the argument P as a goal, using the evaluable predicate **call**. Predicate **call** simply treats its argument as a goal and attempts to satisfy it. We want the first rule to be applicable if P can be shown, and the second to be applicable otherwise. So we say that if Prolog can satisfy **call(P)** it should thereupon abandon satisfying the **not** goal.   The other possibility is that Prolog cannot show **call(P)**.   In this case, it never gets to the cut.   Because the **call(P)** goal failed, backtracking takes place, and Prolog finds the second rule.   Hence the goal **not(P)** will succeed when P is not provable.

As with the first use of "cut", we can replace uses of "cut-fail" with uses of **not**. This involves rather more reorganisation of the program than before, but does not introduce the same inefficiency.   If we were to rewrite our **average_taxpayer** program, it would start off something like:

```
average_taxpayer(X) :-
    not(foreigner(X)),
    not((spouse(X,Y),gross_income(Y,Inc),Inc>3000)),
    gross_income(X,Incl), ...
```

Note that in this example, we have to enclose a whole conjunction of goals inside the **not**. In order to show unambiguously that the commas join the goals into a conjunction (rather than separating multiple **not** arguments), we have enclosed the **not** argument in an extra set of brackets.

4.3.3 Terminating a "generate and test"

Now we come to look at the last major use of "cut" in Prolog programs -- to terminate a "generate and test" sequence.   Very often a program will have parts that conform to the following general model.   There will be a sequence of goals that can succeed in many ways, and which generates many possible solutions on backtracking.   After this, there are goals that check whether a solution generated is acceptable for some purpose.   If these goals fail, backtracking will lead to another solution being proposed.   This will be tested for appropriateness, and so on.   This process will stop when either an acceptable solution is generated (success), or when no more solutions can be found (failure).   We can call the goals that are yielding all the alternatives the "generator" and those that check whether a solution is acceptable the "tester".   Let us consider an example of this.   The following might be part of a program to play "Noughts and Crosses" ("Tic-Tac-Toe").   The program uses the built-in predicates **var** and **arg,** which are fully discussed in Chapter 6.

```
forced_move(Board,Sq) :-
    aline(Squares),
    threatening(Squares,Board,Sq), !.

aline([1,2,3]).
aline([4,5,6]).
aline([7,8,9]).
aline([1,4,7]).
aline([2,5,8]).
aline([3,6,9]).
aline([1,5,9]).
aline([3,5,7]).
```

means only one will be enough threatening two just doing no good!
1
5 6
7 8 9

```
threatening([X,Y,Z],B,X) :- empty(X,B), cross(Y,B), cross(Z,B).
threatening([X,Y,Z],B,Y) :- empty(Y,B), cross(X,B), cross(Z,B).
threatening([X,Y,Z],B,Z) :- empty(Z,B), cross(X,B), cross(Y,B).

empty(Sq,Board) :- arg(Sq,Board,Val), var(Val).
cross(Sq,Board) :- arg(Sq,Board,Val), nonvar(Val), Val = x.
nought(Sq,Board) :- arg(Sq,Board,Val), nonvar(Val), Val = o.
```

In case you haven't come across this game, it involves two players taking turns to occupy squares on a 3x3 board. One player occupies them with pieces marked "o", and the other one with pieces marked "x". The object of the game is to get three of one's own pieces in a (vertical, horizontal or diagonal) line before the other player does. We can number the nine squares on the board as below:

```
1 | 2 | 3
-----------
4 | 5 | 6
-----------
7 | 8 | 9
```

The program is assumed to be looking at the game from the point of view of the player who puts "o"s on the board. The predicate **forced_move** is used to answer the question "Am I forced to put a piece in a particular position?" This will be the case if the "o" player cannot immediately win (we do not deal with this here), but the "x" is threatening to win on his next move. For instance, in the position:

the "o" player is forced to play in square 4, because if he does not, his opponent will be able to fill the line 1-4-7 in his next turn. The program works by trying to find a line, two of whose squares are occupied by crosses, and the other of which is empty. If it can, then the player is forced to move into the empty square. In the clause for **forced_move**, the goal

```
aline(Squares)
```

serves as a "generator" of possible lines. This goal can succeed in many ways -- with **Squares** instantiated as one of the possible lists of square numbers that represent lines. Once a possible line has been suggested, it is necessary to see whether the opponent is threatening to claim this line. This is the purpose of the "tester" goal:

```
threatening(Squares,Board,Sq)
```

In this goal, the variable **Board** is supposed to hold a representation of the current state of the board -- what squares are occupied by what pieces -- and the variable **Sq** becomes instantiated to the number of the square where the "o" player is forced to play (assuming the goal succeeds).

The basic idea of the program is very simple -- **aline** proposes a line, and then **threatening** looks to see whether that line is threatening. If so, the original **forced_move** goal succeeds. Otherwise, backtracking occurs and **aline** comes up with another possible line. Now this is tested also, and maybe backtracking occurs again. If we get to the point when **aline** can generate no more lines, then the **forced_move** goal will correctly fail (there is no forced move). Now consider what happens if this program, as part of a larger system, successfully finds a forced move. **Sq** will become instantiated to the number of the square where the move should be, and this information will be used somewhere else in the program. Suppose that somewhere later a failure occurs, and Prolog eventually tries to resatisfy the **forced_move** goal. Then **aline** will start producing more possible lines to be checked. This makes no sense, because it cannot possibly be useful to find alternative forced moves. If we have found one of them, then we cannot do anything better than carry it out -- failure to do so would guarantee losing the game. Most of the time, there will be no alternative anyway, and **forced_move** will search through all the untried lines in vain, before itself failing. However, in the case of forced moves, we know that even if there is an alternative solution, it cannot be of any use in a context where a failure occurred in spite of the first solution. We can prevent Prolog from wasting time searching for different forced moves by putting a "cut" at the end of the clause. This has the effect of freezing the last successful **aline** solution. Including the "cut" amounts to saying "when I look for forced moves, it is only the first solution that is important".

From the point of view of understanding this use of "cut", it is only necessary to consider the overall structure of this program. However, some of the details are also of interest. The program assumes the board to be represented by a structure with nine components. Each component represents what is occupying the square of the appropriate number. Thus at any time the value for square 4 can be obtained by looking at the fourth argument of the current board structure (we use the built-in predicate **arg** for this). The value is an uninstantiated variable if the square is unoccupied; otherwise it is one of the atoms o and x. We use **var** and **nonvar** to determine whether the square is occupied or not.

↑ variable

Let us look at another example of a program that works by a "generate and test" method. We came across the idea of "integer division" in Section 2.5. Most Prolog systems provide this facility automatically, but here is a program for integer division that only uses addition and multiplication.

```
divide(N1,N2,Result) :-
    is_integer(Result),
    Product1 is Result*N2,
```

$$Result = \left\lfloor \frac{N1}{N2} \right\rfloor$$

see P.62.

76

to prevent infinite loop.

```
    Product2 is (Result+1)*N2,
    Product1 =< N1, Product2 > N1, !.
```

This rule uses the predicate **is_integer** (as defined before) to generate the number **Result** which is the result of "dividing" **N1** by **N2**. So, for instance, the result of dividing 27 by 6 is 4, because

   *4 * 6 is less than or equal to 27, and 5 * 6 is greater than 27*

The rule uses **is_integer** as a "generator", and the rest of the goals provide the appropriate "tester". Now we know in advance that, given specific values of **N1** and **N2**, **divide(N1,N2,Result)** can only succeed for one possible value for **Result**. For although **is_integer** can generate infinitely many candidates, only one will ever get past the tests. We can indicate this knowledge by putting a cut at the end of the rule. This says that if we ever successfully generate a **Result** that passes the tests for being the result of the division, we need never try any more. In particular, we need never reconsider any of the choices that were involved in looking for rules for **divide**, **is_integer** and so on. We have found the only solution, and there is no point in ever looking for another. If we did not put in the cut here, any backtracking would eventually start finding alternatives for **is_integer** again. So we would carry on generating possible values for **Result** again. None of these other values would be the correct result of the division, and so we would continue generating indefinitely.

① *Can hinder possible solution to a quest.*

4.4 Problems with "cut" ②

We have already seen that we must sometimes take into account the way Prolog searches the database and what state of instantiation our goals will have in deciding the order in which to write the clauses of a Prolog program. The problem with introducing cuts is that we have to be even more certain of exactly how the rules of the program are to be used. For, whereas a cut when a rule is used one way can be harmless or even beneficial, the very same cut can cause strange behaviour if the rule is suddenly used in another way. Consider the modified **append** from the last section:

```
    append([],X,X) :- !.
    append([A|B],C,[A|D]) :- append(B,C,D).
```

When we are considering goals like:

```
    append([a,b,c],[d,e],X)
```

and

```
    append([a,b,c],X,Y)
```

the cut is quite appropriate. If the first argument of the goal already has a value, then all the cut does is to reaffirm that only the first rule will be relevant if the value is []. However, consider what happens if we have the goal

```
append(X,Y,[a,b,c])
```

This goal will match the head of the first rule, giving:

```
X=[], Y=[a,b,c]
```

but now the cut is encountered. This will freeze all the choices we have made, and so if we ask for another solution, the answer will be

```
no
```

even though there actually are other solutions to the question.

Here is another interesting example of what can happen if a rule containing a cut is used in an unexpected way. Let us define a predicate **number_of_parents,** which can express information about how many parents somebody has. We can define it as follows:

```
number_of_parents(adam,0) :- !.
number_of_parents(eve,0) :- !.
number_of_parents(X,2).
```

That is, the number of parents is 0 for Adam and Eve, but 2 for everybody else. Now if we are always using our definition of **number_of_parents** to find the number of parents of given people, this is fine. We will get

```
?- number_of_parents(eve,X).

X=0;
no

?- number_of_parents(john,X).

X=2;
no
```

and so on, as required. The cut is necessary to prevent backtracking ever reaching the third rule if the person is Adam or Eve. However, consider what will happen if we use the same rules to verify whether given people have given numbers of parents. All is well, except that we get:

```
?- number_of_parents(eve,2).

yes
```

You should work out for yourself why this happens -- it is simply a consequence of the way

Prolog searches through the database. Our implementation of "otherwise" with a cut simply does not work properly any more. There are two possible modifications we could make to recover from this:

```
number_of_parents(adam,N) :- !, N=0.
number_of_parents(eve,N) :- !, N=0.
number_of_parents(X,2).
```

or

```
number_of_parents(adam,0).
number_of_parents(eve,0).
number_of_parents(X,2) :- X\=adam, X\=eve.
```

Of course, these will still not work properly if we give goals like

```
?- number_of_parents(X,Y).
```
for X is uninstantiated

expecting backtracking to enumerate all the possibilities. So the moral is:

> If you introduce cuts to obtain correct behaviour when the goals are of one form, there is no guarantee that anything sensible will happen if goals of another form start appearing. It follows that it is only possible to use the cut reliably if you have a clear policy about how your rules are going to be used. If you change this policy, all the uses of cut must be reviewed.

Chapter 5. Input and Output

[handwritten annotations in top margin:]
write
read
nl
tab
display
put
[geto
[get
user

[tell
[told
[see
[seen

telling
seeing

Thus far, the only means we have seen of providing information to a Prolog program has been by asking questions of the Prolog system. Also, the only method of finding out· what a variable stands for at some point in the satisfaction of a goal has been by asking a question in such a way that Prolog will print out the answer in the "X = (answer)" form. Much of the time, such direct interaction with questions is all that is required to ensure that a program is working properly. However, for many occasions it is useful to write a Prolog program that initiates a conversation with you by itself. For example, suppose you have a database of world events in the 16th Century, arranged as facts containing dates and headlines. To start with, dates can be represented as integers, and headlines can be represented as lists of atoms. We shall have to enclose some of the atoms in single quotes because they begin with an upper-case letter, and we should not want them to be interpreted as variables:

[handwritten: ≈ is not a variable]

```
event(1505, ['Euclid', translated, into, 'Latin']).
event(1510, ['Reuchlin-Pfefferkorn', controversy, begins]).
event(1523, ['Christian', 'II', flees, from, 'Denmark']).
   .
   .
   .
```

Now if we wish to know about a particular date, we could ask a question as follows:

```
?- event(1505,X).
```

and Prolog would print the reply

[handwritten: deletes the single quotes automatically]

```
X=[Euclid,translated,into,Latin].
```

Representing the history headlines as lists of atoms confers the advantage that "searches" can be made to find out the date when certain key events happened. For example, consider the predicate we shall define, called **when**. The goal **when(X,Y)** succeeds if X is mentioned in year Y according to our history headlines:

```
when(X,Y) :- event(Y,Z), member(X,Z).

?- when('Denmark',D).
```

```
D = 1523
```

One disadvantage of using lists of atoms is that they are awkward to type in, especially if atoms begin with an upper-case letter. Another possibility, which has advantages and disadvantages of its own, is to represent history headlines as lists of characters. From a previous chapter we know that lists of characters can be represented as being between double quotes:

— This will be translated into ASCII codes.

```
event(1511, "Luther visits Rome").
event(1521, "Henry VIII is made Defender of the Faith").
event(1524, "Vasco da Gama dies").
event(1529, "Berquin burnt at Paris").
event(1540, "Reopening of war with Turks").
        .
        .
        .
```

This is easier to type in, but consider asking the question

```
?- event(1524,X).
```

If you try this, Prolog will print out an incomprehensible list of ASCII codes corresponding to the characters in the string to which X is instantiated! Although the list of characters is easy to type in, the question-and-answer sequence is not sufficient to print out a legible answer.

It would be more convenient, instead of asking Prolog questions of this form, to write a program that first asks what date you want to know about, and then prints out the appropriate headline on the computer terminal's display. Headlines could then be represented in any way desired. In order to do these kinds of tasks, Prolog makes available some built-in predicates that print out their arguments on your computer terminal's display. There are also predicates that wait for you to type in text from the computer terminal's keyboard, and instantiate a variable to whatever you typed in. In this way, your program can interact with you, accepting *input* from you, and printing *output* to you. When a program waits for you to type some input from you, we say that it is *reading* the input. Likewise, when a program is printing some output to you, we say it is *writing* the output. In this chapter we describe various methods for reading and writing. One of our examples will be printing headlines from the history database, and we conclude with a program that accepts normal sentences and converts them into a list of constants that can be processed by other programs. This conversion program, called **read_in,** can be used as a "building block" with which to create programs that analyse English language. Such analysis programs are discussed in later chapters, especially Chapter 9.

5.1 Reading and Writing Terms

<u>Writing Terms</u>

Perhaps the most useful way to print some term on the computer terminal's display is to use the predicate **write**. If X is instantiated to a term, then the goal **write(X)** will cause the term to be printed out on the display. If X is not instantiated, a uniquely numbered variable (such as '_253') will be printed. However, if two variables are "sharing" within the same argument of **write** then they will have the same number. The **write** predicate cannot be re-satisfied. It only succeeds once, and it fails if an attempt is made to *re-satisfy* it. Why would it not be a good idea to use **write** to write out the historical headline in our example above? Remember that a string is actually represented as a list of character codes. If we were to **write** out such a list, it would be printed as a sequence of integers, separated by commas, and enclosed in square brackets!

There are two more predicates to introduce, and then we will see our first example using **write**. The built-in predicate **nl** is used to force all succeeding output to be printed on the next line of the display. The name "nl" means "new line". Like **write**, **nl** succeeds only once. Next, the built-in predicate **tab** is used to print a number of blank spaces across the display screen. The goal **tab(X)** succeeds only once, and it causes the cursor on the display to move to the right by X space characters. It is assumed that X is instantiated to an integer. The name **tab** is perhaps a poorly chosen name, because it does not actually have anything to do with the "tab stops" on a standard typewriter or on the display of a computer terminal.

When printing lists, it is helpful for the items of a list to be printed in a way that is easy to understand. Lists that contain other "nested" lists are especially difficult to read, especially when there are structures inside as well. We shall define a predicate **pp** such that the goal **pp(X,Y)** prints out the list (to which X is instantiated) in a helpful way. The name "pp" means "pretty print". The second argument is explained later. Each author of a pretty-print program has his own style of making lists more legible. Just for simplicity, we shall adopt a method where the elements of a list are printed in a vertical column. If the element is itself a list, its elements are printed in a column which is shifted over to the right. This is essentially a "vine diagram" (Chapter 3) on its side. For example, the list **[1,2,3]** is pretty-printed as

```
1
2
3
```

and the list [1,2,[3,4],5,6] is printed as

```
1
2
```

```
    3
    4
  5
  6
```

Notice that we have decided to remove the separating commas and the square brackets. If the element of a list is a structure, we will treat it as though it is an atom. This way we do not have to "get inside" structures to pretty-print their contents. The following program implements the pretty-print method we have specified:

```
pp([H|T],I) :-  !, J is I+3, pp(H,J), ppx(T,J), nl.
pp(X,I) :- tab(I), write(X), nl.

ppx([],_).
ppx([H|T],I) :- pp(H,I), ppx(T,I).
```

Here we see the second argument of **pp** revealed as a column counter. The "top level" goal for printing a list might look like

```
..., pp(L,0), ...
```

which initialises the column counter to 0. The first clause of **pp** handles the special case: if the first argument is a list. If so, we have to set up a new column by increasing the column counter by some amount (3 here). Next, we need to "pretty print" the head of the list, because it might be a list itself. Next, we need to print each element of the tail of the list all in the same column. This is what **ppx** does. And, **ppx** needs to **pp** each element in case it is a list. The second clause of **pp** matches if we wish to pretty-print something that is not a list. We simply indent to the specified column, use **write** to print the term, and print a new line. The first clause of **pp** also needs to terminate each list with a new line, hence the **nl** there.

Notice that we have put the special case for **pp** *before* the catchall boundary condition. If we had put the second clause before the first one, then a list in the first argument of the goal would match with the X in the head of the rule. The result would be to simply **write** the whole list, without benefit of pretty-printing. So, we want the list case to be checked for first. This is why we put the first clause before the second one. The second one is used as a "catchall" rule. Another way to do this would be to put the boundary condition first, and include in its body a goal that fails if the first argument is a list:

```
pp(X,I) :- not(is_list(X)), tab(I), write(X), nl.
pp([H|T],I) :-  J is I+3, pp(H,J), ppx(T,J), nl.

/* ppx as above */

is_list([]).
is_list([_|_]).
```

We needed to define the appropriate predicate **is_list** such that the goal **is_list(X)** succeeds if X is a list. The first fact specifies that the empty list is a list. The second fact specifies that a structure that has a head and a tail is a list.

Let us consider the **event** facts from the beginning of this chapter. Given one of the history headlines represented as a list of atoms, we can use **write** to print out each atom, with a space in between each atom. Consider the predicate **phh** (for "print history headline"):

```
phh([]) :- nl.
phh([H|T]) :- write(H), tab(1), phh(T).
```

So, the following question would print out any history headline that mentions "England":

```
?- event(_,L), member('England',L), phh(L).
```

What'el happen if
L = ['England', fights 'England']

Notice the use of backtracking to search the database. Everytime the **member** goal fails, an attempt is made to re-satisfy **event,** which causes the entire database to be searched top-to-bottom for events that mention the atom 'England'.

The predicate **write** is clever about how it prints a term, because it takes into account what operator declarations have been made. For instance, if we have declared an atom as an infix operator, a term with this atom as functor and two arguments will be printed out with the atom between the two arguments. There is another predicate that behaves in exactly the same way as **write,** except that it ignores any operator declarations that have been made. This predicate is called **display.** The difference between **write** and **display** is illustrated by the following:

```
?- write(a+b*c*c), nl, display(a+b*c*c), nl.

a+b*c*c
+(a,*(*(b,c),c))

yes
```

Notice how **display** has treated the atoms **+** and ***** just like any other atoms for printing out this term. We do not usually want to see our structures printed out in this way, because having operators usually helps us to read program output as well as prepare program input. However, sometimes, if we are not quite sure about the precedences of our operators, using **display** can be quite helpful.

Reading Terms

The predicate **read** will read the next term that you type in from the computer terminal's keyboard. The term must be followed by a dot (.) and a non-printing character such as a space or a RETURN. If X is uninstantiated, the goal **read(X)** will cause the next term to be read, and X to be instantiated to the term. As with the other input/output predicates we have encountered thus far, **read** only succeeds once. If its argument is instantiated at the time it is used as a goal, then the next term will be read, and matched with the argument given to **read**. The goal will succeed or fail, depending on the success of the match.

Using **read,** and **phh** as defined above, we can write a Prolog program to print the historical headlines from the **event** database as follows:

```
hello :-
    phh(['What', date, do, you, 'desire? ']),
    read(D),
    event(D,S),
    phh(S).
```

We have defined a predicate **hello,** having no arguments. When we ask the question

```
?- hello.
```

Prolog will print:

    What date do you desire?

and wait for a response. Suppose we type in:

    1523.

Notice that we need to type in the dot after 1523. This is because the **read** predicate demands that a dot appear. Also, we must type in a RETURN, as usual, to inform the computer that we are finished with that line of text. Prolog will respond:

    Christian II flees from Denmark

Notice also that the first clause of the body of **hello** uses **phh,** even though it is not intended to print a history headline. This simply shows that **phh** suffices also to print *any* list of atoms, no matter where that list came from.

5.2 Reading and Writing Characters

The smallest entity that can be written and read is the character. As we have seen thus far, characters are treated as small integers corresponding to the ASCII code for the character. Prolog has several built-in predicates for reading and writing characters.

Writing.

If X is instantiated to a character (an ASCII code), it will be printed when Prolog encounters the goal **put(X)**. The predicate **put** always succeeds, and it cannot be re-satisfied (it fails when an attempt is made to re-satisfy it). As a "side effect", **put** prints its argument as a character on your terminal's display. For example, we can print the word "hello" in a rather awkward way by:

```
?- put(104),put(101),put(108),put(108),put(111).
hello
```

See p. 246

The result of this conjunction of goals is that Prolog prints the characters h, e, l, l, and o, printing them out under the question as shown above. We have already seen that it is possible to start printing at the beginning of the next line by using the **nl** predicate, which has no arguments. What **nl** actually does is to print some control characters that cause the cursor on your computer terminal's display to move to the beginning of the next line. The question

```
?- put(104),put(105),nl,put(116),put(104),put(101),put(114),put(101).
```

would cause the following to be printed:

```
hi
there
```

Another goal we have seen is **tab(X),** which prints X spaces (ASCII code 32). Of course, X must be instantiated to an integer. Notice that tab(X) could have been defined as:

```
tab(0) :- !.
tab(N) :- put(32), M is N-1, tab(M).
```

We are now able to define a predicate that we shall call **printstring**. If we instantiate X to a list of character codes (a string), **printstring(X)** will print it out using **put** for each element of the list. As in all such programs, the boundary condition is the empty list. This is what we will use to terminate the recursion. Otherwise, we simply use **put** to print the head of the list, and use **printstring** to print the tail of the list:

```
printstring([]).
printstring([H|T]) :- put(H), printstring(T).
```

```
?- printstring("Charles V abdicates at Brussels").

Charles V abdicates at Brussels
```

If we choose to represent a history headline as a string, rather than a list of atoms, such a definition will suffice to print the strings in the **event** database above.

geto (X) — next char (any)
get (X) — next printing char.

Characters may be read from the keyboard by using the goals **get0(X)** and **get(X)**. These goals always succeed if their argument is uninstantiated, and they also cannot be re-satisfied. When they are used, they make the computer wait until some characters have been typed by you. They are slightly different because **get0(X)** will instantiate X to the very next character that is typed, no matter what it is. On the other hand, **get(X)** will skip all *non-printing* characters, and instantiate X to the first *printing* character. As we said in Chapter 2, a printing character is one that makes a mark on the computer terminal's display.

If X is already instantiated, then the goal **get(X)** will skip all non-printing characters and compare the next printing character with whatever X is instantiated to. The goal succeeds or fails depending on the outcome of the test. The goal **get0(X)** compares the next character for equality, and succeeds or fails.   *when X is already instan—*

The next section shows some examples of reading characters. An important consideration is what happens when we need to backtrack over a **get** goal.

5.3   *Reading English Sentences*

We now present the program that reads in a sentence typed at the terminal and converts it to a list of Prolog atoms. The program defines the predicate **read_in** with one argument. The program must know when one word of the input ends and the next begins. In order to know this, it assumes that a word consists of any number of letters, digits, and special characters. Letters and digits are the same as those discussed in Section 2.1, and we will consider the single quote (') and the hyphen (–) to be special characters. Also, the characters

        , ; : ? ! .   *! ?*

are taken to form words on their own. Any other characters just mark space between words. The sentence is deemed to have finished when one of the words ., !, or ? appears. Upper-case letters are automatically converted to lower-case, so that the same word always gives rise to the same atom. As a result of this definition, the program will produce question and answer sequences like:

```
?- read_in(S).
The man, who is very rich, saw John's watch.

    S = [the,man,',',who,is,very,rich,saw,'john''s',watch,'.']
```
                                                        extra.

We have actually inserted extra single-quote characters in this to make it clear what the atoms are.

The program uses the predicate **get0** to read in characters from the terminal. The trouble with **get0** is that, once a character has been read from the terminal by it, that character has "gone for ever", and no other **get0** goal or attempt to resatisfy a **get0** goal will ever get hold of that character again. So we must avoid ever backtracking over a use of **get0** if we want to avoid "losing" the character it reads in. For instance, the following program to read in characters and print them out again, converting 'a's to 'b's (character codes 97 to code 98) will *not work*:

to be instantiated to chara's ASCII

```
go :- do_a_character, go.

do_a_character :- get0(X), X=97, !, put(98).
do_a_character :- get0(X), put(X).
```

This is not a particularly good program anyway, because it will run for ever. However, consider the effect of attempting to satisfy the **do_a_character** goal. If the first **do_a_character** rule reads in an X which is not 97, backtracking then causes the second rule to be tried instead. However, the **get0(X)** goal in the second rule will cause X to be instantiated to the *next* character after the one already found. This is because the satisfaction of the original **get0** goal was an *irreversible* process. So this program would actually fail to print out all the characters. It would even sometimes print out a's.

How does our **read_in** program cope with the problem of backtracking over input? The answer is that we must design it in such a way that it always reads one character ahead, and makes tests on a character inside a different rule to the one where it was read. When a character is found somewhere and cannot be used at that point, it is passed back to the rules that will be able to use it. Hence, our predicate to do with reading a single word, **readword,** actually has three arguments. The first is for the character that was found by whichever rule last satisfied a **get0** goal but could not find a use for the character. The second is for the Prolog atom that will be constructed for the word. The last argument is for the first character that is read after the word. In order to see where a word ends, it is necessary to read up to the next character after it. This character must be passed back, because it might provide the valuable first character of another word.

Here, then is the program:

```
/* Read in a sentence */

read_in([W|Ws]) :- get0(C), readword(C,W,C1), restsent(W,C1,Ws).

/* Given a word and the character after it, read in the
   rest of the sentence */

restsent(W,_,[]) :- lastword(W), !.
restsent(W,C,[W1|Ws]) :- readword(C,W1,C1), restsent(W1,C1,Ws).

/* Read in a single word, given an initial character,
   and remembering what character came after the word */
```

88

```
readword(C,W,C1) :- single_character(C), !, name(W,[C]), get0(C1).
readword(C,W,C2) :-
    in_word(C,NewC), !,
    get0(C1),
    restword(C1,Cs,C2),
    name(W,[NewC|Cs]).
readword(C,W,C2) :- get0(C1), readword(C1,W,C2).

restword(C,[NewC|Cs],C2) :-
    in_word(C,NewC), !,
    get0(C1),
    restword(C1,Cs,C2).
restword(C,[],C).

/* These characters form words on their own */

single_character(44).  /* , */
single_character(59).  /* ; */
single_character(58).  /* : */
single_character(63).  /* ? */
single_character(33).  /* ! */
single_character(46).  /* . */
```
also lastword

```
/* These characters can appear within a word */
/* The second in_word clause converts characters to lower-case */

in_word(C,C) :- C>96, C<123.          /* a b.. z */
in_word(C,L) :- C>64, C<91, L is C+32. /* A B..  Z */
in_word(C,C) :- C>47, C<58.            /* 1 2.. 9 */
in_word(39,39).                        /* ' */
in_word(45,45).                        /* - */

/* These words terminate a sentence */

lastword('.').
lastword('!').
lastword('?').
```

Exercise 5.1:   Explain what each variable in the above program is used for.

Exercise 5.2:   Write a program to read in characters indefinitely, printing them out again with 'a's changed to 'b's.

5.4 Reading and Writing Files

The predicates previously discussed in this chapter were used only for reading from or writing to your computer terminal, but they are actually more general than that. The Prolog system recognises a *current input stream*, from which all input is read. All output is written to the *current output stream*. The computer terminal's keyboard is normally the current input stream, and the terminal's display is normally the current output stream. Often it is useful to read or write *files*, which are sequences of characters on a secondary storage medium. The particular medium depends on your particular computer installation, but nowadays we usually read and write files that are stored on magnetic discs. It is assumed that each file has a *filename* that we use to identify it. In order for this section to be understandable, you should be familiar with the conventions for organising and naming files at your computer installation. In Prolog, filenames are represented as atoms, but we cannot rule out the possibility of further installation-dependent restrictions on the syntax of filenames.

Files have a certain length. That is, they contain a certain quantity of characters. At the end of a file, there is a special marker, called the *end of file marker*. We did not discuss the end of file marker previously, because it is more usual to encounter the end of file marker on a file than on a computer terminal. If a program is reading from a file, the end of file marker can be detected whether the program is reading terms or characters. If a **get0(X)** encounters the end of a file, X will be instantiated to a control character, normally the one with ASCII code 26. If **read(X)** encounters the end of a file, X will be instantiated to some special term that depends on your particular Prolog system. If an attempt is made to read beyond the end of a file, an error is generated.

There is a built-in file called **user.** Reading this file causes input to come from your computer terminal's keyboard, and writing to this file will cause characters to be written on the display. This is the normal mode of operation. When input is from the computer terminal's keyboard, an end of file can be generated by typing the end-of-file control character (ASCII code 26, or control-Z). This will make **get0** and **read** behave as though the end of a file has been encountered.

Writing Files

Terms and characters can be written to files by using exactly the same predicates as discussed earlier. The only difference is that when we wish to write to a file, we must change the *current output stream* to be the file instead of the computer terminal's display. The current output stream is changed by using the **tell** predicate. If X is instantiated to a filename, which must be an atom, the goal **tell(X)** switches the current output stream so that any writing (done by **write, put,** and so forth) will be done to the file, instead of to the computer terminal's display. The **tell(X)** goal succeeds only once (it cannot be resatisfied). Also, when Prolog backtracks over a **tell** goal, *it does not reset the current output to what it was previously.* As well as changing what Prolog considers to be the current output stream, **tell** also performs other operations in certain situations. The first time that we satisfy **tell(X)** for a particular X, Prolog assumes that we want to start a new file with that name. Therefore if X is instantiated to an atom that names a file that already exists, then any characters already in the file will be removed. On the other hand, if X is instantiated to an atom that does not name any existing file, then a file with that name will be created. In either case, the file is now considered *open* (for output). This means that subsequent writing to the file will add characters at the end of the file until we say explicitly that the file is complete (until we *close* the file). At that point, if we try to write to it again, Prolog will assume that we want to write a new version as before. If we try to satisfy **tell(X)** when X is not instantiated,

tell(X)   telling (X).
told

90

or is instantiated to an object other than a filename, then an error occurs. The specific behaviour taken by the Prolog system when an error occurs depends on the particular implementation of Prolog you are using.

The predicate **telling** is used to find out the name of the file that is the current output stream. The goal **telling(X)** succeeds when X is instantiated to the name of the current output file. As you might expect, if X is uninstantiated, then **telling** will instantiate it to the atom that makes the goal succeed.

When all writing to a file has been completed, the predicate **told** will end the file and close it (for output). Also, it will cause the current output to revert to the computer terminal's display. So, a typical sequence of goals to write some characters on a file would be:

```
..., tell(fred), write(X), told, ...
```

If the current output stream is switched without using **told** on the previous file, the previous file will not be closed, but it is still available for writing. This allows you to write to a file at several different times, as in this example:

```
..., tell(X), write(A), tell(user), write(B), tell(X), write(C), told.
```
                                                                    Close X
                    ↳ to terminals

Reading Files

The predicates that Prolog makes available for switching the current input stream are analogues of those discussed above. The goal **see(X)** switches the current input stream to the filename specified. As with **tell,** the goal cannot be resatisfied, and the operation is not undone on backtracking. The first time we satisfy **see(X)** for some file X, that file becomes *open* (for input), and we start at the beginning of the file. Subsequent input continues from where it last left off, until we explicitly *close* the file. After that point, a new attempt to read from the file will open it and start from the beginning as before. The current input stream can be discovered by satisfying **seeing(X),** and the current input stream may be switched back to the computer terminal's keyboard by **seen,** which also closes the file.

Consulting

Reading and writing files is most helpful when our programs deal with more terms than we care to type in by hand each time we want to put them in the database. In Prolog, files are used mainly to store *programs*. If we have the text of a Prolog program in a file, we can read all of the clauses in the file, and put them into the database by using the predicate **consult**. When X is instantiated to the name of a file, the goal **consult(X)** will read Prolog clauses and goals from the file. Most implementations of Prolog have a special notation for **consult,** which allows a list of files to be consulted, one after another. If a list of atoms is given as a Prolog question, then Prolog will consult each file in the list. An example of this notation is:

```
?- [filel, mapper, expert].
```

This behaves as though Prolog were executing a goal consultall(X), were X is the list that we give the question, and where consultall might be defined as follows:

```
consultall([]).
consultall([H|T]) :- consult(H), consultall(T).
```

However, the shorthand list notation reduces effort, and this is especially important when one considers that the very first act that the practising Prolog programmer does is to **consult** a list of files to make available his favourite predicates. The **consult** predicate automatically stops reading clauses when the end of the file is encountered.

Section 6.1 describes **consult** in more detail.

5.5 Declaring Operators

use ?- op(3|; yfx,'+')

Operators are considered in this "input and output" chapter because operators provide syntactic convenience when reading or writing terms. There is no other reason for having operators. Let us first briefly review Section 2.3, and then tell how operators are declared.

The Prolog syntax provides for operators, each having three properties: a *position, precedence,* and *associativity.* The position can be infix, postfix, or prefix (an operator with two arguments can go between them; an operator with one argument can go after or before it). The precedence is an integer whose range depends on the actual Prolog implementation, but we shall assume a range from 1 to 255. The precedence is used to disambiguate expressions where the syntax of the terms is not made explicit through the use of brackets. The associativity is to disambiguate expressions in which there are two operators in the expression that have the same precedence. In Prolog, we associate a special atom with an operator, which specifies its position and associativity. The possible specifiers for infix operators are:

```
xfx   xfy   yfx   yfy
```

To understand these specifiers, it helps to see them as "pictures" of possible uses of the operators. In the pictures, the letter "f" represents the operator and "x" and "y" represent arguments. So in all of the above, the operator must appear *between* two arguments -- that is, it is an infix operator. In accordance with this convention,

```
fx   fy
```

fx fy

are two specifiers for prefix operators (the operator comes *before* its one argument). Also,

xf   yf

are possible specifiers for postfix operators. You may be wondering why there are two letters available for indicating arguments. The choice of "x"s and "y"s in these positions enables associativity information to be conveyed. Assuming that there are no brackets, a "y" says that the argument can contain operators of the same or lower precedence than this operator. On the other hand, an "x" says that any operators in the argument must have a strictly lower precedence than this operator. Consider what this means for the operator +, defined as **yfx**. If we look at

a + b + c

there are two possible interpretations:

(a + b) + c   a + (b + c)

The second of these is ruled out, because it requires the argument *after* the first + to contain an operator of the same precedence (another +). This contradicts the presence of an "x" after the "f" of the specifier.

Thus, in particular, an operator declared **yfx** is left associative. Similarly, an operator declared **xfy** is right associative. If we know the desired associativity of an infix operator we are declaring, this means that the specifier is uniquely determined.

Note that the meanings of "x" and "y" (in terms of what other operators can appear unbracketed in the relevant position) are the same in all the other cases as well. This means that, for instance, the sequence

not not a

not (not (a))

((not (not)) a) X

is legal syntactically if **not** is declared as **fy,** but is illegal if it is declared **fx.**

In Prolog, if we wish to declare that an operator with a given position, precedence, and associativity is to be recognised when terms are read and written, we use the built-in predicate **op.** If **Name** is the desired operator (the atom that we want to be an operator), **Prec** the precedence (an integer within the appropriate range), and **Spec** the position/associativity specifier (one of the above atoms), then the operator is declared by providing the following goal:

?- op(Prec, Spec, Name).

If the operator declaration is legal, then the goal will succeed.

As an example of declaring operators, the following is a complete list of declarations for the "core" operators discussed in this book. Particular implementations of Prolog may have slightly different operators as "standard" ones, and the precedences may be scaled to fit within another range. However, the order of operators within the precedence hierarchy is normally conventional.

```
?-op(255,xfx,':-').
?-op(255,fx,'?-').
?-op(254,xfy,';').
?-op(253,xfy,',').
?-op(250,fx,spy).
?-op(250,fx,nospy).
?-op(60,fx,not).
?-op(51,xfy,'.').          ——— right associative
?-op(40,xfx,is).
?-op(40,xfx,'=..').
?-op(40,xfx,=).
?-op(40,xfx,\=).
?-op(40,xfx,<).
?-op(40,xfx,=<).
?-op(40,xfx,>=).
?-op(40,xfx,>).
?-op(40,xfx,==).
?-op(40,xfx,\==).
?-op(31,yfx,-).
?-op(31,yfx,+).
?-op(21,yfx,/).
?-op(21,yfx,*).
?-op(11,xfx,mod).
```

note = the # is smaller means the precedence is "lower" in the "tree" hence carry out first

(in short = lower first)

Chapter 6. Built-In Predicates

consult(x) ⎤ not   listing (A)
reconsult(x) ⎦ imp.   clause (X,Y)
var(x)   call (X)
nonvar(x)   asserta (x)
atom(x)   assertz (x)
integer(x)   repeat (x)
atomic(x)   retract (x)
                       retractall

In this chapter, we introduce some of the "built-in" predicates that a Prolog system might provide. What do we mean when we say that a predicate is "built-in"? We mean that the predicate's definition is provided in advance by the Prolog system, instead of by your own clauses. Built-in predicates may provide facilities that cannot be obtained by definitions in pure Prolog. Or they may provide convenient facilities just to save each programmer from having to define them himself. We have actually already come across some built-in predicates -- the predicates for reading and writing discussed in Chapter 5. Also, the "cut" could be regarded as a built-in predicate.

The input/output predicates illustrate the fact that a built-in predicate may have "side effects". That is, satisfying a goal involving it may cause changes apart from the instantiation of the arguments. This, of course, cannot occur with a predicate defined in pure Prolog. Another important fact about built-in predicates is that they may expect particular sorts of arguments. For instance, consider the predicate <, defined so that X < Y succeeds if the number X is less than the number Y. Such a relation cannot be defined in Prolog without some "outside help" that knows something about numbers. So < is provided as a built-in predicate, and its definition involves the use of some underlying machine operation for testing the comparative size of numbers (represented as binary patterns, or whatever). What should happen if we introduce a "less than" goal where X is an atom, or even if both X and Y are uninstantiated? The definition in terms of the machine will simply not apply. So we must stipulate that X < Y is only a sensible goal if both X and Y are instantiated to numbers when an attempt is made to satisfy it. What will happen if this condition is not met will depend on the individual Prolog implementation. One possibility is that the goal will simply fail. The other possibility is that an error message will be printed out, and the system will take some appropriate action (like abandoning trying to answer the current question).

6.1 Entering new Clauses

When you write a Prolog program, you will want to tell the system what clauses to use, as well as ask questions about them. You may want to type in new clauses at the terminal, or to tell Prolog to take clauses from a file that you have prepared in advance. In fact, these two operations look the same from Prolog's point of view, because the terminal is seen as just another file, with name **user**. There are two basic built-in predicates for reading in new clauses, **consult** and **reconsult**. In addition, there is a convenient notation for when you want to read in clauses from more then one file -- the list notation. If you are interested, simple definitions in Prolog of **consult** and **reconsult** are actually given in Section 6.4.

consult(X)

The built-in predicate **consult** is meant for those situations when you want the clauses in some file (or to be typed at the terminal) to *augment* those already in the database. The argument must be an atom giving the name of the file the clauses are to be taken from. What characters constitute a legal file name will, of course, depend on your particular computer. Examples of possible **consult** goals for various computers are:

```
?- consult(myfile).
?- consult('/us/qris/pl/chat').
?- consult('lib:iorout.pl').
```

When it has to satisfy a **consult** goal, Prolog reads through the file, adding the clauses it finds at the end of the database. As a result, the new clauses will appear after any already existing clauses for the same predicates. If a question is found in the file, this will be treated just like an ordinary question, except that the answer will not be printed out. It does not usually make sense to interleave questions with new clauses in a file, except to do things like declare new operators and print out helpful messages.

reconsult(X) ← *for correcting programming mistakes*   *because its under reading mode*

The predicate **reconsult** is just like **consult**, except that the clauses read in are taken to *supersede* any existing clauses for the same predicate. Because of this, **reconsult** is appropriate for correcting programming mistakes. If you read in several files of clauses and then discover that there is a mistake in one clause, you may be able to correct it without having to read in all the files again. To do this, you just have to **reconsult** a file containing a correct set of clauses for the predicate in question. You can give the corrected clauses by either typing them at the terminal **(reconsult(user))** *a file* or by editing a file without exiting from Prolog (only possible in some implementations) and then **reconsult** -ing that file. *better* Of course, typing in revised clauses at the terminal will alter what Prolog sees in the *database*, but it will not change the *file* that the original, faulty, clauses came from!

To see how **consult** and **reconsult** work in practice, here is an example Prolog session involving their use. The session starts with the programmer having no clauses in the database.

```
?- append([a,b,c,d],[e],X).
```

96

no ← because there is no append

```
?- consult(user).

append([A|B],C,[A|D]) :- append(A,C,D).     B
append([],X,X).

reverse([],[]).
reverse([A|B],C) :- reverse(B,D), append(D,[A],C).

/* the end of file character (control-Z) is typed here */
yes

?- reverse([a,b,c,d,e],X).

no

?- append([a,b,c,d,e],[f],X).

no

?- append([],[a,b,c],X).

X = [a,b,c]
yes

?- reconsult(user).

append([A|B],C,[A|D]) :- append(B,C,D).
```

replace original append definitions

```
/* the end of file character (control-Z) is typed here */
yes

?- reverse([a,b,c,d],X).

no

?- consult(user).

append([],X,X).
```

added to the end of file.

```
/* the end of file character (control-Z) is typed here */
yes

?- reverse([a,b,c,d,e],X).

X = [e,d,c,b,a]
yes
```

In this session, the programmer starts by entering clauses for the predicates **append** and **reverse** from the terminal. Of course, he could have typed these into a file first and then told Prolog to "consult" that file, but for an example of this small size that might not have been worthwhile. Unfortunately, there is a mistake in the first clause for **append** — the goal contains an A where it should have a B. This mistake is revealed when the system cannot answer his **reverse** and **append** questions. Somehow he realises that his definition of **append** is wrong (in a real session, this would probably happen after use was made of the debugging aids described in Chapter 8). So he decides to supersede his existing definition with a new one, using **reconsult.** Unfortunately, in the new definition, he forgets to specify the boundary condition (the **[ ]** case).   So the program still does not work.   At this point, the original two-clause definition of **append** has been replaced by a new one-clause definition, which is still not complete.   The programmer sees what he has done, and can rectify the situation by simply adding a new clause to the existing definition.   This is achieved with another use of **consult**.   The program now works.

The List Notation

Prolog provides a special notation that makes it more convenient to specify **consult** and **reconsult** goals, especially when you want Prolog to look at more than one file.   The notation involves simply putting the file names (as Prolog atoms) into a list, and giving that list as a goal to be satisfied.   If you want a file to be **consult** -ed, you put the name into the list as it is, and if you want a file to be **reconsult** -ed, you precede the name with a '-' sign.   Thus the question:

```
?- [file1,-file2,'fred.1',-'bill.2'].
```

is exactly equivalent to the longer version:

```
?- consult(file1), reconsult(file2), consult('fred.1'),
   reconsult('bill.2').
```

The list notation is purely a notational convenience, and does not offer any any extra facilities over and above those provided by **consult** and **reconsult**.   Some Prolog implementations may use a different sign than '-' in the list notation, but the effect is the same.

6.2   Success and Failure

In the normal course of executing a Prolog program, a goal succeeds when it can be satisfied, and it fails when there is no way to satisfy it.   There are two predicates that make it more convenient to specify when a goal succeeds or fails.   These are the **true** and the **fail** predicates.

true

This goal always succeeds.   It is not actually necessary, as clauses and goals can be reordered or recombined to obviate any use of **true**.   However, it exists for convenience.

fail
and cause backtracking to take place

This goal always fails.   There are two places where it is helpful.   One place is the "cut fail" combination, which was described in Section 4.3.   A conjunction of goals of the

P.71.

98

form

```
    ..., !, fail.
```

is used to say "if execution proceeds to this point, then one can abandon attempting to satisfy this goal." The conjunction fails due to the **fail**, and the parent goal fails because of the cut.

Another place to use **fail** is where you explicitly want another goal to backtrack through all solutions. You may want to print out all the solutions. For instance,

```
    ?- event(X,Y), phh(Y), fail.
```

would print out all the events in the database of Section 5.1, using **event** and **phh** (and would then fail). See the definition of **retractall** in Section 6.4 for another use of **fail**.

6.3   Classifying Terms

If we wish to define predicates which will be used with a wide variety of argument types, it is useful to be able to distinguish in the definition what should be done for each possible type. At the crudest level, we might wish a different clause to apply if an argument is an integer than if the argument is an atom. Or we might want one clause to apply if the argument is instantiated and another if it is not. The following predicates allow the programmer to put these extra conditions in his clauses.

var(X)

The goal **var(X)** succeeds if X is currently an *uninstantiated* variable. Here is an example of this predicate in use. The following program, which uses the **read_in** predicate defined in Chapter 5, reads in English sentences typed at the terminal and assembles a list of all the words that are used (represented as Prolog atoms), in such a way that each one appears only once in the list. To do this, it keeps a structure that is like an ordinary list, except that it ends in an uninstantiated variable, instead of []. When a word comes along that is not in the list, the variable at the end is made to stand for a piece of list that contains the new word and ends in a new uninstantiated variable. If a sentence typed in consists of a single word followed by a question mark (eg "person?"), the program answers "yes" or "no", according to whether the word has been encountered before, and does not record the word.

```
    go :- readsentences(_).

    readsentences(List) :-
        read_in(Sent),
        continue_from(Sent,List).
```

```
continue_from([bye,'.'],_) :- !.
continue_from([Word,'?'],List) :- !,
    answer_in(Word,List),
    readsentences(List).
continue_from(Sent,List) :-
    all_members(Sent,List),
    readsentences(List).

all_members([],_).
all_members([Word|Words],List) :-
    member(Word,List),
    all_members(Words,List).

member(X,[X|_]).
member(X,[_|List]) :- member(X,List).

answer_in(W,List) :-
    really_in(W,List), !,
    write(yes), nl.
answer_in(_,_) :-
    write(no), nl.

really_in(W,List) :- var(List), !, fail.
really_in(W,[W|_]).
really_in(W,[_|List]) :- really_in(W,List).
```

Originally it is not underlined

The interesting things in this example are the use of **member** and the definition of **really_in**. The idea is that when an attempt is made to satisfy the goal **member(Word,List)** (with Word standing for a word and List standing for the variable-terminated list), the goal will succeed. Moreover, if the word is already in the list, the list will be unchanged. Otherwise, the list will afterwards have the word "tacked onto" its end. This is an unusual use of **member**. The idea is that we are giving it a list that is only partially defined (it ends with an uninstantiated variable). In order to satisfy the goal, Prolog can either find the word in the part of the list that is known, or it can instantiate the end of the list to a list with the word as a member. If the word is not already there, the transition, in terms of "vine diagrams", is from something like:

```
.-------.-------.-------.X (uninstantiated variable)
|       |       |       |
john    went    home    to
```

to

```
.-------.-------.-------.-------.Y (uninstantiated variable)
|       |       |       |       |
john    went    home    to      bed
```

with X instantiated to:

```
.-------Y (uninstantiated variable)
|
bed
```

Now for the predicate **really_in**. We have seen that if we use **member** to see if something is in a list that ends with an uninstantiated variable, the goal will always succeed, instantiating the list as necessary. So we need a special way of seeing if something is *really in* the list. So **really_in** is just like **member**, except that it will never further instantiate the list. It does this by first of all checking whether it has reached the end of the list -- if so, it can fail immediately. To check whether it has reached the end, it uses **var**.

nonvar(X)

The goal **nonvar(X)** succeeds if X is *not* currently an uninstantiated variable. The predicate **nonvar** is therefore the opposite of **var**. Indeed, it could be defined in Prolog by:

```
nonvar(X) :- var(X), !, fail.
nonvar(_).
```

Similar `not(P) :- call(P), !, fail.`
`not(P).`

atom(X) → *actual it mean "Identifier".*

The goal **atom(X)** succeeds if X currently stands for a Prolog atom. As a result, the following behaviour takes place:

✓ ?- atom(23).

no

?- atom(apples).

yes

?- atom('/us/qris/pl.123&').

yes

✓ ?- atom("this is a string").

no

?- atom(X).

no

?- atom(book(bronte,w_h,X)).

no

Something inside of '⊖'
is an atom
but not in " ⟶ "
characters in ASCII

integer(X)

The goal **integer(X)** succeeds if X currently stands for an integer (a whole number). We can use this predicate in the definition of a simple simplifier for arithmetic expressions. Let us assume that we are presented with an expression containing numbers, "unknowns" (like 'x' and 'y') and additions of these. We can represent the numbers by Prolog integers, the unknowns by Prolog atoms and the sum of two expressions by a use of the functor + (with two arguments). Let us also assume that the sum has been "flattened" so that the nesting of subexpressions within expressions is well behaved. Thus we might be presented with:

```
x + 1 + y + 23 + 3 + x + 4
```

(Assuming that + is left associative, this is really (((x+1)+y)+23)...) One form of simplification that could be performed on such an expression would involve all the numbers being added together and the result being put at the front. This would yield:

```
31 + x + y + x
```

from the above example. Here is the definition of a predicate **simplify** which will carry out this simplification.

```
simplify(Expr,Expr1) :-
    simpl(Expr,0,Expr1).

simpl(Expr+A,N,Expr1) :-
    integer(A), !,
    N1 is N+A,
    simpl(Expr,N1,Expr1).
simpl(Expr+A,N,Expr1+A) :-
    atom(A), !,
    simpl(Expr,N,Expr1).
simpl(Rest,N,N1) :-
    integer(Rest), !,
    N1 is Rest+N.
simpl(Rest,0,Rest) :- !.
simpl(Rest,N,N+Rest).
```

[handwritten annotations in margin: "save the expression", "Rest is the last item", and an example worked derivation:
Example: 1+x+y
like: x+y+x → Simpl(x+1+y, 0, Expr1+y)
→ Simpl(x+1, 0, Expr1)
→ Simpl(x, 1, Exp1)
→ Simpl(x, 1, 1+x)]

The definition of **simplify** makes use of another predicate **simpl**. This has an extra argument -- for the "running total" of all the numbers found so far in the expression. The program works its way recursively down the expression, considering each of the things added up in turn. If it is an integer, it is just added on to the running total (clause 1); otherwise it is put onto the result expression (clause 2). When the last thing in the expression is encountered (last three clauses) there are three possibilities. If the last item is an integer, the result (of simplifying this part of the expression) is just the sum of it and the running total. Otherwise, if the running total is 0, the result is just the last item. Otherwise, the result is the expression formed by the addition of the running total to the last item.

atomic(X)

The goal **atomic(X)** succeeds if X currently stands for either an integer or an atom. **atomic** can be defined in terms of **atom** and **integer** by

```
atomic(X) :- atom(X).
atomic(X) :- integer(X).
```

102

6.4 Treating Clauses as Terms

Prolog allows the programmer to examine and alter his program (the clauses that are used to satisfy his goals). This is particularly straightforward, because a clause can be seen as just an ordinary Prolog structure. Therefore Prolog provides "built-in" predicates to allow the programmer to:

- □ Construct a structure representing a clause in the database,

- □ Add a clause, represented by a given structure, to the database,

- □ Remove a clause, represented by a given structure, from the database.

Most operations that involve retrieving information from the database, changing it and adding the result to the database can be performed by the use of these predicates, together with the normal Prolog operations of constructing and decomposing structures. In addition to the examples given here, Section 7.8 shows some of the uses one can make of predicates to add and remove clauses.

Before we look at the relevant built-in predicates, it is important to see just how a Prolog clause can be seen as a structure. For a simple fact, the structure is just the predicate with the arguments. That is, something like

Fact

functor

```
likes(john,X)
```

arguments

can be seen as an ordinary structure, with functor **likes** (with two arguments) and arguments **john** and **X**. A rule, on the other hand, can be seen as a structure whose main functor is ':-' (with two arguments). This functor is declared as an infix operator. The first argument is the head of the clause, and the second is the body. Thus

head   body

Rule

```
likes(john,X) :- likes(X,wine)
```

is really just

```
':-'(likes(john,X),likes(X,wine))
```

-- a perfectly normal structure. Finally, when there is more than one goal in a rule, the goals are considered bound together by the functor ',' (with two arguments). This is also declared as an infix operator. Thus

```
grandparent(X,Z) :- parent(X,Y), parent(Y,Z)
```

is "really" just

```
':-'(grandparent(X,Z), ','(parent(X,Y),parent(Y,Z)) ✓
```

Here now are the predicates that enable the programmer to examine and alter his clauses.

listing(A)

Satisfying a goal of the form **listing(A)**, where **A** is instantiated to an atom, causes all the clauses with the atom as predicate to be written out, as Prolog terms, on the current output file. This is how you check up on what clauses you currently have for some predicate. The exact format of the output will depend on your Prolog implementation. Notice that you will see all the clauses with that atom as predicate, regardless of how many arguments it has. Using **listing** can help you discover a mistake in your program. For instance, in the following example session, the programmer discovers that he has not defined **reverse** properly.

```
?- [test].

test consulted

yes
?- reverse([a,b,c,d],X).

no
?- listing(reverse).

reverse([],[]).

reverse([_44|_45],_38)
    :- reverse(_45,_47),
    appenD(_47,[_44],_38).

yes
```

The listing of the **reverse** clauses reveals that the atom **append** was mis-spelled in the program.

clause(X,Y)

Satisfying a goal of the form **clause(X,Y)** causes X and Y to be matched with the head and body of an existing clause in the database. When an attempt is made to satisfy the goal, X must be instantiated enough so that the main predicate of the clause is known. If there are no clauses for the predicate, the goal just fails. If there is more than one clause that matches, Prolog will pick the first one. In this case, if an attempt is made to resatisfy the goal, the other matching clauses will be picked, one at a time.

104

Notice that, whereas **clause** always has an argument for the body of a clause, not every clause actually has a body. If a clause does not have a body (it is a fact), it is considered to have the dummy body **true**. By providing X's and Y's that are more or less instantiated, you can look for either all the clauses for a given predicate and number of arguments, or all the ones that match some pattern. Thus, for instance:

```
append([],X,X).
append([A|B],C,[A|D]) :- append(B,C,D).

?- clause(append(A,B,C),Y).

A = [], B = _23, C = _23, Y = true;
A = [_23|_24], B = _25, C = [_23|_26], Y = append(_24,_25,_26);
no
```

We can use **clause** to define a version of the **listing** predicate. Let us define **list1** in such a way that, if we try to satisfy a goal **list1(X)** then all the clauses whose heads match X will be printed out. Since the definition of **list1(X)** will involve using **clause** with X as its first argument, we will have to stipulate that X is sufficiently instantiated that the main predicate is known. Here, now, is the definition of **list1**.

```
list1(X) :- clause(X,Y), output_clause(X,Y), write('.'), nl, fail.
list1(X).

output_clause(X,true) :- !, write(X).
output_clause(X,Y) :- write((X :- Y)).
```

When an attempt is made to satisfy a goal **list1(X)**, the first clause causes a search for a clause whose head matches X. If one is found, that clause is printed out and then a failure is generated. Backtracking will reach the **clause** goal and find another clause, if there is one. This will be printed out, a failure will be generated and backtracking will look for another clause. And so on. When there are no more clauses to be found, the **clause** goal will not be able to be resatisfied again, and so will fail. At this point, the second clause for **list1** will be chosen, and so the goal will succeed. As a "side effect", all the appropriate clauses will have been printed out. The definition of **output_clause** says how the clauses will be printed. It looks for the special case of the body **true** and in this case just writes out the head. Otherwise, it writes out the head and the body, put together with the functor :-. Notice the use of the "cut" here -- to say that the first rule is the only valid possibility if the body is **true**. Because this example relies on backtracking, the cut is essential here.

The built-in predicate **clause** can also be used to write a Prolog interpreter in Prolog. That is, we can define what it is to run a Prolog program by something which is itself a Prolog program. Here is the definition of the predicate **call**, in such a way that **call(X)** succeeds as a goal exactly when X succeeds as a goal. In fact, **call** is a built-in predicate (Section 6.7), and is not defined this way at all.

```
call(true) :- !.
```

```
call((G1,G2)) :- !, call(G1), call(G2).
call(Goal) :- clause(Goal,Goals), call(Goals).
```
head match   *body (which are the subgoals)*

The first two clauses deal with the special cases of the goal *true* (which is what **clause** considers to be the "body" of a fact) and a goal which is a conjunction. The last clause covers a simple goal. The procedure is to find a clause whose head matches it (there may be a choice here) and then **call** the goals in the body of that clause. Note that the above definition will not cope with programs using built-in predicates, because such predicates do not have clauses in the usual sense.

asserta(X), assertz(X)
beginning   *end*

The two built-in predicates **asserta** and **assertz** allow one to add new clauses to the database. The two predicates act in exactly the same way, except that **asserta** adds a clause at the *beginning* of the database, whereas **assertz** adds a clause at the *end* ('a' is the first letter of the alphabet, and 'z' is the last). In a goal **asserta(X)**, X must be already instantiated to something representing a clause; indeed, as for **clause**, it must be sufficiently instantiated that the main predicate can be established. It is important to stress that the action of adding a clause to the database is *not* undone when backtracking takes place. Therefore, once we have used **asserta** or **assertz** to add a new clause, that clause will only be removed if we explicitly say so (using **retract**, discussed below).

Let us see an example of one of these predicates in action. There follows a definition of the predicate **consult**. Of course, **consult** is provided as a built-in predicate in most Prolog systems. Nevertheless, it is interesting to see how we could define it in Prolog if we wished to.

```
consult(File) :-
    seeing(Input),
    see(File),
    repeat,
    read(Term),
    process(Term),
    seen,
    see(Input), !.
```
backtracking until EOF

```
process(Term) :- end_of_file_mark(Term), !.
process((?- Q)) :- !, call(Q), !, fail.
process(Clause) :- assertz(Clause), fail.
```
if call(Q) succeed then do nothing. otherwise try next process

There are several interesting points about this definition, apart from the use of **assertz**. Firstly, the goal **seeing(Input)** and its partner **see(Input)** are just to ensure that, however the definition of **consult** is used, the current input file will not be different afterwards from what it was before. Secondly, we have used the predicate **end_of_file_mark** without defining it. **end_of_file_mark(X)** is supposed to succeed only if X is what would be the result of a **read** that encountered the end of a file (see Section 5.4). Different Prolog implementations have different terms to represent "end of file", and so the predicate **end_of_file_mark** would have to be defined differently for different implementations. One possible definition would be:

```
end_of_file_mark((?-end)).
```

The point of the definition of **process** is to cause an appropriate action to be taken for each term read from the input file. The definition is such that it only succeeds when the term is actually the end of file mark. Otherwise a failure occurs after the appropriate action and backtracking goes back to the **repeat** goal. Note the importance of the "cut" at the end of the **consult** definition. This cuts out the choice introduced by the **repeat**, and hence allows backtracking to go back further than the original **consult** choice. A final point -- if a term read from the file represents a question (second clause for **process**) an attempt is made to satisfy the appropriate goal using the **call** built-in predicate (Section 6.7).

retract(X)

The built-in predicate **retract** enables a program to remove clauses from the database. The predicate takes a single argument, representing a term that the clause is to match. The term must be sufficiently instantiated that the predicate of the clause can be determined (as for **asserta, clause,** etc). When an attempt is made to satisfy a goal **retract(X),** X is matched with the first clause in the database that it can be matched with, and that clause is removed. When an attempt is made to resatisfy the goal, Prolog searches on from that clause, looking for another one that will match. If it finds one, the same thing happens as before. If an attempt is made to resatisfy it again, the search continues for another appropriate clause. And so on. Note that, once a clause has been removed it is never reinstated, even when backtracking tries to resatisfy the **retract** goal. If at any time the search cannot find any more matching clauses, the goal fails.

Because the argument X is matched with a clause as it is removed, it is possible to see exactly which clause has been removed, even if X originally stood for something with lots of uninstantiated variables in it. So one can use **retract** to duplicate the function of **clause,** in the case that one wants to remove the clause after finding it. This is how it is used in the definition of **gensym** (Section 7.8).

As an example of the use of **retract,** here is the definition of a useful predicate called **retractall.** When the goal **retractall(X)** is satisfied, all the clauses whose heads match X are removed from the database. Because the definition uses **retract,** X cannot be uninstantiated, for otherwise the predicate of the clause could not be determined. In the definition, we must deal with the two cases of a clause whose head matches X -- a clause with no body (a fact) and a clause with a body (a rule). We have to provide different arguments to **retract** in order to get at these two types of clauses. The definition uses the fact that, if we allow a **retract** goal to backtrack, eventually all the clauses matching the argument will be removed.

```
retractall(X) :- retract(X), fail.
retractall(X) :- retract((X:-Y)), fail.
retractall(_).
```

As an example of the predicate **retractall** in use, here is a definition in Prolog of the predicate **reconsult**. The meaning of **reconsult** is essentially the same as that of **consult**, except that any clauses read are taken to *supersede* existing clauses for the same predicate, rather than add to them (see Section 6.1).

```
reconsult(File) :-
    retractall(done(_)),
    seeing(Old),
    see(File),
    repeat,
    read(Term),
    try(Term),
    seen,
    see(Old), !.

try(X) :- end_of_file_mark(X), !.
try(?-Goals) :- !, call(Goals), !, fail.
try(Clause) :-
    head(Clause,Head),
    record_done(Head), assertz(Clause), fail.

record_done(Hd) :- done(Hd), !.
record_done(Hd) :-
    functor(Hd,Func,Num),
    functor(Proc,Func,Num),
    asserta(done(Proc)),
    retractall(Proc), !.

head((A:-B),A) :- !.
head(A,A).
```

This definition actually looks very similar to what we had for **consult**, with **try** taking the place of the predicate **process**. The main difference is the use in the definition of **record_done**. The idea behind this is that, when the first clause for a given predicate appears in a file, all the existing clauses for that predicate must be removed before the new one is added. We must not remove clauses when later ones for that predicate appear, because then we will be removing clauses that have just been read in. How can we tell whether a clause is the first one in the file for its predicate? The answer is that we keep a record in the database of which predicates we have so far found clauses for in the file. This is done through the predicate **done**. When the first clause for a predicate, for instance **foo** with two arguments, appears, the existing clauses are removed, and the new clause is added to the database. In addition, the fact

```
done(foo(_,_)).
```
is added to database

108

is added. When a later clause for the predicate appears, we will be able to see that the old clauses have already been removed, and so we can avoid accidentally removing new clauses. It is important for the definition that we don't add something like:

```
done( foo(a,X) ).
```

because then the argument of **done** will not necessarily match the head of an incoming clause for **foo**. The pair of goals:

```
..., functor(Hd,Func,Num), functor(Proc,Func,Num), ...
```

have the effect of making Proc stand for a structure with the same functor as the head Hd, but with variables as its arguments (see Section 6.5).

Exercise 6.1: Write a version of **list1** that displays the clauses in a nicer format, using indentation and multiple lines, rather than just all squashed onto one line.

6.5 Creating and Accessing Components of General Structures

Normally when we want to talk about a structure of a certain kind in a Prolog program, we do so by just "mentioning" such a structure. For instance, consider the following definition of the predicate **evaluate**.

```
evaluate(A+B,Res) :-
    evaluate(A,Res1),
    evaluate(B,Res2),
    Res is Res1+Res2.
evaluate(A-B,Res) :-
    evaluate(A,Res1),
    evaluate(B,Res2),
    Res is Res1+Res2.
evaluate(A,A) :-
    integer(A).
```

If we give Prolog a goal for the predicate **evaluate**, with the first argument instantiated to an expression made up of integers and '+'s and '-'s, it will instantiate the second argument to the number obtained by evaluating the expression. Thus we will get interactions like:

```
?- evaluate(3+(2-4)+5-6,X).

X = 0
```

In this definition, we knew that there were only two possible types of structure (apart from numbers) that might appear in the first argument position. So we just mentioned them in separate clauses for the predicate. If we wanted to allow another kind of structure, for instance with the functor * with two arguments, we could just add another clause. For this program, we can always anticipate exactly what structures will appear. However, this will not always be the case. What would happen if we wanted to write a program that took *any structure* as its first argument and displayed it on the terminal, as in the following example?

```
?- output(mother(fred,mary)).
the mother of fred is mary

yes

?- output(difference(6,2,4)).
the difference of 6 and 2 is 4

yes

?- output(a+(b+c)).
the + of a is (b+c)

yes

?- output([a,b,c]).
the . of a is [b,c]

yes
```

$$\therefore [a \mid L] = [a,b,c]$$
$$\Rightarrow L = [b,c]$$

In case the pattern of these examples is not yet clear, the purpose of **output** is to produce output in the following format:

the *functor* of *all arguments but one* is *last argument*

That is, the functor of the argument is displayed after the word 'the'. Then comes the word 'of', followed by all the arguments but one (separated by the word 'and'). Finally come the word 'is' and the last argument. It is not clear from the examples what should happen when the structure has fewer than 2 arguments. But that need not bother us for now. The important point is that we want this program to work *whatever* kind of structure (with at least two components) we give it. One possibility, of course, is to provide a clause for every functor we can possibly think of. But this is a task that we will never finish, because there are infinitely many of them! The way to write this kind of program is to use built-in predicates that perform operations on *general* structures. We will now describe some of these -- the predicates **functor, arg** and '=..'. We will also describe a predicate that works on *general* atoms, the predicate *name*.

functor(T,F,N)

T is instantiated
T is uninstantiated

The predicate **functor** is defined in such a way that **functor(T,F,N)** means "T is a structure with functor F and arity (number of arguments) N". It can be used in basically two ways. In the first way, T is already instantiated. The goal fails if T is not an atom or a structure. If T is an atom or structure, F is matched with the functor and N is matched with the number giving the arity (number of arguments) of the functor. Note that in this context, an atom is considered to be like a structure with arity 0. Here are some examples of goals

110

involving **functor:**

```
?- functor(f(a,b,g(Z)),F,N).

   Z = _23, F = f, N = 3

?- functor(a+b,F,N).

   F = +, N = 2

?- functor([a,b,c],F,N).

   F = ., N = 2          a , [b,c]

?- functor(apple,F,N).

   F = apple, N = 0

?- functor([a,b,c],'.',3).

no

?- functor([a,b,c],a,Z).

no
```

In fact, **functor** is just what we need for the first part of the definition of **output**. One of the first things that the clauses for **output** must do is cause the functor of the argument to be found and printed out. As we will see, the definition starts out:

```
output(S) :- functor(S,Fn,_),
    write('the '), write(Fn), ...
```

Before we can give the rest of the definition, we need to show how the arguments of a general structure can be obtained. This is what the predicate **arg**, described in the next section, is for.

structure

Before we go on to look at **arg**, we should consider the second possible use for **functor**. This occurs when the first argument of the goal (T) is uninstantiated. In this case, both of the others must be instantiated -- specifying a functor and a number of arguments respectively. A goal of this form will always succeed, and as a result T will become instantiated to a structure with the functor and number of arguments provided. So this is a way of *creating general structures*, given a specification in terms of a functor and its number of arguments. The arguments of such a structure created by **functor** are uninstantiated variables. Hence the structure will match any other structure with the same functor and number of arguments. We can use this facility to make an improved version of a predicate defined in the last section. We defined the predicate **list1** in such a way that goals for it would cause the clauses for given predicates to be displayed on the terminal. As we remarked there, this facility is actually already provided more conveniently by the built-in predicate **listing**. The trouble with **list1** is that we had to specify a predicate by giving a structure with the right functor and variables as its arguments. Thus to get the clauses for **sentence** with 14 arguments, we would have laboriously to type:

```
?- list1(sentence(_,_,_,_,_,_,_,_,_,_,_,_,_,_)).
```

Now that we know about **functor**, we can use it to create this structure for us. We can now define a new predicate **list2** (this time with two arguments), as follows:

```
list2(Functor,Arity) :- functor(Struct,Functor,Arity), list1(Struct).
```

Now we just need to specify the functor and the number of arguments. We can achieve the effect of the last question by simply:

```
?- list2(sentence,14).
```

This saves a lot of typing!

A common use of **functor** to create a structure is when we wish to make a "copy" of an existing structure with new variables as the arguments of the principal functor. We can encapsulate this use in the definition of a predicate **copy**, as follows:

```
copy(Old,New) :-
    functor(Old,F,N),
    functor(New,F,N).
```

Copy same structure.

Here, two **functor** goals occur adjacently. If the **copy** goal has the first argument instantiated and the second uninstantiated, then the following will happen. The first **functor** goal will involve the first possible use of the predicate (because the first argument will be instantiated). Hence F and N will become instantiated to the functor and number of arguments of this existing structure. The second **functor** goal uses the predicate in the second way. This time the first argument is uninstantiated, and the information in F and N is used to *construct* the structure New. This is a structure involving the same functor and number of arguments as Old, but with variables as its components. Thus we would get interactions like:

N = 2

```
?- copy(sentence(np(n(john)),v(eats)),X).
```
F

```
X = sentence(_23,_24)
```
F N1 N2

We used a combination of **functor** goals in this way in the definition of **reconsult** in Section 6.4.

arg(N,T,A)

The predicate **arg** must always be used with its first two arguments instantiated. It is used to get hold of a particular argument of a structure. The first argument of **arg** specifies the number of the argument required. The second specifies the structure that the argument

112

is to be found inside. Prolog finds the appropriate argument and then tries to match it with the third **arg** argument. Thus **arg(N,T,A)** succeeds if the Nth argument of T is A. Let us look at some goals involving **arg**.

```
?- arg(2,related(john,mother(jane)),X).

   X = mother(jane)

?- arg(1,a+(b+c),X).

   X = a

?- arg(2,[a,b,c],X).

   X = [b,c]

?- arg(1,a+(b+c),b).

   no
```

— with only two arguments .(a, [b,c])

Now that we have introduced **arg**, we can provide the complete definition of our predicate **output**:

```
output(S) :- functor(S,Fn,_),
   write('the '), write(Fn), write(' of '),
   output_all_but_one(S), write(' is '),
   output_last_arg(S), nl.

output_all_but_one(S) :- functor(S,_,0), !.
output_all_but_one(S) :- functor(S,_,Ar),
   N is Ar-1, o_args(1,N,S).

o_args(N1,N2,_) :- N1>N2, !.
o_args(N1,N1,S) :- !, arg(N1,S,A), write(A).
o_args(N1,N2,S) :- arg(N1,S,A), write(A),
   write(' and '), N3 is N1+1, o_args(N3,N2,S).

output_last_arg(S) :- functor(S,F,N),
   (N=0; (arg(N,S,A),write(A))), !.
```

or

Let us look at another example where **functor** and **arg** are used together. We use them to define the relation of *substitution*. This enables us to see what a term will look like if all occurrences in it of a second term are substituted by another term. We introduce a predicate **substitute** with four arguments. The first two specify what is to be substituted for what. The second two give the term inside which substitution will take place and the term that will result after the substitution. We can read **substitute(A,B,C,D)** as saying "the result of substituting A for B inside C is D". Thus:

```
?- substitute(john,mary,father(mary),X).

   X = father(john)

?- substitute(b,a,[a,b,c,d,e],X).
```

```
X = [b,b,c,d,e]
```

Here is the definition of **substitute**.

```
substitute(New,Old,Old,New) :- !.
substitute(New,Old,Val,Val) :- atomic(Val), !.
substitute(New,Old,Val,NewVal) :-
    functor(Val,Fn,N),
    functor(NewVal,Fn,N),
    subst_args(N,New,Old,Val,NewVal).

subst_args(0,_,_,_,_) :- !.
subst_args(N,New,Old,Val,NewVal) :-
    arg(N,Val,OldArg),
    arg(N,NewVal,NewArg),
    substitute(New,Old,OldArg,NewArg),      → recursive
    N1 is N-1,
    subst_args(N1,New,Old,Val,NewVal).  ← check for each arguments
```

Again, we use **functor** and **arg** in the definition of **substitute** because we do not know in advance what structures will be given. Nevertheless, we want to be able to look down into the arguments, whatever structures they are.

Sometimes we will want to use **functor** and **arg** when the possible structures *are* known. This is because there may be so many arguments that it is inconvenient to specify them every time. Consider an example where we use structures to represent books. We might have a component for the title, the author, the publisher, the date of publication, and so on. Let us say that the resulting structures have 14 components. We might write the following useful definitions:

```
is_a_book(book(_,_,_,_,_,_,_,_,_,_,_,_,_,_)).

title(book(T,_,_,_,_,_,_,_,_,_,_,_,_,_),T).
author(book(_,A,_,_,_,_,_,_,_,_,_,_,_,_),A).
    .
    .
    .
```

In fact, we can write these much more compactly as:

```
is_a_book(X) :- functor(X,book,14).

title(X,T) :- is_a_book(X), arg(1,X,T).
author(X,A) :- is_a_book(X), arg(2,X,T).
    .
    .
    .
```

univ

X =.. L

functor and **arg** provide one way of creating and accessing arguments of general structures. The predicate =.. (pronounced "univ" for historical reasons) provides an alternative way, which is useful if you want to obtain the arguments of a structure all together, or if you want to construct a structure, given a list of arguments. **X =.. L** means "L is the list consisting of the functor of X followed by the arguments of X". Such a goal can be used in two ways, in the same way that a **functor** goal can. If X is instantiated, Prolog creates the appropriate list and tries to match it with L. Alternatively, if X is uninstantiated, the list will be used to construct an appropriate structure for X to stand for. In this case, the head of L must be an atom (it will become the functor of X). Here are some examples of =.. goals:

```
?- foo(a,b,c) =.. X.

   X = [foo,a,b,c]

?- append([A|B],C,[A|D]) =.. L.

   A = _2, B = _3, C = _4, D = _5,
   L = [append,[_2|_3],_4,[_2|_5]]

?- [a,b,c,d] =.. L.

   L = ['.',a,[b,c,d]].

?- (a+b) =.. L.

   L = [+,a,b].

?- (a+b) =.. [+,X,Y].

   X = a, Y = b.

?- [a,b,c,d] =.. [X|Y].

   X = '.', Y = [a,[b,c,d]]

?- X =.. [a,b,c,d].

   X = a(b,c,d).

?- X =.. [append,[a,b],[c],[a,b,c]].

   X = append([a,b],[c],[a,b,c])
```

Here is another definition of **substitute**, using =..

more concise

```
substitute(New,Old,Old,New) :- !.
substitute(New,Old,Val,Val) :- atomic(Val), !.
substitute(New,Old,Val,NewVal) :-
    Val =.. [Fn|Args],
    subst_args(New,Old,Args,NewArgs),
    NewVal =.. [Fn|NewArgs].
```

```
subst_args(_,_,[],[]) :- !.
subst_args(New,Old,[Arg|Args],[NewArg|NewArgs]) :-
    substitute(New,Old,Arg,NewArg),
    subst_args(New,Old,Args,NewArgs).
```

good!

name(A,L)

Whereas **functor, arg** and **=..** are for creating and accessing general *structures*, the predicate **name** is for dealing with general *atoms*. **name** relates an atom to the list of characters (ASCII codes) that make it up. This can be used either to find the characters for a given atom, or to find the atom that has some given characters. **name(A,L)** means that "the characters for the atom A are the list L". If the argument A is instantiated, Prolog creates the list of characters and tries to match them with L. Otherwise Prolog uses the list L to make an atom for A to stand for. Example uses of **name** are as follows:

```
?- name(apple,X).

    X = [97,112,112,108,100]

?- name(X,[97,112,112,108,100]).

    X = apple

?- name(apple,"apple").

yes

?- name(apple,"pear").

no
```

As an example of **name** in use, let us assume that we are representing English words as atoms. We might want to capture the relationship between a noun in its singular and plural forms. One way to do this would be to write a clause for each noun:

```
plural_form(aardvark,aardvarks).
plural_form(abacus,abacuses).
plural_form(abattoir,abattoirs).
```
屠場
```
    .
    .
    .
plural_form(zygote,zygotes).
```
撮合豹子

This would be very laborious and time consuming. It is much better to provide a *general rule* for plural forms, and just specify the exceptions separately. We can do this by using the **name** predicate, thus:

```
plural_form(abacus,abacuses) :- !.
    .
    .
    .
```

116

```
plural_form(yeoman,yeomen) :- !.

plural_form(Sing,Plur) :-
    name(Sing,List1),
    append(List1,"s",List2),
    name(Plur,List2).
```

6.6 Affecting Backtracking

There are two built-in predicates that affect the normal sequence of events that happens during backtracking. Basically, **!** removes possibilities for the resatisfaction of goals, and **repeat** makes new alternatives where there were none before.

!

The "cut" symbol can be viewed as a built-in predicate that "freezes" certain choices that the Prolog system has made. For more details about the "cut", see Chapter 4.

repeat

The built-in predicate **repeat** is provided as an extra way to generate multiple solutions through backtracking. In most Prolog systems, it is 'built-in' -- that is, it is not defined in Prolog, but in the implementation language. Nevertheless, it behaves exactly as if it is defined with the following:

```
repeat.
repeat :- repeat.
```

What is the effect of this if we put **repeat** as a goal in one of our rules? First of all, the goal will succeed, because of the fact which is the first piece of information about **repeat**. Secondly, if backtracking reaches this point again, Prolog will be able to try an alternative -- the rule that is provided as the second piece of information. When it uses this rule, another goal **repeat** is generated. Since this matches the first fact, we have succeeded again. If backtracking reaches here again, Prolog will again use the rule where it used the fact before. To satisfy the extra goal generated, it will again pick the fact as the first option. And so on. In fact, the goal **repeat** will be able to succeed infinitely many times on backtracking. Note the importance of the order of the information here (What would happen if the fact appeared after the rule?).

Why is it useful to generate goals that will always succeed again on backtracking? The reason is that they allow one to build out of rules that have no choices in them rules that do have choices. And we can make them generate different values each time.

Consider the built-in predicate **get0**, which is described in Chapter 5. If Prolog comes across a goal **get0(X)** it takes this as an instruction to look at the next character (letter, digit, space or whatever) that has been input to the system and to try and match the integer representation of this character with whatever value X has. If it will match, the goal succeeds; otherwise it fails. There is no choice involved -- **get0** always only considers the character which comes next at the time it is invoked. The next time a goal involving **get0** is invoked, it will find the character after this, but again there will be no choice. We can define a new predicate **new_get** as follows:

```
new_get(X) :- repeat, get0(X).
```

Cannot be resatisfied.

by ?-;

The predicate **new_get** has the property that it generates the values of all the next characters (in the right order) one by one as its alternative solutions. Why is this? When we first call **new_get(X)**, the subgoal **repeat** succeeds and the subgoal **get0(X)** succeeds with the value of the next character associated with X. When we backtrack, the last place where there was a choice is in the satisfaction of **repeat**. So Prolog forgets everything it has done since then and succeeds in establishing **repeat** in another way. It now has to look at the subgoal **get0(X)** again. By now, the "next character" is the one after what we last saw, and so X ends up with the second character as its value.

We can use our definition of **new_get** to define another useful predicate. The predicate **get** is normally provided as a built-in predicate in Prolog systems. When Prolog finds a goal **get(X)**, it treats this as an instruction to read characters until it finds the next proper printing character (not a space, newline or whatever). It then tries to match the integer representation of this character with X. We can write an approximate definition of **get** as follows:

```
get(X) :- new_get(X), X>32.
```

To understand this definition, one must realise that the printing characters all have integer values above 32, whereas the others all have values 32 or less. What happens when we try to satisfy **get(X)**? First of all, **new_get(X)** matches X against the next character coming in. If the value is less than or equal to 32, the next goal will fail, and **new_get** will have to generate the next character as the next possible solution. This will then be compared to 32, and so on. Eventually, **new_get** will find a printing character, the comparison will succeed, and the value of this character will be returned as the result of **get**.

Exercise 6.2: The above definition of **get** will not necessarily work if we invoke the goal **get(X)** when X is already instantiated. Why is this? *Example = get(33)   B↑   A↑*

One trouble with **repeat** is that it always has a choice to redo when backtracking reconsiders it. So backtracking will never be able to reconsider choices made earlier than the last call of **repeat** unless we manage to cut out the choice in some way. Because of this, the above definitions should be rewritten as:

```
new_get(X) :- repeat, get0(X).

get(X) :- new_get(X), X>32, !.
```
         new_get(X), X>32, !, X=Y.

(Note that this definition will still only work if we attempt to satisfy **get(X)** with X uninstantiated) Because of the problem of backtracking over **repeat** choices, everything using **new_get** should be responsible for cutting out the choice as soon as the character generated is satisfactory for its purposes. In particular, the following definition of a predicate to type out the contents of a file needs the cut so that once the end of file has been reached (taken to be character code 26 here), backtracking never causes an attempt to read more characters.

                    read   write
```
type(File) :- see(File), tell(user),
              new_get(X), put(X),
              X=26, !, seen.
```

6.7 Creating Complex Goals

In rules and questions of the form **X :- Y** or **?- Y,** the term appearing as Y may consist of a single goal, or a conjunction of goals, or a disjunction of goals. Furthermore, it is possible to have variables as goals, and to satisfy a goal when the goal actually fails by using **not**. The predicates described in this section provide ways to specify more complicated ways of expressing goals.

X , Y

The ',' operator specifies a conjunction of goals. This operator was introduced in Chapter 1. Where X and Y are goals, the goal **X,Y** succeeds if X succeeds and if Y succeeds. If X succeeds and then Y fails, then an attempt is made to re-satisfy X. If X fails, then the entire conjunction fails. This is the essence of backtracking. The operator , is left associative, which means that

```
    X, Y, Z
```

means

```
    (X , Y) , Z
```

X ; Y

The ';' operator specifies a disjunction of goals (X or Y). When X and Y are goals, the goal **X;Y** succeeds if X succeeds or if Y succeeds. If X fails, then an attempt is made to satisfy Y. If Y then fails, the entire disjunction fails. We can use the ; operator to express alternatives *within the same rule*. For instance, let us say that something is a person if it is either Adam or Eve, or if it has a mother. We can express this in a single rule as follows:

```
person(X) :- (X=adam;  X=eve; mother(X,Y)).
```
check P.47

In this rule, we have actually specified three alternatives. However, as far as Prolog is concerned, this breaks down into two alternatives, one of which itself introduces two alternatives. Because ; is declared as a right associative **(xfy)** operator, the goal in the clause is actually the same as:

```
';'( X=adam, ';'(X=eve,mother(X,Y)) )
```

So the first possibility is that X is Adam. The second possibility involves the two alternatives that X is Eve or X has a mother.

We can put disjunctions anywhere where we can put any other kind of goal in Prolog. However, it is advisable to add extra brackets to avoid confusion about how the operators ; and , interact. We can usually replace a use of disjunction with a use of several facts and rules, possibly involving the definition of an extra predicate. For instance, the above example is exactly equivalent to:

```
person(adam).
person(eve).
person(X) :- mother(X,Y).
```

The effect of a "cut" includes "freezing" any choices made because of disjunctions since the rule was matched (Chapter 4). Because of this, there are some cases where a program with "cuts" cannot be translated into one without disjunctions. However, in general you are not recommended to use ; excessively. Refer to Chapter 8 for warnings on how injudicious use of ';' may lead to programs that are difficult to understand.

call(X)

It is assumed that X is instantiated to a term that can be interpreted as a goal. The **call(X)** goal succeeds if an attempt to satisfy X succeeds. The **call** goal fails if an attempt to satisfy X fails. At first sight, this predicate may seem redundant, because one might ask why the argument of **call** shouldn't simply appear by itself as a goal? For instance, the goal

```
..., call(member(a,X)), ...
```

can always be replaced by

```
..., member(a,X), ...
```

However, if we are *constructing* goals by using the '=..' operator or its friends, then it is possible to call goals that have a functor that is *unknown* at the time you type in your program. In the definition of **consult** in Section 6.4, for instance, we want to be able to treat any term read after a ?– as a goal. Assuming that P, X, and Y are instantiated to a functor and arguments appropriately, **call** can be used as follows:

```
..., Z =.. [P,X,Y], call(Z), ...
```

The above line can be thought of as a way of expressing the following sort of call, which is *not correct syntax* in the standard version of Prolog we are using in this book:

```
..., P(X,Y), ...
```

However, some versions of Prolog do permit the use of variable functors in goals.

not(X)

It is assumed that X is instantiated to a term that can be interpreted as a goal. The **not** goal succeeds if an attempt to satisfy X fails. The **not** goal fails if an attempt to satisfy X succeeds. In this way, **not** is rather like **call**, except that the success or failure of the argument, interpreted as a goal, is reversed.

What is the difference between the following two questions?

```
/* 1 */     ?- member(X,[a,b,c]), write(X).

/* 2 */     ?- not(not(member(X,[a,b,c]))), write(X).
```

One might be tempted to say that there is no difference, because in question 2, **member(X,[a,b,c])** succeeds, so **not(member(X,[a,b,c]))** fails, and so **not(not(member(X,[a,b,c])))** succeeds. This is partly right. However, the first question would cause the atom 'a' to be written, and the second goal would cause an *uninstantiated variable* to be written. This is what happens when an attempt is made to satisfy the first goal of the second question above:

1.   The **member** goal succeeds, instantiating **X** to **a**.

2.   An attempt is made to satisfy the first **not** goal, and it fails because the **member** goal, its argument, succeeded. Now remember that when a goal fails, any variables that became instantiated, such as X in the example, must now "forget" what they stood

for. Hence X becomes uninstantiated.

3. An attempt is made to satisfy the second **not** goal, and it succeeds, because its argument (**not(member...)**) failed. X is still uninstantiated.

4. An attempt is made to satisfy the **write** goal, with X uninstantiated. The uninstantiated variable, as described in Section 6.9, is printed in a special way.

i.e. —39

6.8 Equality

This section deals briefly with the various built-in predicates for testing and making things equal in Prolog.

X = Y

def: X = X.

When Prolog encounters a goal **X = Y** it attempts to make X and Y equal by matching them together. If it can match them, the goal succeeds (and X and Y may have become more instantiated). Otherwise the goal fails. A fuller discussion of this predicate is given in Section 2.4.

X \= Y

The **\=** predicate is the opposite of the **=** predicate in terms of success and failure. That is, **X \= Y** succeeds if **X = Y** fails, and vice versa. If the goal **X \= Y** succeeds (X and Y could not be matched), the instantiation of X and Y will not have been changed at all. If **\=** happened not to be a built-in predicate, we could define it in Prolog, thus:

```
X \= Y :- X=Y, !, fail.
X \= Y.
```

X == Y

The predicate **==** represents a much stricter equality test than **=**. That is, if **X == Y** ever succeeds then **X = Y** does as well. On the other hand, this is not so the other way round. The way that **==** is more strict is by the way it considers variables. The **=** predicate will consider an uninstantiated variable to be equal to anything, because it will match anything. On the other hand, **==** will only consider an uninstantiated variable to be equal to *another uninstantiated variable that is already sharing with it*. Otherwise the test will fail. So we get the following behaviour:

```
?- X == Y.
```

```
no

?- X == X.

    X = _23

?- X=Y, X==Y.

    X = _23, Y = _23

?- append([A|B],C) == append(X,Y).

no

?- append([A|B],C) == append([A|B],C).

    A = _23, B = _24, C = _25
```

Here is a little program that makes use of the == predicate. The idea is that the computer has a model of a tiny world, eg the objects on a table top. It has 10 descriptions of objects, but it does not know how many different objects there really are. Thus, for instance, "the object on the far left" may be describing the same thing as "the red object". This program is to help organise the knowledge about what descriptions refer to the same object. It carries out a "conversation" with the programmer, who tells it which descriptions are "equal" and can also ask it questions. Here is a sample conversation:

```
?- converse.

1 = 3.
ok
2 = 8.
ok
6 = 4.
ok
2 = 10.
ok
10 = 4.
ok
7 = 3.
ok
?- 6 = 2.
yes
?- 7 = 1.
yes
?- 3 = 8.
no
  .
  .
  .
```

The first six inputs from the programmer state "equalities" between descriptions. Thus, 1 = 3 means that description 1 refers to the same object as description 3. The last three inputs ask questions. The program can show that 6 = 2 because 6 = 4, 4 = 10 and 10 = 2. Here is the program.

(handwritten: √ be any functor of 10 components)

```
converse :-
    functor(W,world,10),
    proceed(W).

proceed(W) :-
    read(Command),
    answer(Command,W),
    proceed(W).

answer(N1=N2,W) :-
    N1=<11, N2=<11, !,
    arg(N1,W,Var),
    arg(N2,W,Var),
    write(ok), nl.
answer((?-N1=N2),W) :-
    N1=<11, N2=<11, !,
    arg(N1,W,V1),
    arg(N2,W,V2),
    say_equal(V1,V2).
answer(Other,W) :-
    write('eh?'), nl.

    say_equal(V1,V2) :- V1==V2, !, write(yes), nl.
    say_equal(V1,V2) :- write(no), nl.
```

(handwritten: loop)

(handwritten: — always of form { N1 = N2 / or ?- N1 = N2 / or other)

The program knows the descriptions by the numbers 1 to 10, and it represents the world by a structure with 10 components, one component corresponding to each description. In its model at any stage, each argument of the **world** functor is an uninstantiated variable. If two descriptions are found to refer to the same object, the two corresponding variables are matched together (the built-in predicate **arg** is used to access the appropriate component). In order to tell whether two descriptions are "equal", the program just has to test whether the two variables share, using **==**. The properties of sharing are just like those of equality (for instance, if A shares with B and B shares with C then A shares with C). Therefore the program will automatically know about "equalities" that follow from what it has been told.

X \== Y

This predicate is to **==** as \= is to =. That is, a goal involving it succeeds exactly when the same goal for **==** would fail, and vice versa. Again, we could imagine it defined in Prolog, thus:

(handwritten: def)

```
X \== Y :- X == Y, !, fail.
X \== Y.
```

6.9 Input and Output

The predicates made available for reading and writing characters and terms were descibed in Chapter 5. Here we summarise each one.

get0(X)

This goal succeeds if X can be matched with the next character encountered on the current input stream. get0 succeeds only once (it cannot be re-satisfied). The operation of moving to the next character is not undone on backtracking, because there is no way to put a character back onto the current input stream.

get(X) $X > 32$ (i.e $>= 33$)

This goal succeeds if X can be matched with the next printing character encountered on the current input stream. Printing characters have an ASCII code that is greater than 32. Any non-printing characters are skipped. get succeeds only once (it cannot be re-satisfied). The operation of get, is not undone on backtracking, because there is no way to put a character back onto the current input stream.

skip(X)

This goal reads and skips over characters from the current input stream until a character is found that matches with X. skip succeeds only once.

read(X)

This goal reads the next term from the current input stream and matches it with X. read succeeds only once. The term must be followed by a dot (.), which does not become a part of the term, and at least one non-printing character. The dot is removed from the current input stream.

put(X)

This goal writes the integer X as a character on the current output stream. put succeeds only once. An error occurs if X is not instantiated.

nl

Writes a control sequence to the current output stream that causes a "new line". On a computer display, all characters after the use of nl appear on the next line of the page. nl succeeds only once.

tab(X)

Writes a quantity of X "space" characters to the current output stream. An error occurs if X is not instantiated. **tab** succeeds only once.

write(X)

?- write("ab") → [97,98]
?- write('ab') → ab   p.104

This goal writes the term X to the current output stream. **write** succeeds only once. Any uninstantiated variables in X are written as uniquely numbered variables beginning with an underscore, such as '_239'. Sharing variables within the same argument to **write** have the same number when they are printed out. The predicate **write** takes account of current operator declarations when it prints a term. Thus an infix operator will be printed out between its arguments, for instance.

?- write([1,2,3]) → [1,2,3]
?- write(([1,2,3])) → ([1,2,3])

display(X)

The predicate **display** works in exactly the same way as **write**, except that it ignores any operator declarations. When **display** is used, any structure is printed out with the functor first and the arguments in brackets afterwards.

op(X,Y,Z)

This goal declares an operator having precedence X, position/associativity Y, and name Z. The position/associativity specification is taken from the following set of atoms:

prefix postfix
fx fy xf yf xfx xfy yfx yfy
                     right left.

If the operator declaration is legal, then **op** will succeed. See Section 5.5 for more details.

6.10 Handling Files

The predicates that Prolog makes available for altering the current input and current output streams were introduced in Chapter 5. Here we summarise each one.

see(X)

This goal opens file X, if it is not already open, and defines the current input stream to originate from file X. An error occurs if X is not instantiated, or if X names a file that does not exist.

seeing(X)

This goal succeeds if the name of the current input stream matches with X, and fails otherwise.

seen   ~~back to terminal~~

This goal closes the current input stream, and defines the current input stream to be the user's computer terminal's keyboard.

tell(X)

This goal opens file X, if it is not already open, and defines the current output stream to write into the file. An error occurs if X is not instantiated. The first time **tell** is used on a file not already open, if X names a file that does not exist, then a file of that name is created. Otherwise, if X names a file that exists, then the previous contents of the file are destroyed.

telling(X)

This goal succeeds if X matches with the name of the current output stream, and fails otherwise.

told

This goal closes the current output stream, causing an end-of-file marker to be written on the file. The current input stream reverts to the user's computer terminal's display.

6.11 Evaluating Arithmetic Expressions

Arithmetic was first discussed in Section 2.5. Here we summarise the use of the **is** operator, and what operators are available for constructing arithmetic expressions.

X is Y

Y must be instantiated to a structure that can be interpreted as an arithmetic expression as described in Section 2.4. First, the structure instantiated for Y is evaluated to give an integer, called the *result*. If X is uninstantiated, then X becomes instantiated to the result, and the **is** succeeds. If X is already instantiated, then X and the result are compared for equality, and the **is** succeeds or fails on the basis of the test. The operators that can be used to make up the structure on the right-hand side of an **is** are as follows:

X + Y

The addition operator, an infix operator of precedence 31. When evaluated by **is**, its result is the numerical sum of its two arguments. The arguments must be instantiated to structures that evaluate to integers.

X - Y

The subtraction operator, an infix operator of precedence 31. When evaluated by **is**, its result is the numerical difference of its two arguments. The arguments must be instantiated to structures that evaluate to integers.

X * Y

The multiplication operator, an infix operator of precedence 21. When evaluated by **is**, its result is the numerical product of its two arguments. The arguments must be instantiated to structures that evaluate to integers.

X / Y

The integer division operator, an infix operator of precedence 21. When evaluated by **is**, its result is the numerical *quotient* of its two arguments. The arguments must be instantiated to structures that evaluate to integers.

X mod Y

The integer remainder operator of precedence 11. When evaluated by **is**, its result is the integer *remainder* that is generated when X is divided by Y. The arguments must be instantiated to structures that evaluate to integers.

6.12 Comparing Numbers *6 predicates*

Six predicates are provided for comparing numbers. These predicates were first presented in Section 2.5 when we discussed arithmetic. Each predicate is an infix operator having two arguments, and having a precedence of 40.

X = Y

The *equality* operator, described in Section 6.8, also succeeds when two integer arguments are the same.

X \= Y

The *inequality* operator of Section 6.8 also holds for integers, succeeding when the two arguments are not the same integer.

X ≤ Y

The *less than* operator succeeds when the left-hand integer argument is less than the right-hand integer argument. Both arguments must be instantiated.

X > Y

The *greater than* operator succeeds when the left-hand integer argument is greater than the right-hand integer argument. Both arguments must be instantiated, or an error occurs.

X >= Y

The *greater than or equal to* operator succeeds when the left-hand integer argument is greater than or equal to the right-hand integer argument. Both arguments must be instantiated.

X =< Y

The *less than or equal to* operator succeeds when the left-hand argument is less than or equal to the right-hand argument. Both arguments must be instantiated. Notice that the predicate is spelled as =< rather than <=, so that <= is free to be used as an operator that looks like an arrow.

6.13 Watching Prolog at Work

This section describes the built-in predicates that enable you to watch your program as it runs. We will only describe the built-in predicates here, and refer you to Chapter 8 for a more detailed discussion of debugging and tracing.

trace

The effect of satisfying the goal **trace** is to turn on *exhaustive tracing*. This means that afterwards you will get to see every goal that your program generates at each of the four main *ports*.

notrace

The effect of the goal **notrace** is to stop exhaustive tracing from now on. However, any tracing due to the presence of spy points will continue.

spy P   *fx*

The predicate **spy** is used when you want to pay special attention to goals involving some specific predicates. You do this by setting *spy points* on them. The predicate is defined as a prefix operator, and so you do not need to put brackets round the argument. The argument can be any of the following:

- An atom. In this case, a spy point is put on all predicates with this atom, however many arguments are used. Thus if we had clauses for **sort** with both two and three arguments, the goal **spy sort** would cause spy points to be set on both sets of clauses.

- A structure with a single numerical argument. This specifies a predicate with the functor of the structure and the number of arguments given in the argument. Thus **spy sort(2)** would cause spy points to be set on goals for the predicate **sort** with two arguments. *# of arg.*

- A list. In this case, the list must be terminated with **[]**, and each element of the list must itself be an allowable argument to **spy**. Prolog will put spy points in all the places specified in the list. Thus **spy [sort(2),append(3)]** would cause spy points to be set on **sort** with two arguments and **append** with three.

debugging

The built-in predicate **debugging** allows you to see which spy points you currently have set. The list of spy points is printed out as a side-effect of the goal **debugging** being satisfied.

nodebug — *remove all spy points*

The goal **nodebug** causes all your current spy points to be removed.

nospy *P*

Like **spy**, **nospy** is a prefix operator. **nospy** is more selective than **nodebug**, because you can specify exactly which spy points you wish to have removed. You do this by providing an argument in exactly the same form as for **spy**. Thus the goal **nospy [reverse(2),append(3)]** will remove any spy points on **reverse** with two arguments and **append** with three arguments.

Chapter 7. More Example Programs

Each section of this chapter deals with a particular application of Prolog programming. We suggest that you read all of the sections in this chapter. Do not be concerned if you do not understand the purpose of a program because you are not acquainted with the particular application. For example, only those readers who have been introduced to Calculus will appreciate the value of symbolic differentiation. Read it anyway, because the program for finding symbolic derivatives demonstrates how to use pattern matching to transform one kind of structure (an arithmetic expression) into another one. What is important is to gain an understanding of programming techniques available to the Prolog programmer, regardless of the particular application.

We hope that we have included enough applications to satisfy most tastes. Naturally, all of the applications deal with areas that suit Prolog's way of representing the world. You will *not* find how to calculate the flow of heat through a square metal pipe, for example. It is possible to solve such problems using Prolog, but the expressiveness and power of Prolog is not shown to advantage on problems which are essentially repetitious calculations over arrays of numbers. We would like to be able to discuss large Prolog programs, such as those that are used by Artificial Intelligence researchers for understanding natural language. Unfortunately, the aims of a book like this one preclude discussion of programs that are longer than a page of text and which would appeal only to a specialised audience.

7.1   A Sorted Tree Dictionary

Suppose we wish to make associations between items of information, and retrieve them when required. For example, an ordinary dictionary associates a word with its definition, and a foreign language dictionary associates a word in one language with a word in another language. We have already seen one way to make a dictionary: with facts. If we wanted to make an index of the performance of horses in the British Isles during the year 1938, we could simply define facts `winnings(X,Y)` where X is the name of the horse, and Y is the number of guineas (a unit of currency) won by the horse. The following database of facts could serve as part of such an index:

```
        .
        .
        .
    winnings(abaris,582).
    winnings(careful,17).
```

```
winnings(jingling_silver,300).
winnings(maloja,356).
    .
    .
    .
```

If we wanted to find out how much was won by **maloja,** we would simply ask the right question, and Prolog would give us the answer:

```
?- winnings(maloja,X).

X=356
```

Remember that when Prolog searches through a database to find a matching fact, it starts at the top of the database and works its way down. This means that if our dictionary database is arranged in alphabetical order, as is the one above, then Prolog will take a short amount of time to find the winnings for **ablaze,** and it will take longer to find the winnings for **zoltan.** Although Prolog can look through its database much faster than you could look through a printed index, it is silly to search the index from beginning to end if we know that the horse we are looking for is at the end. Also, although Prolog has been designed to search its database quickly, it is not always as fast as we would wish. Depending on how large your index is, and depending on how much information you have stored about each horse, Prolog might take an uncomfortably long amount of time to search the index.

For these reasons and others, computer scientists have devoted much effort into finding good ways to store information such as indices and dictionaries. Prolog itself uses some of these methods to store its own facts and rules, but it is sometimes helpful to use these methods in our programs. We describe one such method for representing a dictionary, called the *sorted tree.* The sorted tree is both an efficient way of using a dictionary, and a demonstration of how lists of structures are helpful.

A sorted tree consists of some structures called *nodes*, where there is one node for each entry in the dictionary. Each node has four components. It contains the two associated items of information, rather like **winnings,** above. One of these items, called the *key*, is the one whose name determines its place in the dictionary (the name of the horse in our example). The other is used to store any other information about the object involved (the winnings in our example). In addition, each node contains a tail (like the tail of a list) to a node containing a key whose name is alphabetically *less than* the name of the key in the node itself. Furthermore, the node contains *another* tail, to a node whose name is alphabetically *greater* than the key in the node. Let us use a structure called **w(H,W,L,G)** (w is short for "winnings") where H is the name of a horse (an atom) used as the key, W is the amount of guineas won (an integer), L is a structure with a horse whose name is less than H's, and G is a structure with a horse whose name is greater than H's. If there are no structures for L and G, we will leave them uninstantiated. Given a small set of horses, the structure might look like this when written as a tree:

```
                      w(massinga, 858,  ,  ).
                            /  \
                           /    \
                          /      \
           w(braemar, 385,  , _ )      w(panorama, 158,  , _ )
                        /                        /
                       /                        /
                      /                        /
          w(adela, 588, _ , _ )      w(nettleweed, 579, _ , _ )
```

Represented as a structure in Prolog, and indented so as not to be too wide to fit on the page, this would look like:

```
w(massinga,858,
    w(braemar,385,
        w(adela,588,_,_),
        _),
    w(panorama,158,
        w(nettleweed,579,_,_)
        _)
    ).
```

Now given a structure like this, we wish to "look up" names of horses in the structure to find out how many guineas they won during 1938. The structure would have the format w(H,W,L,G) as above. The boundary condition is when the name of the horse we are looking for is H. In this case, we have succeeded and need not try any alternatives. Otherwise, we must use **aless**, defined in Chapter 3, to decide which "branch" of the tree, L or G, to "look up" recursively. We use these principles to define the predicate **lookup**, for which **lookup(H,S,G)** means that horse H, when "looked up" in index S (a **w** structure), won G guineas:

```
lookup(H, w(H,G,_,_), G) :- !.
lookup(H, w(H1,_,Before,_), G) :-
    aless(H,H1),
    lookup(H,Before,G).
lookup(H, w(H1,_,_,After), G) :-
    not(aless(H,H1)),
    lookup(H,After,G).
```

If we use this predicate to search a sorted tree, in general we examine fewer horses than if we arranged them in a single list, and searched that from start to finish.

There is a suprising and interesting property of this **lookup** procedure: if we look for the name of a horse which is not in the structure, then whatever information we supplied about the horse when we used **lookup** as a goal *will be instantiated* in the structure when **lookup** returns from its recursion. In other words, the interpretation of **lookup** in this question

```
?- lookup(ruby_vintage,S,X).
```

→
→ *Lookup (ruby_vintage, After, X)*
  After = w(ruby_vintage, X, _, _).
    X = _45

is

> *Construct a structure, instantiated to S, such that* `ruby_vintage` *is "paired" with* X.

So, `lookup` is inserting new components in a partially specified structure. We can therefore use `lookup` repeatedly to create a dictionary. For instance,

```
?- lookup(abaris,X,582), lookup(maloja,X,356).
```

would instantiate X to be a sorted tree with two entries. The actual means by which `lookup` functions for both storing and retrieving components takes advantage of what you should know already about Prolog, so we urge you to work this out by yourself. Hint: when `lookup(H,S,G)` is used in a conjunction of goals, the "changes" made to S only hold *over the scope of S*.

Exercise 7.1: Experiment with the `lookup` predicate to determine what difference it makes to insert items in the dictionary in a different order each time. For example, what does the dictionary tree look like when entries have been inserted in the order: **massinga, braemar, nettleweed, panorama?** In the order: **adela, braemar, nettleweed, massinga?**

7.2 Searching a Maze

It is a dark and stormy night. As you drive down a lonely country road, your car breaks down, and you stop in front of a splendid palace. You go to the door, find it open, and begin looking for a telephone. How do you search the palace without getting lost, and know that you have searched every room? Also, what is the shortest path to the telephone? It is just for such emergencies that maze-searching methods have been devised.

In many computer programs, such as those for searching mazes, it is useful to keep lists of information, and search the list if some information is needed at a later time. For example, if we decide to search the palace for a telephone, we might need to keep a list of the room numbers visited so far, so we don't go round in circles visiting the same rooms over and over again. What we do is to write down the room numbers visited on a piece of paper. Before entering a room, we check to see if its number is on our piece of paper. If it is, we ignore the room, since we must have been to it previously. If the room number is not on the paper, we write down the number, and enter the room. And so on until we find the telephone. There are some refinements to be made to this method, and we will do so later when we discuss graph searching. But first, let's write down the steps in order, so we know what problems there are to solve:

1. Go to the door of any room.

2. If the room number is on our list, ignore the room and go to Step 1. If there are

no rooms in sight, than "backtrack" through the room we went through previously, to see if there are any other rooms near it.

3. Otherwise, add the room number to our list.

4. Look in the room for a telephone.

5. If there is no telephone, go to Step 1. Otherwise we stop, and our list has the path that we took to come to the correct room.

We shall assume that room numbers are constants, but it does not matter whether they are integers or atoms. First, we can solve the problem of how to look up room numbers on the piece of paper by using the **member** predicate defined in Section 3.3. Now we can get on with the problem of searching the maze. Let us consider a small example, where we are given the floor plan of a house, with letters labelling the different rooms, like this:

Notice that gaps in the walls are meant to represent doors, and that room "a" is simply a representation of the space outside the house. There are doors from rooms a to b, from c to d, from f to e, and so forth. The facts about where there are doors can be represented as Prolog facts:

```
d(a,b).
d(b,e).
d(b,c).
d(d,e).
d(c,d).
d(e,f).
d(g,e).
```

Notice that the information about doors is not redundant. For example, although we have said that there is a door between room g and room e, we have not said that there is a door between room e and room g: we have not asserted **d(e,g)**. To get around this problem of representing two-way doors, we could write a duplicate **d** fact for each door, reversing the arguments. Or, we could make the program recognise that each door fact can be interpreted in two ways. This is the alternative that we choose in the program that follows.

To go from one room to another, we must recognise one of two cases:

□ we are in the room we want to go to, or

□ we have to pass through a door, and recognise these cases again (recursively).

Consider the goal go(X,Y,T), which succeeds if it is possible to go from room X to room Y. The third argument T is our piece of paper that we carry, that has a "trail" of the room numbers that we have visited so far.

The boundary condition for going from room X to room Y is if we are already at room Y (X is Y). This is represented as the clause:

```
go(X,X,T).
```

Otherwise we choose some adjoining room, call it Z, and see if we have been to it before. If we haven't, then we "go" from Z to Y, adding Z to our list. All of this is represented as the following clause:

```
go(X,Y,T) :- d(X,Z), not(member(Z,T)), go(Z,Y,[Z|T]).
```

> To "go" from X to Y, not passing though the rooms on T, find a door from X to anywhere (Z), ensure that Z is not already on the list, and "go" from Z to Y, using the list T with Z added to it.

There are three ways that failures can occur in the use of this rule. First, if there is no door from X to anywhere. Second, if the door we choose is on the list. Third, if we cannot "go" to the Z we chose because it fails deeper in the recursion. If the first goal d(X,Z) fails, then it will cause any use of go to fail. At the "top level" (not a recursive call), this means that there is no path from X to Y. At lower levels, it simply means we must backtrack to find a different door.

The program as stated treats each door as a "one-way" door. If we assume that having a door from room a to room b is just the same as having a door from room b to room a, then we must make this explicit, as indicated above. Instead of supplying a duplicate fact for each d fact but with the arguments reversed, there are two ways to put this information in the program. The most obvious way is to add another rule:

```
go(X,X,T).
go(X,Y,T) :- d(X,Z), not(member(Z,T)), go(Z,Y,[Z|T]).
go(X,Y,T) :- d(Z,X), not(member(Z,T)), go(Z,Y,[Z|T]).
```

136

Or, the semicolon operator (meaning "or") can be used:

```
go(X,X,T).
go(X,Y,T) :- (d(X,Z) ; d(Z,X)), not(member(Z,T)), go(Z,Y,[Z|T]).
```

Now for finding the telephone. Consider the goal **hasphone(X)** which succeeds if room X has a telephone. If we want to say that room g has a telephone, we simply write our database with **hasphone(g)** in it. Supposing we start at room a, the question we ask to find the path to the telephone is:

```
?- go(a,X,[]), hasphone(X).
```

Initialising the third argument to the empty list means that we start with a "clean piece of paper". This can be changed to provide variety: the question *find the telephone without entering rooms d and f* would be expressed in Prolog as

```
?- go(a,_,[d,f]).
```

In Section 7.9 we will describe some general graph searching procedures, including some attempts at finding the shortest path through a graph.

Exercise 7.2: Annotate the above program so that it will print messages such as "entering room Y" and "found telephone in room Y" with the appropriate room numbers filled in.

Exercise 7.3: Can alternate paths be found by this program? If so, where do you put the "cut" goal to prevent more than one path from being found?

Exercise 7.4: What determines the order in which rooms are searched?

7.3 The Towers of Hanoi

The "Towers of Hanoi" is a game played with three poles and a set of discs. The discs are graded in diameter, and fit onto the poles by means of a hole cut through the centre of each disc. Initially all the discs are on the left-hand pole, as shown here:

The object of the game is to move all of the discs onto the centre pole. The right-hand pole can be used as a "spare" pole, a temporary resting place for discs. Each time a disc is moved from one pole to another, two constraints must be observed: only the top disc on a pole can be moved, and no disc may be placed on top of a smaller one.

Many people who play this game never actually discover the quite simple strategy which will correctly play the Towers of Hanoi game with three poles and *N* discs. To save you the effort of finding it, we reveal it here:

□   The boundary condition occurs when there are no discs on the source (the left-hand) pole.

□   Move *N*-1 discs from the source pole to the spare pole (the right-hand one), using the destination as a spare. Notice that this is a recursive move.

□   Move a single disc from the source pole to the destination pole. At this point our program will print a message informing us of the move.

□   Finally, move *N*-1 discs from the spare to the destination, using the source as the spare.

The Prolog program that implements this strategy is defined as follows. We define a predicate **hanoi** having one argument, such that **hanoi(N)** means to print out the sequence of moves when N discs are on the source pole. Of the two **move** clauses, the first one is the boundary condition as described above, and the second clause implements the recursive cases. The predicate **move** has four arguments. The first argument is the number of discs to be moved. The other three represent the poles which are the source, destination and spare for moving the discs. The predicate **inform** uses **write** to print out the names of the poles that are involved in moving a disc.

```
hanoi(N) :- move(N,left,centre,right).

move(0,_,_,_) :- !.
move(N,A,B,C) :-
    M is N-1,
    move(M,A,C,B),
    inform(A,B),
    move(M,C,B,A).

inform(X,Y) :- write([move,a,disc,from,the,X,pole,to,the,Y,pole]), nl.
```

138

7.4 Improved Parts Inventory

In Chapter 3 we discussed a program for printing a list of parts required in constructing an assembly when given an inventory of parts. In the improved program described in this section, we take into account how many of each part is required, by accumulating the quantities of parts required as we descend from assemblies to their constituents. The improved program also handles duplicates properly: the **collect** procedure removes duplicates, while summing up the quantities of each part required, before the answer is printed out.

The structure of the inventory database is identical to that described in Chapter 3. An assembly is represented as a list of structures of the form **quant(X,Y)**, where X is the name of some part (a basic part or an assembly), and Y is the quantity of such parts needed.

Each predicate of the modified program, together with a description of its purpose, is listed here:

partlist(A): prints out a list of all of the basic parts required, and the quantities of each, for the construction of assembly A.

partsof(N,X,P): P is a list of structures **quant(Part,Num)** giving the part name **Part** and the quantity **Num** of each required for the construction of N X's. N is an integer and X is an atom which is the name of some part.

partsoflist(N,S,P): P is a list of structures **quant(Part,Num)** as above, required for the construction of the sum of all the members of the list S, given that N such lists are required. N is an integer, S is a list of **quant** structures.

collect(P,A): P and A are lists of **quant** structures. A is a list with the same members of P except that there are no duplicate parts, and for any duplicates in P, the quantity of that part in A is the sum of all the corresponding quantities in P. We use **collect** to collect several descriptions of collections of like parts. For instance, "3 screws, 4 cushions and 4 screws" is collected to form "7 screws and 4 cushions".

collectrest(X,N,L,O,N): L and O are lists of **quant** structures. O is the list of all the members of L except for those which have X as their part. X is an atom which is the name of some part. N is the sum of all the quantities of X in list L, added to M. M is an integer that is used to accumulate the quantity of X's in L, and is passed down to each call of **collectrest**. At the end of the recursion, which is caught by the boundary condition, M is returned as N.

printpartlist(P): P is a list of **quant** structures, printed one structure per line of output. The **put(9)** prints the ASCII code 9, which is a horizontal tab motion.

append is what we have seen many times before.

The complete Prolog program is as follows:

```
partlist(T) :- partsof(1,T,P), collect(P,Q), printpartlist(Q).

partsof(N,X,P) :- assembly(X,S), partsoflist(N,S,P).
partsof(N,X,[quant(X,N)]) :- basicpart(X).

partsoflist(_,[],[]).
partsoflist(N,[quant(X,Num)|L],T) :-
    M is N * Num,
    partsof(M,X,Xparts),
    partsoflist(N,L,Restparts),
    append(Xparts,Restparts,T).

collect([],[]).
collect([quant(X,N)|R],[quant(X,Ntotal)|R2]) :-
    collectrest(X,N,R,O,Ntotal),
    collect(O,R2).

collectrest(_,N,[],[],N).
collectrest(X,N,[quant(X,Num)|Rest],Others,Ntotal) :-
    !,
    M is N + Num,
    collectrest(X,M,Rest,Others,Ntotal).
collectrest(X,N,[Other|Rest],[Other|Others],Ntotal) :-
    collectrest(X,N,Rest,Others,Ntotal).

printpartlist([]).
printpartlist([quant(X,N)|R]) :-
    tab(4), write(N), put(9),write(X),nl,printpartlist(R).
```

(handwritten annotations: "facts" pointing to assembly(X,S); "head", "tail", "result" pointing to partsoflist clauses; "head of head / tail . tail!" pointing to collect clause)

7.5 List Processing

In this section we shall describe some basic predicates that are useful for manipulating lists. Because Prolog makes arbitrary data structures available to you, lists may not take on the omnipresent rôle that they do in other computer languages such as LISP and POP-2. Whether or not your programs will make use of lists, it is always important to understand how the predicates defined in this section work, because they employ principles that can be applied to manipulating any kind of data structure.

Finding the last element of a list: the goal **last(X,L)** succeeds if element X is the last element of list L. The boundary condition is when there is only one element in L. The first rule checks for this. The usual kind of recursive case forms the second rule.

```
last(X,[X]).
last(X,[_|Y]) :- last(X,Y).

?- last(X,[talk,of,the,town]).
X=town
```

2 *Checking for consecutive elements:* the goal **nextto(X,Y,L)** succeeds if elements X and Y are consecutive elements of list L. Due to the way variables work, either X, or Y, or both could be uninstantiated when an attempt is made to satisfy the goal. The first clause, which checks for the boundary condition, must also assume that there are more elements in the list after X and Y. This is why the anonymous variable appears, holding down the tail of the list.

```
nextto(X,Y,[X,Y|_]).
nextto(X,Y,[_|Z]) :- nextto(X,Y,Z).
```

3 *Appending lists:* We have seen this example before, but more explanation will not hurt. The goal **append(X,Y,Z)** succeeds when Z is a list constructed by appending Y to the end of X. For example,

```
?- append([a,b,c],[d,e,f],Q).

Q=[a,b,c,d,e,f]
```

It is defined as follows:

```
append([],L,L).
append([X|L1],L2,[X|L3]) :- append(L1,L2,L3).
```

The boundary condition occurs when the first argument is the empty list. This is because appending the empty list to a list does not change the list. Furthermore, we will gradually approach the boundary condition because each recursion of **append** removes an element from the head of the first argument. The following points illustrate the principle of the second rule:

- The first element of the first list (X) will always be the first element of the third list.

- The tail of the first list (L1) will always have the second argument (L2) appended to it to form the tail (L3) of the third argument.

- The best way to accomplish the appending described in the previous point is to use **append** itself!

- As we are removing the head from the first argument, it will be gradually reduced to the empty list, and then the boundary condition will succeed.

Notice that any two of the arguments of **append** can be instantiated, and **append** will instantiate the third argument to the appropriate result. This property, which we might call "reversible programming", is true of many of the predicates defined in this chapter. Because of the flexibility of **append,** we can actually define several other predicates in terms of it:

```
last(El,List) :- append(_,[El],List).     ✓
next_to(Ell,El2,List) :- append(_,[Ell,El2|_],List).
member(El,List) :- append(_,[El|_],List).
```

fantastic!

Reversing a list: the goal **rev(L,M)** succeeds if the result of reversing the order of elements in list L is list M. The program uses a standard technique, where we reverse a list by appending its head to the reverse of its tail. And, what better way to reverse the tail than to use **rev!** The boundary condition is when the first argument is reduced to the empty list, in which case the result is also the empty list.

```
rev([],[]).
rev([H|T],L) :- rev(T,Z), append(Z,[H],L).
```

Notice that we have enclosed H in square brackets in the second argument of **append.** This is because H was selected as the head of the first argument, and the head of a list is not necessarily a list. Of course, the tail of a list is always a list. For a more efficient implementation of **rev,** we can incorporate the appending into the clauses for **rev:**

```
rev2(Ll,L2) :- revzap(Ll,[],L2).

revzap([X|L],L2,L3) :- revzap(L,[X|L2],L3).
revzap([],L,L).
```

The second argument of **revzap** is used to hold the "answer so far". Whenever a new piece of the answer is discovered, the "answer so far" passed to the rest of the program is the old one combined with the new piece of information. At the end, the last "answer so far" is passed back to be the answer in the original goal. A similar technique is used in the definition of **integer_name** in Section 7.8

Deleting one element: the goal **efface(X,Y,Z)** removes the first occurrence of element X from list Y, giving a new "effaced" list Z. If there is no such element X in the list Y, the predicate fails. The boundary condition is when we have found the element. Otherwise, we recur on the tail of Y.

```
efface(_,[],[]).
efface(A,[A|L],L) :- !.
efface(A,[B|L],[B|M]) :- efface(A,L,M).
```

It is easy to add a clause so that the predicate does not fail when the second argument becomes reduced to the empty list. The new clause, which recognises a new boundary condition, is **efface(_,[],[]).**

*Deleting **all** occurrences of an element:* the goal **delete(X,Ll,L2)** constructs a list L2 by

142

deleting all the elements X from list L1. The boundary condition is when L1 is the empty list, meaning that we have recurred down the entire length of the list. Otherwise, if X is in the list, then the result is the tail of the list, and we delete from that as well. The final case is if we have seen something *other than* X in the second argument -- we simply recur.

```
delete(_,[],[]).
delete(X,[X|L],M) :- !, delete(X,L,M).
delete(X,[Y|L1],[Y|L2]) :- delete(X,L1,L2).
```

Substitution: this is quite similar to **delete,** except instead of deleting a desired element, we substitute some other element in its place. The goal **subst(X,L,A,M)** will construct a new list M made up from elements of list L, except that any occurrences of X will be replaced by A. There are three cases. The first one is the boundary condition, exactly as for **delete.** The second one is in case an X is found in the second argument, and the third is in case something *other than* X is found.

$$X \to A$$
$$L \to M$$

```
subst(_,[],_,[]).
subst(X,[X|L],A,[A|M]) :- !, subst(X,L,A,M).
subst(X,[Y|L],A,[Y|M]) :- subst(X,L,A,M).
```

Sublists: list X is a sublist of list Y if every item in X also appears in Y, consecutively, and in the same order. The following goal would succeed:

```
sublist([of,the,club],[meetings,of,the,club,shall,be,called]).
```

The **sublist** program requires two predicates: one to find a matching first element, and one to ensure that the remainder of the first argument matches element-for-element with the remainder of the second argument:

```
sublist([X|L],[X|M]) :- prefix(L,M), !.
sublist(L,[_|M]) :- sublist(L,M).

prefix([],_).
prefix([X|L],[X|M]) :- prefix(L,M).
```

Mapping: a powerful technique is the ability to convert one list into another list by applying some function to each element of the first list, using the successive results as the successive members of the second list. Our program in Chapter 3 for changing one sentence into another is an example of mapping. We say that we are "mapping one sentence into another".

3.4 p.48

Mapping is so useful that it justifies a section of its own. Furthermore, becase lists in Prolog are simply special cases of structures, we will postpone discussion of mapping lists until the section on mapping structures, which is later in this chapter. Mapping appears in other guises also. Section 7.11, on symbolic differentiation, describes a way to map arithmetic expression onto other ones.

7.6 Representing and Manipulating Sets

The *set* is one of the most important data structures used in Mathematics, and operations with sets find some applications in computer programming as well. A set is a collection of elements, rather like a list, but it does not make sense to ask "where" or "how many times" something is an element of a set. Thus, the set {1,2,3} is the same as the set {1,2,3,1}, because all that matters is whether a given item is an element of the set or not. Sets may also have other sets as members. The most fundamental operation on a set is to determine whether some element is *a member of* some given set.

It should come as no suprise that a convenient representation for sets is as lists. A list can contain arbitrary elements including other lists, and it is possible to define a membership predicate over lists. However, when we represent a set as a list, we will arrange that the list only has one element for each thing that belongs to the set. Dealing with lists without duplicated elements simplifies some operations like removing elements. So we will deal only with lists without duplicates. The predicates described in this section expect and maintain this property.

It is usual to define the following operations over sets -- we shall include the usual mathematical notation for those who are accustomed to it:

set membership: X ∈ Y
X is a member of some set Y if X is one of the elements of Y.
Example: a ∈ {c,a,t}

subset: X ⊆ Y
Set X is a subset of set Y if every element of X is also an element of Y. Y may contain some elements that X does not.
Example: {x,r,u} ⊆ {p,q,r,s,t,u,v,w,x,y,z}

disjoint: X ⊄ Y
Set X is disjoint from set Y if no element of X is a member of Y.
Example: {c,a,t} ⊄ {d,o,g}

intersection: X ∩ Y
The intersection of sets X and Y is the set containing those elements which are members of X *and* which are members of Y.
Example: {r,a,p,i,d} ∩ {p,i,c,t,u,r,e} = {r,i,p}

union: X ∪ Y

The union of sets X and Y is the set consisting of members from X, or Y, or both.
Example: {a,b,c} ∪ {c,d,e} = {a,b,c,d,e}

These are the basic operations that are normally used to manipulate sets. We can now write Prolog programs to implement each one. The first basic operation, membership, is the same **member** predicate that we have seen several times before. However, the definition of **member** that we use does not contain the "cut" symbol in the boundary case so that we can generate successive elements of the list by backtracking:

```
member(X,[X|_]).
member(X,[_|Y]) :- member(X,Y).
```

Next, a predicate **subset** for which **subset(X,Y)** will succeed if X is a subset of Y. The second fact in the definition embodies the mathematical notion that the empty set is a subset of every set. In Prolog, this notion turns into a way of checking the boundary condition on the first argument, since we recur on its tail:

```
subset([A|X],Y) :- member(A,Y), subset(X,Y).
subset([],Y).
```

Next, a predicate **disjoint**, for which the goal **disjoint(X,Y)** will succeed if X is disjoint from Y. Here is where it is important to take advantage of the behaviour of **member** as defined above. Notice we have given **not** a conjunction of goals in this example. In the first goal, because Z is uninstantiated, **member** will cause a member of X to be chosen. When backtracking occurs (because **member(Z,Y)** fails), then the first goal will choose *another* member of X. This is a spendid example of what some people call "non-deterministic" programming:

```
disjoint(X,Y) :- not(( member(Z,X), member(Z,Y) )).
```

Next, the most complicated example, **intersection**. The goal **intersection(X,Y,Z)** will succeed if the intersection of X and Y is Z. Here is where we have to assume that the lists contain no duplicated elements.

```
intersection([],X,[]).
intersection([X|R],Y,[X|Z] :-
   member(X,Y),
   !,
   intersection(R,Y,Z).
intersection([X|R],Y,Z) :- intersection(R,Y,Z).
```
(not) member(X, Y).

Finally, **union**. The goal **union(X,Y,Z)** will succeed if the union of X and Y is Z.

Notice that **union** looks rather like an arranged marriage between **intersection** and **append**:

```
union([],X,X).
union([X|R],Y,Z) :- member(X,Y), !, union(R,Y,Z).
union([X|R],Y,[X|Z]) :- union(R,Y,Z).
```

This completes our repertoire of set-processing predicates. Although sets may not feature in the kind of programming you intend to do, it is worthwhile to study these examples to obtain a clear understanding of how you can make recursion and backtracking work for you.

7.7 Sorting

Sometimes it is helpful to sort a list of elements into order. If the elements of the list are integers, we can use the '<' operator to decide whether two integers are in order. The list [1,2,3] is sorted into order because the predicate '<' succeeds for each consecutive pair of integers in the list. If the elements are atoms, we can use **aless** as discussed in Chapter 3. The list [alpha,beta,gamma] is sorted into order because the predicate **aless** succeeds for each consecutive pair of atoms in the list. In Section 7.9 we shall use the sorting predicates developed in this section to "score" the possible paths to take though a maze in order to find the shortest path.

Computer scientists have developed many techniques for sorting a list into order when given some predicate that tells us whether consecutive elements are in order. We will show Prolog programs for four such sorting methods: naive sort, insertion sort, bubble sort, and Quicksort. Each program will use a predicate **order** which can be replaced by '<' or **aless** or any other predicate you desire, depending on what kind of structure you are sorting. We assume that the goal **order(X,Y)** will succeed if objects X and Y are in the desired order, that is, if X is less than Y in some sense.

One way of sorting numbers into ascending order is first to generate some permutation of the numbers, and then test to see if the resulting list of numbers is in ascending order. If they are not, then we generate some other permutation of the numbers. This method is known as the naive sort.

```
sort(L1,L2) :- permutation(L1,L2), sorted(L2), !.

permutation(L,[H|T]) :-
    append(V,[H|U],L),
    append(V,U,W),
    permutation(W,T).
permutation([],[]).

sorted(L) :- sorted(0,L).

sorted(_,[]).
```

N<H

```
sorted(N,[H|T]) :- order(N,H), sorted(H,T).
```

The predicate **append** is defined as before. In this program, the predicates have the following meanings. **sort(L1,L2)** means that L2 is the list which is the sorted version of L1. **permutation(L1,L2)** means that L2 is a list consisting of all the elements of list L1 in one of the many possible orders -- this is a "generator", in the terminology of Section 4.3. Predicate **sorted(L)** means that the numbers in the list are sorted into increasing order -- this is a "tester".

The goal of finding the sorted version of a list consists in generating a permutation of the elements and testing to see if it is sorted. If it is, we have found the unique answer. Otherwise we must carry on generating permutations. This is not a very efficient way of sorting a list.

In the *insertion sort* method, each item of the list is considered one at a time, and each item is inserted into a new list in the appropriate position. If you play card games, then you probably use this method when you sort your hand, picking up one card at a time. The goal **insort(X,Y)** succeeds when list Y is a sorted version of list X. Each element is removed from the head of the list and passed to **insortx**, which inserts the element in the list and returns the modified list:

```
insort([],[]).
insort([X|L],M) :- insort(L,N), insortx(X,N,M).

insortx(X,[A|L],[A|M]) :- order(A,X), !, insortx(X,L,M).
insortx(X,L,[X|L]).                     A<X
```

A convenient way to obtain a more general-purpose insertion sorting predicate is to use the ordering predicate as an argument of **insort**. We use the '=..' predicate as discussed in Chapter 6:

↑ P. 114

```
insort([],[],_).
insort([X|L],M,O) :- insort(L,N,O), insortx(X,N,M,O).

insortx(X,[A|L],[A|M],O) :-
        P =.. [O,A,X],
        call(P),
        !,
        insortx(X,L,M,O).
insortx(X,L,[X|L],O).
```

will be instantiated to some kind of ordering!

Then we can use goals like **insort(A,B,'<')** and **insort(A,B,aless)** without requiring a predicate named **order**. This technique can be applied to the remainder of the sorting algorithms in this section.

The *bubble sort* checks the list to see if two adjacent elements are out of order. If so, then they are exchanged. This process is repeated until no more exchanges are necessary.

bubble sort

Whereas the insertion sort makes elements "sink" down to the appropriate level, the bubble sort is so named because it makes elements "float" up to the appropriate level.

```
busort(L,S) :-
    append(X,[A,B|Y],L),
    order(B,A),
    append(X,[B,A|Y],M),
    busort(M,S).
busort(L,L).

append([],L,L).
append([H|T],L,[H|V]) :- append(T,L,V).
```

← will try all the combinations [A,B] in list L.

— compare P.71

Notice that the **append** predicate is the same as we have seen before, and that in this example it must be able to backtrack on each solution found. Hence, a "cut" does not appear in the first clause. This is another example of what some people call "non-deterministic" programming, because we are using **append** to select, in an undetermined way, members of list L. It is the responsibility of **append** to ensure that the set of selection from L is complete.

Quicksort, a more sophisticated sorting method due to C.A.R. Hoare, is suitable for sorting large lists. To implement Quicksort in Prolog we first need to split a list consisting of head H and tail T into two lists L and M such that:

□ all the elements of L are less than or equal to H

□ all the elements of M are greater than H, and

□ the order of elements within L and M is the same as in [H|T].

Once we have split the list, we Quicksort each list (this is the recursive part), and append M onto the back of L. The goal **split(H,T,L,M)** splits the list [H|T] into L and M as described above:

```
split(H,[A|X],[A|Y],Z) :- order(A,H), split(H,X,Y,Z).
split(H,[A|X],Y,[A|Z]) :- order(H,A), split(H,X,Y,Z).
split(_,[],[],[]).
```

The Quicksort program is now:

```
quisort([H|T],S) :-
    split(H,T,A,B),
    quisort(A,Al),
    quisort(B,Bl),
    append(Al,[H|Bl],S).
```

It is also possible to build the **append** into the sorting program, giving the alternative predicate:

```
quisortx([H|T],S,X) :-
    split(H,T,A,B),
```

Quisortx ([H|T],S,X) :-
split (H,T,A,B),
Quisortx (A,S,[H|Y]),
Quisortx (B,Y,X).

Quisortx ([ ],X,X).

(handwritten annotations: ?- quisortx(L, S, []) *;* ? *;* this Y will not be instantiated before this Y gets instaniated. *;* stupid! *;* good assignment *)*

```
quisortx(A,S,[H|Y]),
quisortx(B,Y,X).
quisortx([],X,X).
```

In this case the third argument is used as a temporary work area, and it will be filled with the empty list when **quisortx** is used as a goal.

More information on sorting can be found in Volume 3 (Sorting and Searching) of *The Art of Computer Programming* by Donald Knuth, published in 1973 by Addison-Wesley. Hoare's Quicksort method is described in his paper in *Computer Journal* 5 (1962), pages 10 to 15.

Exercise 7.5: Verify that, when given a known list as L1, **permutation(L1,L2)** will generate all the permutations of L1 (once each) as the alternative values of L2. In what order are the solutions generated?

Exercise 7.6: Quicksort works best on large lists because it converges to a solution more rapidly. However, the amount of work done at each recurrence of **qsort** is more than the other methods, because it must use **split**. So, perhaps when sorting small lists, then qsort's recursive calls could be replaced by calls to some other sorting method, say insertion sort. Develop a "hybrid" sorting program that uses Quicksort to sort the large partitions (the lists made by the **split** predicate), but switches to another sorting method when the size of the partition becomes sufficiently low that the insertion sort can be used. Hint: since **split** has to look at every element of the list anyway, then it can be used to compute the length of a list.

7.8 Assert and Retract: Random, Gensym, Findall.

In all of the programs discussed so far, we have used the database only to store facts and rules that define predicates. It is possible to use the database to store ordinary structures, such as the structures that are constructed as a program executes. Until now, we have been passing such structures from one predicate to another by using arguments. However, a good reason for storing information in the database, rather than passing it around through arguments, is that sometimes a piece of information may be needed by many parts of a program, and that the alternative would involve something like one or two extra arguments to most predicates. In this section we describe three predicates that take advantage of the database for storing structures that have a lifetime that extends further than is convenient for using variables. The three programs are **random**, which generates a pseudorandomly chosen integer each time it is called; **findall**, which generates a list of all the structures that make a given predicate succeed, and **gensym**, which generates atoms with unique names.

Random

The goal **random(R,N)** instantiates N to a randomly chosen integer between 1 and R.

The method of choosing a random integer is to use a congruential method, using a "seed" that is initialised to an arbitrary integer. Each time a random integer is desired, the answer is computed using the existing seed, and a new seed is determined, and stored until the next time that a random integer is desired. We use the database to store the seed between calls to **random**. After the seed is used, we retract the old information about its structure. Then, the new seed is computed, and new information is asserted. The initial seed is simply a fact in the database, with functor **seed** having one component, the integer value of the seed.

```
seed(13).

random(R,N) :-
   seed(S),
   N is (S mod R) + 1,
   retract(seed(S)),
   NewSeed is (125 * S + 1) mod 4096,
   asserta(seed(NewSeed)), !.
```

We can take advantage of the semantics of **retract** to simplify the definition of **random** in the following way:

```
random(R,N) :-
   retract(seed(S)),
   N is (S mod R)+1,
   NewSeed is (125*S+1) mod 4096,
   asserta(seed(NewSeed)), !.
```

To print out a lot of random numbers between 1 and 10, all that is required is:

```
?- repeat, random(10,X), write(X), nl, fail.
```

Prolog will, of course, never finish answering this question.

Gensym

The predicate **gensym** provides a way of generating new Prolog atoms. If we have a program that is assimilating information about the world (perhaps by understanding English sentences about it), we have the problem of dealing with the situation when a new object is discovered. A natural way to represent an object is with a Prolog atom. If the object has not been encounted before, we must ensure that the atom we assign to it does not accidentally coincide with the one representing some other object. That is, we require the ability to generate a new atom. We might as well require that the atom have some mnemonic significance as well, so that we can understand the program's output. If we were representing students, say, a reasonable solution would be to name the first student **student1**, the second **student2**, the third **student3**, and so on. Then if in addition we had to represent teachers, we could pick atoms **teacher1**, **teacher2**, **teacher3** and so on to represent them.

The function of **gensym** is to generate new atoms from given *roots* (like **student** and teacher). For each root, it remembers what number was last used, so that next time it is asked to generate an atom from that root it can guarantee that it will be different from the ones generated before. Thus, the first time the question:

```
?- gensym(student,X).
```

is asked, the answer is

```
X = student1
```

The next time, the answer will be

```
X = student2
```

and so on. Note that these different solutions are not generated on backtracking (gensym(X,Y) can never be resatisfied), but are generated by *subsequent goals* involving the predicate.

The definition of **gensym** makes use of the subsidiary predicate **current_num**. It is by putting facts about **current_num** into the database (and also by removing facts that are no longer applicable) that **gensym** keeps track of which number to use next with a given root. **current_num(Root,Num)** means that the last number used with root **Root** was **Num**. That is, the last atom generated for this root had the characters derived from **Root** followed by those derived from **Num**. The normal course of action when Prolog tries to satisfy a **gensym** goal is that the last **current_num** fact about the given root is removed from the database, 1 is added to the number involved and a new **current_num** fact is added to replace it. Meanwhile, the new number is used as the basis for generating an atom. It is very convenient to keep the **current_num** information in the database. The only alternative would be to have every predicate directly or indirectly involved in a **gensym** carry the information about current numbers in extra arguments.

The last few clauses of this program define the predicate **integer_name**, which is used to derive a list of characters from a number. The atoms created by **gensym** are made up by using the built-in **name** predicate to make an atom whose characters consist of the characters of the root followed by the characters of the number. Some Prolog implementations use a version of the **name** predicate which will perform the functions of **integer_name**, but it is quite instructive to see how it can be defined in Prolog. One fact that is used implicitly in the definition is that the ASCII character codes for the digits 0, 1, 2, etc are 48, 49, 50, etc in that order. Therefore, in order to convert from a number less than 10 to its character, one only has to add 48. To get the list of characters for a number greater than 9 is more complex. We can easily get hold of the last digit of a number, because this is simply the remainder on division by 10 (the number **mod** 10). It is therefore easy to generate the characters of a number in reverse order -- we just keep on finding the last digit, getting hold of the rest of the number (the result of integer division by 10), finding its last digit, and so on. The Prolog definition of this would be:

```
reverse_chars(N,[C]) :- N<10, !, C is N+48.
reverse_chars(N,[C|Cs]) :-
    C is (N mod 10) + 48,
    N1 is N/10.
    reverse_chars(N1,Cs).
```

[handwritten: Say N => 5 / C = 5+48 / N1 = 2   ([2.5])]

To get the characters in the right order, we adopt a neat trick. We introduce an extra argument to the predicate, expressing the list of characters *generated so far*. Using this argument, we can find the characters in reverse order, as above, but put together the list in the right order. This works as follows. Assume we have the number 123. We start with the "list built so far" []. First, the number 3 is discovered and converted into the character code 51. We then invoke a recursive **integer_name** goal, to find the characters of 12. The "list so far" given to this goal is made up of the character generated put on the front of the original "list so far" -- it is the list [51]. The second **integer_name** goal generates the character 50 (for the 2) and tries to satisfy **integer_name** again, this time with the number 1 and the "list so far" [50,51]. This final goal succeeds and, because the number was less than 10, gives the answer [49,50,51]. This answer is passed up through the arguments of the various **integer_name** goals and forms the answer of the original question -- what are the characters corresponding to 123?

[handwritten: [49,50,51]]

Here, now, is the program.

```
/* Create a new atom starting with a root provided and
   finishing with a unique number */

gensym(Root,Atom) :-
    get_num(Root,Num),
    name(Root,Name1),
    integer_name(Num,Name2),
    append(Name1,Name2,Name),
    name(Atom,Name).

get_num(Root,Num) :-
    /* this root encountered before */
    retract(current_num(Root,Num1)), !,
    Num is Num1+1,
    asserta(current_num(Root,Num)).
/* first time for this root */
get_num(Root,1) :- asserta(current_num(Root,1)).

/* Convert from an integer to a list of characters */

integer_name(Int,List) :- integer_name(Int,[],List).
integer_name(I,Sofar,[C|Sofar]) :-
    I<10, !, C is I+48.
integer_name(I,Sofar,List) :-
    Tophalf is I/10,
    Bothalf is I mod 10,
    C is Bothalf+48,
    integer_name(Tophalf,[C|Sofar],List).
```

[handwritten: See p.55. name(X, [97,99]) -> X = ac]

[handwritten: extra. (Same idea as Quisortx) p.148]

Findall

In some applications it is helpful to determine all of the terms that satisfy some predicate. For example, we might want to make a list of all of the children of Adam and Eve using the **parents** predicate of Chapter 1 (and assuming we had a database of **parents** facts). For this we could use a predicate called **findall,** which we shall define below. The goal **findall(X,G,L)** constructs a list L consisting of all of the objects X such that the goal G is satisfied. G is an ordinary structure, except that **findall** treats it as a Prolog goal. Also, X will appear somewhere inside G. So, G can be instantiated to a Prolog goal of arbitrary complexity. Here is how we could find out all the children of Adam and Eve:

```
?- findall(X, parents(X,eve,adam), L).
```

The variable L would be instantiated to a list of all of the X's that satisfy **parents(X,eve,adam).** All that **findall** needs to do is to repeatedly attempt to satisfy its second argument, and each time it succeeds it should take whatever X is instantiated to, and put it in the database. When the attempt to satisfy the second argument finally fails, then we go back and collect all of the X's that we put into the database. The resulting list is returned as the third argument. If the attempt to satisfy the second argument *never* succeeds, then the third argument will be instantiated to the empty list. To put items into the database, we use the **asserta** predicate, which inserts structures *before* those that have the same functor. To put an item X in the database, we supply it as a component of the functor called **found.** The Prolog clauses for **findall** are as follows:

```
findall(X,G,_) :-
    asserta(found(mark)),
    call(G),
    asserta(found(X)),
    fail.
findall(_,_,L) :- collect_found([],M), !, L = M.

collect_found(S,L) :- getnext(X), !, collect_found([X|S],L).
collect_found(L,L).

getnext(X) :- retract(found(X)), !, X \== mark.
```

The **findall** predicate first adds a special marker to the facts for **found,** in the form of a structure with functor **found** and component **mark** This special marker serves to mark the place in the database before which all of the X's satisfying G in this use of **findall** will be asserted. Next, an attempt is made to satisfy G, and each time it succeeds, then X is inserted in the database by supplying it as a component to the **found** functor. The **fail** forces backtracking to occur, attempting to re-satisfy G (**asserta** only succeeds once). When G finally fails, backtracking will force the first **findall** clause to fail, and an attempt will be made to satisfy the second one. The second clause calls **collect_list** to retract each found structure back out of the database, inserting its component in a list. The **collect_list** predicate puts each element into a variable that holds the "list so far", the trick revealed when explaining **gensym** above. As soon as the component **mark** is encountered, **getnext** fails, so the second clause of **collect_found** is satisfied, which shares its second argument (the result) with its first (the collected list).

Notice that the presence of the **found(mark)** in the database indicates a particular use of **findall**. This means that **findall** can be used recursively -- any occurrence of **findall** used within the second argument of another **findall** will be treated correctly.

In Section 7.9 we develop a program that uses **findall** to construct a list of all of the descendants of a node in a graph. This is used to implement a breadth-first graph searching program.

Exercise 7.7: Write a Prolog program that defines the predicate **random_pick**, for which the goal **random_pick(L,E)** instantiates E to a randomly chosen element of list L. Hint: Use the random number generator and define a predicate that returns the *N*th element of a list.

Exercise 7.8: Given the goal **findall(X,G,L)**, what happens when there are uninstantiated variables not sharing with X in G?

7.9 Searching Graphs

Graphs are networks of nodes connected by arcs. For example, a map can be seen as a graph, in which the nodes are villages and the arcs are roads connecting the villages. If you want to find the shortest journey between two villages, you have to solve the problem of finding the shortest path between nodes of a graph.

The easiest way to represent a graph is by using a database of facts to represent the arcs between nodes of a graph. For example, the graph consisting of the following pattern of nodes and arcs can be represented as facts as shown:

```
      a ———— b ———— c
      |        |        |
  d – e ———— f ————+
      |        |
      g ————— h
```

```
a(g,h).  a(g,d).  a(e,d).  a(h,f).  a(e,f).
a(a,e).  a(a,b).  a(b,f).  a(b,c).  a(f,c).
```

So to go from node g to node a, we could take the path g,d,e,a or g,h,f,e,a or even g,d,e,f,c,b,a. If we had a directed graph, then the predicate a would be interpreted such that **a(X,Y)** means that there is an arc from X to Y, but not necessarily from Y to X. In this section, we shall assume that all graphs are undirected -- that is, they do not contain any "one-way streets". This is the same assumption as we made in Section 7.2 when searching the maze.

The easiest program for searching a graph represented as above is the following:

```
go(X,X).
go(X,Y) :- (a(X,Z);a(Z,X)), go(Z,Y).
```

Unfortunately, it is possible for this program to get into a loop. This is why, as before we use list T to keep a "trail" of the nodes we have visited at any particular recurrence of the predicate:

depth first

```
go(X,X,T).
go(X,Y,T) :- (a(X,Z);a(Z,X)), not(member(Z,T)), go(Z,Y,[Z|T]).
```

This program, developed in Section 7.2, does what is called a "depth first" search, because at first only one of the neighbours of a node in the graph is considered. The other neighbours are ignored until later failure causes backtracking to the node so another neighbour can be considered.

A "neighbours first" search occurs when a program considers all of the immediate neighbours of a node, and then chooses one of the neighbours to search. This is different from a "breadth-first" search, which we discuss later. We can implement neighbour-first search by using **findall** to obtain all of the immediate neighbours of a node. Next, we use a function to apply the search predicate to each of the neighbours. To make the program easier to read, we shall define a predicate **goodnode** that avoids the "one-way" street problem, and checks if we have visited the node before. The goal **goodnode(X,Y,T)** will succeed only if there is a arc from X to Y or Y to X, and if Y is not already a member of T.

neighbours first with a flavor of depth first and breadth first.

```
goodnode(X,Y,T) :- ( a(X,Y) ; a(Y,X) ), not(member(Y,T)).

go(X,X,_).
go(X,Y,T) :-
    findall(Z, goodnode(X,Z,T), D),
    go_all(D,Y,T).

go_all([H|_],Y,T) :- go(H,Y,[H|T]).
go_all([_|L],Y,T) :- go_all(L,Y,T).
```

The first **go** clause checks for the boundary condition, when we wish to go to the node where we already are. The second **go(X,Y,T)** clause first finds all of the immediate neighbours that pass the **goodnode** test, and then puts them all into list D. The next goal searches via one of these neighbours. The predicate **go_all** is designed to fail when it reaches the end of the list of nodes to search. Notice that we must *not* put in a clause **go_all([],_,_)**, because this would cause **go_all** to succeed when it has finished with its list. The reason we make **go_all** fail is so that it can cause backtracking to occur either if there are no neighbours or if we have run out of neighbours to examine. The **go_all** predicate has two clauses. The first one applies **go** to the head of the list, and the second one recursively applies **go_all** to the tail of the list in the way to which we are accustomed.

Suppose we have what is called a "labelled" graph, where each arc has some item of information associated with it. In a road map, for example, each road could have associated with it the distance between the villages that the road connects. A simple addition to the database can represent labelled graphs -- we simply add a third argument. Now, the fact **a(X,Y,Z)** means that there is an arc from X to Y with "label" Z. Let's use road maps again. The following database represents a road map of towns in Northern England. The distances given are in units of miles:

```
a(newcastle,carlisle,58).
a(carlisle,penrith,23).
a(darlington,newcastle,40).
a(penrith,darlington,52).
a(workington,carlisle,33).
a(workington,penrith,39).
```

Now that there are distances involved in traversing the map, it becomes interesting to see if we can write a program that could find the shortest path between two towns. We shall use a strategy called "best first search". In fact, a best-first program will not necessarily find the shortest path, but let's see what it does for us in this case. Now that we have a neighbour-first search strategy, all we have to do is to *sort* the list of immediate neighbours so that the *nearest* neighbour is searched first. The list of neighbours must contain not only the name of a neighbour (a town name), but also a distance. For convenience we can represent the neighbour list as a list of structures of the form **desc(X,Y),** were X is the name of a town to try, and Y is how far away it is from our current position. A best-first search program, which sorts the neighbour list before trying each neighbour is:

```
go(X,X,_).
go(X,Y,T) :-
    findall(desc(Z,Dist), goodnode(X,Z,Dist,T), D),
    insort(D,D1),
    go_all(D1,Y,T).

goodnode(X,Y,D,T) :- ( a(X,Y,D) ; a(Y,X,D) ), not(member(Y,T)).

go_all([desc(H,_)|_],Y,T) :- go(H,Y,[H|T]).
go_all([_|L],Y,T) :- go_all(L,Y,T).

insort([H|T],S) :- insort(T,L), plugin(H,L,S).
insort([],[]).

plugin(desc(Town,Dist),[desc(Town2,Dist2)|T],[desc(Town2,Dist2)|L]) :-
    Dist2 < Dist,
    !,
    plugin(desc(Town,Dist),T,L).
plugin(X,L,[X|L]).
```

The resulting program is pretty much the same as before, except that we have accounted for the neighbour list having **desc** structures in it. We have also added a version of the insertion sort predicate that was discussed in Section 7.7. Since the program always searches routes starting from the nearest neighbour first, we might expect the first route found always to be the shortest one. However, when applied to the database of Northern England above, we find that this "best first" strategy finds the *worst* path between Workington and Newcastle. Why? The neighbours of Workington are Carlisle (33 miles) and Penrith (39 miles), so the next move is to Carlisle. For Carlisle we can go to Newcastle (58) or Penrith (23), so it chooses Penrith. From Penrith we can go back to Workington (discarded by **goodnode**) or to Darlington (52). We must go to Darlington, and then on to Newcastle (40). The total journey is 33+23+52+40 = 148 miles.

From looking at a map (or at the database given above), the best journey is to go from Workington to Carlisle to Newcastle, for a total of 91 miles. The "best first" strategy fails to find this route first, because it is "short sighted" enough to immediately choose the nearest neighbour, regardless of how far off course the neighbour is from the goal. However, "best-first" does not always perform this poorly.

An alternative method for searching graphs is the "breadth first" strategy. This involves keeping a list of all the alternative nodes that have to be followed, not just the neighbours of a single node. Here is a program for a "breadth first" search of an unlabelled graph. The program does not check for loops in the path by using a "trail" list, but it finds a solution if there is one to be found.

```
go(X,Y) :- go1([X],Y).

go1(L,D) :- member(D,L), !.
go1(L,D) :- go2(L,[],M), go1(M,D).

go2([],L,L) :- !.
go2([N|Ns],Sf,L) :-
    findall(D,(a(N,D);a(D,N)),Ds),
    addon(Ds,Sf,Sf1),
    go2(Ns,Sf1,L).

addon([],L,L).
addon([N|Ns],L,M) :- member(N,L), !, addon(Ns,L,M).
addon([N|Ns],L,M) :- addon(Ns,[N|L],M).
```

Exercise 7.9: Modify the above programs so that the database is searched for all paths between two given towns, and the total distance for each path is printed out.

Information about how to search graphs using more effective heuristics than "best first" is available in books on Artificial Intelligence. For example: *Problem Solving Methods in Artificial Intelligence*, by Nils Nilsson, published in 1971 by McGraw-Hill; and *Artificial Intelligence*, by Patrick Winston, published in 1977 by Addison-Wesley.

7.10 Sift the Two's and Sift the Three's

> Sift the Two's and sift the Three's:
> The Sieve of Erastosthenes.
> When the multiples sublime,
> The numbers that remain are Prime.
>
> Anon.

A *prime number* is a number that has no whole number divisors except 1 and itself. For instance, the number 5 is prime, but the number 15 is not, because it has the whole number 3 as a divisor. If you want to generate prime numbers, then one of the best ways is called the Sieve of Erastosthenes. This method for sifting for primes up to the integer N works as follows:

1. Put all the numbers between 2 and N into the "sieve".

2. Select and remove the smallest number remaining in the sieve.

3. Include this number in the primes.

4. Step though the sieve, removing all multiples of this number.

5. If the sieve is not empty, repeat steps 2 through 5.

To translate these rules into Prolog, we define a predicate **integers** to generate a list of integers, a predicate **sift** to examine each element of the sieve, and a predicate **remove** to create a new sieve by removing multiples of the selected number from the sieve. This new sieve is passed back to **sift**. The predicate **primes** is the top-level goal such that **primes(N,L)** instantiates L to the list of primes lying in the range from 1 to N inclusive:

```
primes(Limit,Ps) :- integers(2,Limit,Is), sift(Is,Ps).

integers(Low,High,[Low|Rest]) :-
    Low =< High, !, M is Low+1, integers(M,High,Rest).
integers(_,_,[]).

sift([],[]).
sift([I|Is],[I|Ps]) :- remove(I,Is,New), sift(New,Ps).

remove(P,[],[]).
remove(P,[I|Is],[I|Nis]) :-
    not(0 is I mod P),
    !,
    remove(P,Is,Nis).
remove(P,[I|Is],Nis) :- 0 is I mod P, !, remove(P,Is,Nis).
```

remove mult. of I from Is to get New

Is = (2 3 4 5 6)

158

Continuing in this arithmetical vein, here are Prolog programs for the recursive formulation of Euclid's algorithms for finding the greatest common divisor and the least common multiple of a pair of integers. The goal gcd(I,J,K) succeeds when the greatest common divisor of I and J is K. The goal lcm(I,J,K) succeeds when the least common multiple of I and J is K:

```
gcd(I,0,I).
gcd(I,J,K) :- R is I mod J, gcd(J,R,K).

lcm(I,J,K) :- gcd(I,J,R), K is (I*J)/R.
```

Notice that due to the way of computing remainders, these predicates are not 'reversible' -- variables I and J must be instantiated in order for the predicates to work.

Exercise 7.10: The three numbers X, Y and Z are said to form a *Pythagorean triple* if the square of Z is equal to the sum of the squares of X and Y (Z*Z = X*X + Y*Y). Write a program to generate Pythagorean triples, that is, define a predicate **pythag** such that asking

```
?- pythag(X,Y,Z).
```

and asking for alternative solutions gives us as many different Pythagorean triples (X, Y, Z) as we desire. Hint: Make use of predicates like **is_integer** of Chapter 4.

7.11 *Symbolic Differentiation*

In mathematics, symbolic differentiation is an operation that converts an arithmetic expression into another arithmetic expression called the *derivative*. Suppose U and V stand for arithmetic expressions (such as $2 \cdot x + y$); x stands for a variable in an expression; and c stands for a constant (such as 2). The *derivative of* U *with respect to* x is written as dU/dx, and it is defined recursively by applying the following conversion rules to the expression U. The two boundary conditions come first, and the arrow is read as "is converted to":

```
dc/dx    →   0

dx/dx    →   1

d(-U)/dx  →   -(dU/dx)

d(U+V)/dx  →   dU/dx + dV/dx

d(U-V)/dx  →   dU/dx - dV/dx

d(c·U)/dx  →   c · dU/dx

d(U·V)/dx  →   U · dV/dx + V · dU/dx

d(U/V)/dx  →   d(U·V⁻¹)/dx
```

$X \wedge Y : X$ to the power Y
$\sim X : $ negative X

$$d(U^c)/dx \; \to \; c \cdot U^{c-1} \cdot dU/dx$$

$$d(\log_e U)/dx \; \to \; U^{-1} \cdot dU/dx$$

This set of conversion rules is easily translated to Prolog, because we can represent arithmetic expressions as structures, and use operators as the functors of the structures. We can also take advantage of the pattern-matching that occurs when a goal matches against the head of a rule. Let us consider a goal **d(E,X,F)** that succeeds when the derivative of expression E with respect to constant X is the expression F. Although the +, −, *, and / operators have built-in declarations, we shall have to declare a ^ operator, where X^Y is read as "X to the power Y", and a unary ~ operator, where ~X means "negative X". Operator declarations are used simply to make the syntax of expressions easier to read. For example, the following questions might be asked of **d** after it is defined:

```
?- d(x+1,x,X).

X = 1+0

?- d(x*x-2,x,X).

X = x*1+1*x-0
```

Notice that simply transforming one expression into another using the rules does not necessarily render the result in a simplified form, but a simplifier can be written as a separate task (Section 7.12). The differentiation program consists of the extra operator declarations plus a line-by-line translation of the above conversion rules into Prolog clauses:

```
?- op(10,yfx,^).
?- op(9,fx,~).

d(X,X,1) :- !.            Only one match to this clause
d(C,X,0) :- atomic(C).
d(~U,X,~A) :- d(U,X,A).
d(U+V,X,A+B) :- d(U,X,A), d(V,X,B).
d(U-V,X,A-B) :- d(U,X,A), d(V,X,B).
d(C*U,X,C*A) :- atomic(C), C \= X, d(U,X,A), !.   else
d(U*V,X,B*U+A*V) :- d(U,X,A), d(V,X,B).
d(U/V,X,A) :- d(U*V^(~1),X,A).
d(U^V,X,V*W*U^(V-1)) :- atomic(V), C \= X, d(U,X,W).
d(log(U),X,A*U^(~1)) :- d(U,X,A).
```

Notice the two places where the cuts occur. The first cut ensures that a the derivative of a variable with respect to itself matches *only* with the first clause, eliminating the second clause as a possibility. Secondly, there are two clauses for multiplication, the first one dealing with a special case. If the special case succeeds, the general case must be eliminated as a possibility.

As pointed out above, the solutions generated by this program are far from simplified. For example, any occurrence of **x*1** may as well be written as **x,** and any occurrence of, for example **x*1+1*x−0** may as well be written as **2*x** The next section describes an algebraic simplifier that can be used to simplify arithmetic expressions is very much the same way as the derivatives were derived above.

7.12 *Mapping Structures and Tree Transformation*

If we copy a structure component–by–component to form a new structure, we say that we are *mapping* one structure into another. It is usual to make a slight modification to each component as we copy it, as was done when we changed one sentence into another sentence in Chapter 3. In that example, sometimes we wanted to copy a word in the sentence exactly as it appeared in the original sentence, and sometimes we wanted the new copy to be a changed word. We used the following program to *map* the first argument of **alter** into its second argument:

```
alter([],[]).
alter([A|B],[C|D]) :- change(A,C), alter(B,D).
```

Since mapping is such a general–purpose operation, we can define a predicate **maplist** such that the goal **maplist(P,L,M)** succeeds by applying the predicate P to each element of a list L to form a new list M. We assume that P has two arguments, such that the first argument is the "input" element, and the second argument is the modified element to be inserted into M:

```
maplist(_,[],[]).
maplist(P,[X|L],[Y|M]) :-
    Q =.. [P,X,Y],
    call(Q).
    maplist(P,L,M).
```

There are several points to note about this definition. First, the definition consists of a boundary condition (the first clause) and a general recursive case (the second clause). The second clause uses the '=..' operator, pronounced "univ", to form a goal from the given predicate (P), the input element (X), and the variable that P is assumed to instantiate to form the modified element (Y). Next, an attempt is made to satisfy Q, which will result in Y being instantiated, forming the head of the second argument to this call of **maplist**. Finally, the recursive call maps the tail into the tail.

The predicate **alter** can be replaced by using **maplist**. Assuming that **change** is defined as in Chapter 3, **maplist** would be used as follows:

```
?- maplist(change,[you,are,a,computer],Z).

Z=[i,[am,not],a,computer]
```

A simplification of **maplist** results in **applist,** which simply applies some predicate, assumed to have one argument, to each member of a list. No new list is created:

```
applist(_,[]).
applist(P,[X|L]) :-
    Q =.. [P,X],
    call(Q),
    applist(P,L).
```

Notice that the predicate **printstring** of Chapter 5 could have been replaced by a goal of the form **applist(put,L),** where L is the string to be printed.

Mapping is not restricted to lists, but can be defined for any kind of structure. For example, consider arithmetic expressions made up of functors such as * and +, each having two arguments. Suppose we wanted to map one expression into another, removing all multiplications by 1 in the process. One way to describe this algebraic simplification would be to define a fact **s(Op,La,Ra,Ans)** which means that if we have an expression consisting of an operator Op with a left argument La and right argument Ra, then a simplified form is the expression Ans. The facts for removing multiplications by 1 would look like this, with two facts accounting for the commutativity of multiplication:

```
s(*,X,1,X).
s(*,1,X,X).
```

So, given an expression of the form **1*X**, this table of simplifications could tell us to map it into whatever X is. Let us see how we can use this in a program.

To *simplify* an expression E using such a table of simplification rules, we need to first *simplify* the left-hand argument of E, then *simplify* the right-hand argument of E, and then see if E is in our table. [the simplified expressions are in the table] If it is, we make the new expression whatever the table indicates. Since we recursively simplify the sub-components of E, E will be in a simplified state when it is time to see if it is in the table. At the "leaves" of the expression tree there are integers or atoms. These are simplified into themselves. As above, we can use '=..' to separate E into its functor and components:

```
simp(E,E) :- atomic(E), !.
simp(E,F) :-
    E =.. [Op, La, Ra],
    simp(La,X),
    simp(Ra,Y),
    s(Op,X,Y,F).
```

So, **simp** maps expression E into expression F, using the facts found in a simplification table. What happens if no simplification can be made? To prevent **s(Op,X,Y,F)** failing, we must have a 'catchall' rule at the end of each operator's part of the simplification table. The following simplification table includes rules for addition and multiplication, and shows the catchall rule for each operator included:

```
s(+,X,0,X).
s(+,0,X,X).
s(+,X,Y,X+Y).       /* catchall for + */
s(*,_,0,0).
s(*,0,X,0).
s(*,1,X,X).
s(*,X,1,X).
s(*,X,Y,X*Y).       /* catchall for * */
```

With the 'catchall' rules present, there is now a choice of how to simplify some expressions. For instance, with 3+0, we can either use the first fact, or we can employ the 'catchall' for +. Because of the way the facts are ordered, Prolog will always try the special case rules before the 'catchall's. Thus the first solution to **simp** will always be a true simplification (if there is one). However, alternative solutions will not be in the simplest possible form.

Another simplification used in computer-aided algebra is known as *constant folding*. The expression 3*4+a can have the constants 3 and 4 'folded' to form the expression 12+a. The folding rules can be added to the appropriate parts of the simplification table above. The rule for addition is

```
s(+,X,Y,Z) :- integer(X), integer(Y), Z is X+Y.
```

The rules for the other arithmetic operations are similar.

In commutative operations such as multiplication and addition, the simplifications described above may have different effects on expressions that are written differently but are algebraically equivalent. For example, if a folding rule is available for multiplication, then the **simp** predicate will faithfully map 2*3*a into 6*a, but a*2*3 or 2*a*3 will be mapped into themselves. To see why this is, think about what the expressions look like as trees:

```
2*3*a =       *
            / \
           *   a
          / \
         2   3


a*2*3 =
              *
            / \
           *   3
          / \
         a   2
```

The first tree can have its bottom-most multiplication folded from 2*3 into 6, but the second tree has no sub-tree that can be folded. Because multiplication is commutative, adding the following rule to the table will suffice for this particular case:

```
s(*,X*Y,W,X*Z) :- integer(Y), integer(W), Z is Y*W.
```

A more general algebra system can be constructed simply be adding more **s** clauses, instead of adding more "programming" to **simp**.

more rules not more program

Chapter 8. Debugging Prolog Programs

By this point you will have used and modified many of the example programs described earlier, and you will have written programs of your own. The problem of what to do when your program does not behave as expected is now relevant. Problems with programs are known as "bugs", and the process of removing bugs from programs is known as "debugging". We believe that a convenient approach to programming is what could be described as "preventative programming". To paraphrase an old proverb, *an ounce of careful programming is worth a pound of debugging*. In this chapter we shall attempt to describe some techniques for debugging, but we shall start with a discussion of how to try to prevent bugs from infesting your programs. We realise that such a problem is unsolved in general, but we simply wish to convey some informal techniques that have helped other Prolog programmers.

As with any creative activity, be it musical composition, literature, or architecture, computer programming offers a multitude of methods for expressing how to *represent* and *manipulate* the objects and relationships that are found in a particular problem. In general, there will be a number of ways to represent or manipulate some item of information in a program. Every time the programmer decides to use one of the ways in the program, we say that the programmer has made a *design decision*.

Novices faced with the task of making design decisions for the first time often feel confused. An understanding of the choices available will help them, and it is important for a tutor to explain programming techniques in general. This is because the art of making design decisions in programming is a discipline in its own right. We attempted to give the flavour of this problem in Section 1.1 when we discussed the different ways to interpret clauses. This is a matter of *representing* objects and relationships. Also, in Section 7.7 the problem also became apparent when we described three different ways to sort a list of objects. This is a matter of different ways to *manipulate* objects and relationships.

We hope that this book provides help about making design decisions in two ways. First, by containing a number of example programs, it should convey some idea of the solutions that practising programmers have obtained. Second, this chapter should provide some advice and direction that is specific to Prolog.

8.1 Laying out Programs

Assuming that the programmer has decided how to represent and manipulate the objects and relationships in the problem, the next step is to ensure that the layout and syntax of the program is clear and easily read. The collection of clauses for a given predicate is called a *procedure*. In the examples in this book, you may have noticed that each clause in a procedure has started on a new line, and there is one blank line between procedures. For example, one way to define the set equality predicate (representing sets as lists) is to use three predicates, each of which is defined by a two-line procedure:

```
eqset(X,X) :- !.
eqset(X,Y) :- eqlist(X,Y).

eqlist([],[]).
eqlist([X|Ll],L2) :- delete(X,L2,L3), eqlist(Ll,L3).

delete(X,[X|Y],Y).
delete(X,[Y|Ll],[Y|L2]) :- delete(X,Ll,L2).
```

This is not necessarily the best definition of set equality, but it points out how to lay out procedures. Notice that the clauses for each procedure are grouped together, and procedures are separated by a blank line. Notice also that the body of each rule is short enough to fit on one line. Another convention that is adopted by many Prolog programmers is to write each clause on a single line if the entire clause will fit on a line. Otherwise, write the head of the clause and the ':-' on the first line, and write each goal of a conjunction indented on a separate line. For example, a program to generate all permutations of a list:

```
permute([],[]).
permute(L,[H|T]) :-
    append(V,[H|U],L),
    append(V,U,W),
    permute(W,T).
```

The definition uses a backtracking **append,** so that another permutation Y is generated from X each time an attempt is made to re-satisfy **permute(X,Y).** What we should notice here is the way the conjuncts in the second clause are laid out on the page.

The main point is to decide on consistent conventions, whatever the conventions may be. In general, it is wise to add comments, to group terms appropriately, to use round brackets when in doubt about operator precedences, and to use plenty of white space (spaces and blank lines) in consistent ways. Comments should indicate how the arguments of a structure (or clause) are interpreted: what order they come in, and what data structures (constants or structures) are expected to fill each argument. Also, it is wise to write comments on the way that variables are expected to become instantiated as the clause becomes satisfied.

For more global organisation of the program, it is helpful to divide the program into reasonably self-contained parts, for example, where all of the list processing procedures would appear in the same file. A Prolog procedure that uses more than about five to ten rules may be hard to read, so consider whether it can be broken up naturally by the definition of some subsidiary predicates. If a program uses many facts, such as the simplification rules in Section 7.12, then all of the facts should belong together in the same file. A lot of facts is generally easier to read than a lot of rules, and although even a few rules may be difficult to understand, many pages of a particular fact can be understood because the semantics of facts are less complex.

Another issue that affects the ease in which Prolog programs can be read is the use of semicolon ("or") and exclamation ("cut"). The problems with over-using "cut" were introduced in Chapter 4. You should always consider whether it may be worthwhile avoiding a ; by defining extra clauses. For instance, the following program:

```
nospy(X) :-
    check(X,Functor,Arity,A), !,
    ( spypoint(_,Functor,A), !,
      ( deny(spypoint(Head,Functor,Arity),_),
      makespy(Head,Body),
      deny(Head,Body),
      write('Spy-point on '), prterm(Functor,Arity),
      write(' removed.'), nl,
      fail
          ; true
      )
              ; write('There is no spy-point on '),
                   write(X), put(46), nl
    ),
    !.
```

is much harder to understand than:

```
nospy(X) :-
    check(X,Functor,Arity,A), !,
    try_remove(X,Functor,Arity,A).

try_remove(_,Functor,Arity,A) :-
    spypoint(_,Functor,A), !,
    remove_spy(Functor,Arity,A).
try_remove(X,_,_,_) :-
    write('There is no spy-point on '),
    write(X), put(46), nl, !.

remove_spy(Functor,Arity,A) :-
    deny(spypoint(Head,Functor,Arity),_),
    makespy(Head,Body),
    deny(Head,Body),
    write('Spy-point on '), prterm(Functor,Arity),
    write(' removed.'), nl, fail.
remove_spy(_,_,_).
```

which does exactly the same thing. When you really do want to use "or", it is helpful to arrange the conjunction of goals so that the "or" stands out from the rest of the goals, and to place brackets around the goals so that the scope of the "or" is made explicit.

Throughout the book, we have emphasised the importance of thinking of many problems in terms of boundary conditions together with a general rule. Whenever possible, we write boundary conditions before all the other clauses of a procedure. This makes it easy to see what the boundary conditions are, and also provides some measure of protection against circular definitions. However, there are some cases where it is desirable to place the boundary condition after the other clauses of a procedure. Obviously, "catchall" rules, as seen several times previously, need to be placed at the end of the procedure.

When reading a Prolog procedure, it is helpful to look *each time* for the following key properties of the procedure.

- Look at how each predicate and variable in the procedure is *spelled*. Mis-spelling is a common mistake.

- Look for the *number of arguments* of each functor that is mentioned in the procedure. Ensure if the number of arguments (and their order) is consistent with your design decisions.

- Locate all of the *operators* in the clauses, and determine their precedence, associativity, and where their arguments are. You can determine this from operator declarations and the presence of brackets. When in doubt, add extra brackets. Also, to check whether an operator behaves in the way you expect, try printing out some sample terms using **display**.

- Notice the *scope* of each variable, and locate all the like-named variables within the scope. Notice which variables will "share" when one of them becomes instantiated. Notice whether variables in the head of the clause appear in the body of the clause.

- Try to determine what variables are instantiated or uninstantiated at the time the clause will be used.

- Locate the clause(s) that constitute the boundary condition(s). Determine whether all the conceivable boundary conditions have been accounted for.

Once you can "dissect" a procedure in this way, your understanding of the procedure will improve.

8.2 Common Errors

In this section we list a number of problems that both beginning and experienced Prolog programmers encounter. The problems fall into two categories: errors of *syntax*, and errors of *control flow*.

Once the programmer has decided what program to write, and how to lay it out on the printed page (or terminal display screen), there is the problem of getting the program into a file or typing it straight into the top level of a Prolog system. The main problem encountered here is ensuring that the *syntax* of the program is correct. Here we list a number of common syntactic errors. If these errors are not detected by the programmer, Prolog may provide an error message when an attempt is made to **consult** the program.

☐ A common syntax error is forgetting to add the dot '.' at the end of a clause. A dot must also always follow any term that is read by the **read** predicate. You must also leave at least one "white space" character after the dot. So beware of ending a disc file with the dot of the last clause -- make sure that there is a 'return' at the very end.

☐ Some special characters belong in pairs. There are the round brackets '(' and ')' for bracketing terms and clauses, the square brackets '[' and ']' for the list notation, and the curly brackets '{' and '}' for the grammar rule notation (Chapter 9). Also, the double quote (") for denoting strings, and the single quote (') for atoms, belong in pairs. The composite brackets '/*' and '*/' surround comments. Ensure that there are neither too few or too many of each kind of bracket.

☐ Beware of mis-spelled words, especially the names of built-in predicates. These can cause unexpected failures, because mis-spelled predicates are unlikely to match with any clauses in the database. Or, they may unexpectedly match with clauses that happen to have the same name as the mis-spelled one.

☐ Operators are another source of possible errors. Use round brackets when in doubt, to make the associativity of an operator explicit. Use **display** to experiment with the operators you have defined.

☐ The list notation: beginners may have difficulty with the following questions:
How do [a,b,c] and [X|Y] match? *(X is instantiated to a, and Y is instantiated to [b,c])*.
Do [a] and [X|Y] match? *(Yes. X is instantiated to a, and Y is instantiated to [])*.
Do [] and [X|Y] match? *(no)*.
Is [X,Y|Z] meaningful? *(yes)*.
Is [X|Y,Z] meaningful? *(no)*.
Is [X|[Y|Z]] meaningful? *(Yes, it is the same as [X,Y|Z])*.
How do [a,b] and [A|B] match? *(A is instantiated to a, and B is instantiated to [b])*.

Is there more than one way to match them? *(No, never)*.

When dealing with lists, or any other structure for that matter, it is important to stress the helpfulness of the "tree diagrams" that we introduced in Chapter 2.

Even if you are certain that a program is free from syntax errors, the program can still exhibit unexpected behaviour when an attempt is made to satisfy goals in the program. Typical symptoms are a program which seems to run without stopping (an "infinite loop"), the response **no** appearing unexpectedly, or variables being instantiated to unexpected terms. Usual sources of errors are:

☐   Circular definitions, which were mentioned in Chapter 3.

☐   Not enough boundary conditions, or some other underspecification of the problem.

☐   Useless procedures that redefine built-in predicates.

☐   Supplying the wrong number of arguments to a functor. This is not considered a syntax problem because the number of arguments of a functor depends on what the functor is used for.

☐   Unexpectedly reaching the end of a file when using the **read** predicate.

Beware of the following fallacies about the nature of backtracking:

☐   *Fallacy:* One of the reasons for backtracking is so that Prolog can return to a previous match and do it again in some other way. *Fact:* When Prolog searches the database in an attempt to match a goal against something in the database (a fact or the head of a rule), the match either succeeds or fails. Prolog does not backtrack to a "match" and try to match another way, because there is only one way to match a particular goal with a particular clause in the database.

☐   *Fallacy:* The list notation [X|Y] can match against any segment of a list, and can take apart lists in several different ways. The behaviour of **append(X,Y,[a,b,c,d])** is due to this. *Fact:* In [X|Y], X matches only the head of a list, and Y matches only the tail.

170

8.3   Another Control Flow Model

There are different ways of looking at the method by which Prolog attempts to satisfy goals. We have dealt with some of these in Chapters 1, 2, and 4. Another way of looking at the "flow of satisfaction" is the *box model*, due to our colleague Lawrence Byrd. • This section describes the box model, which is an aid to debugging. You should be familiar with the box model before you start to use the Prolog debugging facilities.

When the **trace** facility is used, the Prolog system prints out information about the sequence of goals in order to show where the program has reached in its execution. However, in order to understand what is happening, it is important to understand when and why the goals are printed. In a conventional programming language, the key points of interest are the entries to and exits from functions. But Prolog is a non-determinate language, and this introduces the complexities of backtracking. Not only are clauses entered and exited, but backtracking can suddenly reactivate them in order to generate an alternative solution. Furthermore, the cut symbol '!' indicates what goals are committed to having only one solution. One of the major confusions that novice programmers face is what actually occurs when a goal fails and the system suddenly starts backtracking. We hope this has been adequately explained in the previous chapters. However, the previous chapters discussed not only control flow, but also how variables are instantiated, how goals match against clause heads in the database, and how subgoals are satisfied. The box model only makes explicit the control flow through clauses, which is what the **trace** facility displays.

Let us look at an example Prolog procedure, seen surrounded by a box:

```
CALL +-----------------------------------------+ EXIT
 -->  |       descendant(X,Y) :-                |  -->
      |          offspring(X,Y).                |
      |                                         |
      |       descendant(X,Z) :-                |
      |          offspring(X,Y),                |
      |          descendant(Y,Z).               |
FAIL  |                                         | REDO
 -->  |_____|  -->
```

This simple example derives descendants of a person, provided that there are **offspring** facts in the database, such as

```
offspring(abraham,ishmael).
offspring(abraham,isaac).
offspring(isaac,esau).
       .
       .
       .
```

In the box, the first clause states that Y is a descendant of X if Y is an offspring of

X, and the second clause states that Z is a descendant X if Y is an offspring of X and if Z is a descendant of Y. In the diagram we have drawn a box around the whole procedure and added some labelled arrows which indicate the control flow in and out of the box. There are four such arrows which we shall look at in turn.

CALL. This arrow represents the initial invocation of the procedure. When an attempt is made to satisfy a goal of the form **descendant(X,Y)**, control passes through the CALL port of the descendant box with the intention of matching a component clause and then satisfying any subgoals in the body of that clause. Notice that this is independent of whether such a match is possible -- the box is CALLed, and then such matters are worried about. Textually we can imagine moving our finger to the code for **descendant** when meeting a call to **descendant** in some other part of the code.

EXIT. This arrow represents a successful return from the procedure. This occurs when the initial goal has been matched with one of the component clauses and any subgoals have been satisfied. Control now passes out of the EXIT port of the **descendant** box. Textually we stop following the code for **descendant** and go back to the place we came from.

REDO. (meaning "do again") This arrow indicates that a subsequent goal has failed and that the system is backtracking in an attempt to find alternatives to previous solutions. Control passes through the REDO port of the **descendant box.** An attempt will now be made to resatisfy one of the component subgoals in the body of the clause that last succeeded; or, if that fails, to match the original goal with an alternative clause and then try to satisfy any subgoals in the body of this new clause. Textually we follow the code backwards up the way we came looking for new ways of succeeding, possibly dropping down on to another clause and following that if necessary.

FAIL. This arrow represents a failure of the initial goal, which might occur if no clause is matched, or if subgoals are never satisfied, or if any solution produced is always rejected by later processing. Control now passes out of the FAIL port of the **descendant** box and the system continues to backtrack. Textually we move our finger back to the code which called this procedure and keep moving backwards up the code looking for alternative matches.

In terms of this model, the information we get about the procedure box is only the control flow through these four ports. This means that at this level we are not concerned with which clause matches, and how any subgoals are satisfied, but rather we only wish to know the initial goal and the final outcome. However, it can be seen that whenever we are trying to satisfy subgoals, what we are actually doing is passing through the ports of their respective boxes. If we were to follow this, then we would have complete information about the control flow inside the descendant procedure box. We shall go on to consider an example, but first we should point out that the box we have drawn round the procedure should really be seen as an invocation box. That is to say, we will have a different box for each different invocation of the procedure (each time we try to satisfy **descendant(X,Y)** for some X and Y). Obviously, with something like a recursive procedure, we are going to have lots of different CALLs and EXITs in the control flow but these will be for different invocations. Since this might get confusing we shall give each invocation box a unique integer identifier. Furthermore, since each invocation of a clause means that all the variables in the clause will be new ones, we have given each use of a variable a unique name formed by appending an integer to the original variable name.

Let us now take a look at an example. We shall use the **descendant** procedure we have been looking at, and we shall follow the control flow through all of the ports of this procedure and of the **offspring** procedure. First let us reproduce the program within boxes:

```
          +------------------------------------------------------+
CALL |                                                        |  EXIT
---> |   descendant(X,Y) :-                                   |  --->
     |      +--------------------+                            |
     |  --> |                    | -->                        |
     |      | offspring(X,Y)     |                            |
     |  <-- |                    | <--                        |
     |      +--------------------+                            |
     |                                                        |
     |   descendant(X,Z) :-                                   |
     |      +--------------------+   +--------------------+   |
     |  --> |                    | --> |                  | --> |
     |      | offspring(X,Y)     |   | descendant(Y,Z)    |   |
     |  <-- |                    | <-- |                  | <-- |
     |      +--------------------+   +--------------------+   |
<--- |                                                        |  <---
FAIL |                                                        |  REDO
          +------------------------------------------------------+


          +----------------------------------+
     CALL |                                  |  EXIT
     ---> |                                  |  --->
          |   offspring(abraham,ishmael)     |
          |   offspring(abraham,isaac)       |
          |   offspring(isaac,esau)          |
          |   offspring(isaac,jacob)         |
          |                                  |
     <--- |                                  |  <---
     FAIL |                                  |  REDO
          +----------------------------------+
```

It is important that you try to follow the trace we are about to look at by physically tracing along the arrows entering and leaving the above boxes. This will show how it is possible to follow the execution in terms of up-and-down movement in the program text. Backtracking is followed by moving your finger back up the code; every goal you meet can be seen as a REDO in the trace. If this goal can be resatisfied then we come out at the EXIT port and travel down the text as normal, trying again to satisfy all the following goals. If the goal fails then we come out at the FAIL port and keep going backwards looking for another alternative. The fact that we are following all the previously executed goals back the way we came, means that it is very easy to see where another alternative is found.

To begin this example, we shall ask the following question:

?- descendant(abraham,ANS), fail.

The first goal in the question is followed by a **fail.** This purpose of this is to force all possible backtracking behaviour out of the **descendant** procedure. The command as a whole can therefore never succeed. However, the point of this trace is to observe the execution flow induced by the failure of the second goal (the **fail**). We begin with the question, which is enclosed in a box as the other goals are:

Control first passes through the CALL port of the **descendant** box. This is invocation number 1.

```
(1) CALL: descendant(abraham,ANS)
(2) CALL: offspring(abraham,ANS)
```

We have matched the first clause of the **descendant** procedure and this results in the control flow passing through the CALL port of **offspring.**

```
(2) EXIT: offspring(abraham,ishmael)
```

Immediate success on the first clause, and control passes out through the EXIT port.

```
(1) EXIT: descendant(abraham,ishmael)
```

And thus we have satisfied the first **descendant** clause.

```
(3) CALL: fail
(3) FAIL: fail
(1) REDO: descendant(abraham,ishmael)
```

Then we try to satisfy **fail,** and, as might be expected, this succeeds, causing *failure.* Control passes out of the FAIL port of **fail** and we are now backtracking, moving in the opposite direction from before, looking for alternatives. When we REDO **descendant** we are in exactly the same place as when we left except for the direction of movement. Hence the instantiation state of the goal. If you wish to know the original state of the goal, then look back to the CALL port corresponding to this invocation number.

```
(2) REDO: offspring(abraham,ishmael)
(2) EXIT: offspring(abraham,isaac)
```

We REDO **offspring** and drop down onto the next clause thus producing an alternative solution.

```
(1) EXIT: descendant(abraham,isaac)
(4) CALL: fail
(4) FAIL: fail
(1) REDO: descendant(abraham,isaac)
```

Again, **fail** causes us to reject this solution and to start backtracking. Notice that this was a completely new invocation of **fail**.

```
(2) REDO: offspring(abraham,isaac)
(2) FAIL: offspring(abraham,ANS)
```

This time, **offspring** cannot offer us another match and so we continue backtracking with control passing out through the FAIL port.

```
(5) CALL: offspring(abraham,Y)
```

What has happened here is that we have dropped down onto the second **descendant** clause and this is a completely new **offspring** invocation corresponding to the first subgoal.

```
(5) EXIT: offspring(abraham,ishmael)
(6) CALL: descendant(ishmael,ANS)
```

This provides a solution with which we now recursively call **descendant**. This gives us a new invocation of **descendant**.

```
(7) CALL: offspring(ishmael,ANS)
(7) FAIL: offspring(ishmael,ANS)
(8) CALL: offspring(ishmael,Y2)
(8) FAIL: offspring(ishmael,Y2)
(6) FAIL: descendant(ishmael,ANS)
```

Ishmael has no offspring (in this example), and so the **offspring** subgoals in both **descendant** clauses fail, thus failing the **descendant** goal.

```
(5) REDO: offspring(abraham,ishmael)
```

Back we go for an alternative.

```
(5) EXIT: offspring(abraham,isaac)
(9) CALL: descendant(isaac,ANS)
(10) CALL: offspring(isaac,ANS)
(10) EXIT: offspring(isaac,esau)
```

We get a new invocation of **descendant** and the **offspring** subgoal succeeds.

```
(9) EXIT: descendant(isaac,esau)
(1) EXIT: descendant(abraham,esau)
(11) CALL: fail
```

```
(11) FAIL: fail
(1) REDO: descendant(isaac,esau)
(9) REDO: descendant(isaac,esau)
```

This provides a final solution to the initial question, but the **fail** forces backtracking again and so back we come along the REDO paths.

```
(10) REDO: offspring(isaac,esau)
(10) EXIT: offspring(isaac,jacob)
(9) EXIT: descendant(isaac,jacob)
(1) EXIT: descendant(abraham,jacob)
```

The **offspring** subgoal has another alternative which produces another result for the initial **descendant** goal. As can be seen, this is Abraham's last possible descendant, however there is a certain amount of work left to be done. Let us continue to follow the control flow as it backtracks unsuccessfully back to the beginning.

```
(12) CALL: fail
(12) FAIL: fail
(1) REDO: descendant(abraham,jacob)
(9) REDO: descendant(isaac,jacob)
(10) REDO: offspring(isaac,jacob)
(10) FAIL: offspring(isaac,ANS)
(13) CALL: offspring(isaac,Y3)
```

We are now trying the second clause for **descendant**.

```
(13) EXIT: offspring(isaac,esau)
(14) CALL: descendant(esau,ANS)
```

Recur again.

```
(15) CALL: offspring(esau,ANS)
(15) FAIL: offspring(esau,ANS)
(16) CALL: offspring(esau,Y4)
(16) FAIL: offspring(esau,Y4)
(14) FAIL: descendant(esau,ANS)
(13) REDO: offspring(isaac,esau)
(13) EXIT: offspring(isaac,jacob)
(17) CALL: descendant(jacob,ANS)
```

Try jacob.

```
(18) CALL: offspring(jacob,ANS)
(18) FAIL: offspring(jacob,ANS)
(19) CALL: offspring(jacob,Y5)
(19) FAIL: offspring(jacob,Y5)
(17) FAIL: descendant(jacob,ANS)
(13) REDO: offspring(isaac,jacob)
(13) FAIL: offspring(isaac,Y3)
(9) FAIL: descendant(isaac,ANS)
(1) FAIL: descendant(abraham,ANS)
```

```
no
```

And that's the end of that. We hope that this exhaustive example has provided an understanding of the control flow involved in the execution of a Prolog program. You should have noticed that for any invocation there is always only one CALL and FAIL, although there may be arbitrarily many REDOs and corresponding EXITs. It is the initial call which introduces the invocation and it is here that we first see the new invocation numbers. In the next section this model is used to show how the behaviour of a more complicated example -- **append** -- can be traced.

If you followed the steps above by tracing along the arrows linking the boxes in the code then you will have a good idea of the sense in which this is a 'textual processor' model of Prolog. The execution of the program can be directly followed in the program text.

Exercise 8.1: In the above model, no mention is made of how the cut goal 'I' is handled. Extend the model to account for the action of cut.

8.4 Tracing and Spy Points

When you find that your program doesn't work (because it generates an error, just says "no" or produces the wrong answer), you will want to find out quickly where the mistakes are so that you can correct them. This section describes a set of built-in predicates that allow you to "watch" your program running. Using these, you can give your program the same task again, and watch to see where it starts going wrong. What you will see is how the program progresses through the ports of the box model, in the same way as we saw how **descendent** behaved in the last section. The exact facilities that the debugging predicates provide will depend on the particular Prolog implementation, but the following should give some guide about the sorts of options, so that you can make sense of what your system provides. In any case, you are strongly advised to consult the documentation for your Prolog system before you start using these facilities.

The basic principle behind tracing and spy points is that the programmer is informed about the satisfaction of certain goals that arise in the running of his program. The programmer can decide, first, what goals he wishes to be informed about, and second, how much he wants to interact with their satisfaction. The first decision involves deciding what combination of *exhaustive tracing* and *spy points* he will use. Basically, exhaustive tracing involves information being given about *all* goals, and spy points enable the programmer to get only information about certain predicates that he has specified. However, these options can be mixed in various ways. Section 6.13 outlines the relevant built-in predicates that are of use here. To set a spy point on a predicate, we use predicate **spy** (and to remove a spy point, we use **nospy**). To start exhaustive tracing, we use **trace** (and to turn it off, we use **notrace**).

The second decision involves deciding on the level of *leashing* that is to be used. In unleashed tracing, information about the goals is displayed on the terminal and the program keeps on running. In leashed tracing, as well as the information being displayed, the programmer is asked at each point what he wishes to do. He can then specify changes in the level of tracing, alterations from the normal flow of the program and various other options. Your Prolog system may provide an independent choice of leashed or unleashed tracing at each of the four *ports* for a goal:

□   When an attempt is first made to satisfy the goal -- when the goal is encountered for the first time (the CALL port).

□   When the goal has successfully been satisfied (the EXIT port),

□   When an attempt is about to be made to resatisfy the goal (the REDO port), and

□   When the goal is about to fail, because all attempts to resatisfy it have failed (the FAIL port).

For instance, a reasonable choice would be to specify that CALL and REDO ports are leashed and EXIT and FAIL ports are unleashed. We gave a more detailed description of these four stages of the satisfaction of goals in Section 8.3.

Now let us consider the information that is given to you at a port of a goal you are interested in. First of all, the goal itself is shown, together with an indication of which port is involved and perhaps an invocation number. If tracing at this port is unleashed, this is all that is provided. Otherwise, Prolog will also ask you to specify one of a set of options about what should be done next. A session with exhaustive, unleashed tracing would look something like:

```
?- [user].

append([],Y,Y).
append([A|B],C,[A|D]) :- append(B,C,D).

/* type the end of file character here */
yes

?- append([a],[b],X).

CALL append([a],[b],_43)
CALL append([],[b],_103)
EXIT append([],[b],[b])
EXIT append([a],[b],[a,b])

X = [a,b];
```

```
REDO append([a],[b],[a,b])
REDO append([],[b],[b])
FAIL append([],[b],_103)
FAIL append([a],[b],_43)

no

?- append(X,Y,[a]).

CALL append(_37,_38,[a])
EXIT append([],[a],[a])

X = [], Y = [a];

REDO append([],[a],[a])
CALL append(_93,_38,[])
EXIT append([],[],[])
EXIT append([a],[],[a])

X = [a], Y = [];

REDO append([a],[],[a])
REDO append([],[],[])
FAIL append(_93,_38,[])
FAIL append(_37,_38,[a])

no
```

Here, all four ports of all goals are being shown on the terminal. However, the programmer is not given any chance to make the program pause at any point, change the amount of tracing half way through or affect the way it runs in any other way. These facilities are what leashed tracing provides.

Before we go on to discuss leashed tracing, we should make some remarks about how Prolog shows your goals when you are tracing. Now, actually the way your goals are shown by the tracing facilities is not necessarily the same as if they were output using **write**. This is because you are allowed to provide your own special purpose definitions for showing the goals in your program. You can use this facility to output some of the common structures used in your program in ways that are clearer or more concise than **write** would normally produce. The way the facility works is as follows. The standard way of printing your goals is actually by using the built-in predicate **print**, with one argument. **print** works as if it is defined as follows:

```
print(X) :- portray(X), !.
print(X) :- write(X).
```

Now, the predicate **portray** is not a built-in predicate, and so you can provide clauses for it yourself. If your clauses allow the goal **portray(X)** to be satisfied for one of your goals X, then it will be assumed that that provides all the necessary output. Otherwise, the goal will be output using **write** instead. So if for some reason you did not want to ever see the third arguments of **append** goals, you could make sure of this by providing the clause:

```
portray( append(A,B,C) ) :-
    write('append('), write(A), write(','),
    write(B), write(','),
    write('<foo>)').
```

Whenever a goal X involving **append** occurs, this clause will cause the goal **portray(X)** to succeed, and so it will provide the only output. For a goal involving any other predicate, **portray(X)** will fail, and X will be output using **write**. If the above clause was in the database, part of the above example session would look like the following:

```
?- append([a],[b],X).

CALL append([a],[b],<foo>)
CALL append([],[b],<foo>)
EXIT append([],[b],<foo>)
EXIT append([a],[b],<foo>)

X = [a,b];

REDO append([a],[b],<foo>)
REDO append([],[b],<foo>)
FAIL append([],[b],<foo>)
FAIL append([a],[b],<foo>)

no
```

Now for a discussion of leashed tracing. If you have specified leashed tracing at some port you will be asked to specify what should be done next when such a port is reached. This will look something like the following at the terminal:

```
?- append([a],[b],X).

CALL append([a],[b],_43) ?
```

The program stops after typing out the '?'. You are now supposed to reply by specifying one of a set of possible options. If the option you specify involves the program continuing as usual, it will then run on as far as the next leashed port for a predicate being traced, and again ask you, with something like:

```
CALL append([],[b],_103) ?
```

One of the options is likely be to cause a list of available options to be displayed at the terminal. Here are some of the options that may be available:

Examining the goal

The first set of options involve looking at the goal in various ways. As we have seen, the standard is for a goal to be shown using **print,** which gives your **portray** clauses a chance to show things in a special way. However, you may start to have doubts about the correctness of your **portray** clauses, or just want to see a goal written in the normal way for a change. Hence Prolog will allow you to either **write** or **display** the current goal as a possible option. In this case, the program will not run any further, but you will be asked for another option that will specify how the program should continue. A typical interaction might be:

```
?- append([a],[b],X).

CALL append([a],[b],<foo>) ? write
CALL append([a],[b],_103) ?
```

Usually you will only want to use **write** as an alternative way of looking at a goal. You might want to use **display** when the goal involves many operators, and you have forgotten what their various precedences are. In such a case, **display** will enable you to see the nesting of functors unambiguously.

Examining the Ancestors

The *ancestors* of a goal are those goals to which its satisfaction will eventually contribute. Thus every goal has an ancestor which is one of the goals in the original question -- the one that it is helping to satisfy. Also, whenever a rule is used, each of the goals introduced by the rule body has as an ancestor the goal that matched the rule head. Let us look at some examples of ancestors. Consider the following simple program to reverse a list (described in Section 7.5):

```
rev([],[]).
rev([H|T],L) :- rev(T,Z), append(Z,[H],L).

    append([],X,X).
    append([A|B],C,[A|D]) :- append(B,C,D).
```

If we ask the initial question:

```
?- rev([a,b,c,d],X).          (A)
```

then, because of the second clause, there will be two subgoals to satisfy. Each of these has the goal in the question as its immediate ancestor. The subgoals are:

```
rev([b,c,d],Z)            (B)
append(Z,[a],X)           (C)
```

Since the second clause will be used again to satisfy (B), again two subgoals will be introduced.

```
rev([c,d],Z1)             (D)
append(Z1,[a],Z)          (E)
```

These will have as their ancestors goals (A) and (B). Note that goal (C) is not an ancestor of these, because they are only contributing immediately to the satisfaction of (B), which contributes to the satisfaction of (A). Goals (D) and (E) are not contributing in any way to the satisfaction of (C). When the satisfaction of this question has progressed fairly far, a goal of the form:

```
append([c],[b],Y)
```

will appear. At this stage, the goal and its ancestors might be displayed as follows:

```
(1) rev([a,b,c,d],_49)          (Goal A)
(2) rev([b,c,d],[d|_50])        (Goal B)
(3) append([d,c],[b],[d|_51])
(4) append([c],[b],_52)
```

Before you read any further, you should make sure that you understand why these are all ancestors of the goal, and why there are not any more ancestors. There is one peculiarity with the way the ancestors are shown here, which may be reflected in your Prolog system. There are two possible ways of printing out an ancestor -- as it was when an attempt was first made to satisfy it, or as it stands now, with any variables as they are now instantiated. Here we have adopted the second course. When the goal (B) was first encountered, the second argument of **rev** was uninstantiated. However, that argument is shown with a value in the ancestor list. This is because by now the variable that was in that position has become instantiated -- by now we have found out that the first element of the reverse of [b,c,d] is d.

By looking at the ancestors of the current goal, you can get a fair idea what your program is up to, and why is is doing what it is. One of the options that a Prolog system may provide at a leashed port of a goal is for some of the current ancestors to be printed out. So if your program seems to be spending a lot of time somewhere and you suspect that it may be in a loop, a good strategy is to interrupt the execution, turn on full tracing and then take a look at the ancestors to see where you are.

Altering the degree of tracing

Another set of options that may be available at a leashed port concerns changing how much tracing is going on. Some of the more coarse controls that you can exercise are:

☐   Removing all spy points. This has the same effect as invoking the goal **nodebug** (Section 6.13).

☐   Turning exhaustive tracing off. This has the same effect as invoking the goal **notrace**

(Section 6.13)

□   Turning exhaustive tracing on. This has the same effect as invoking the goal **trace** (Section 6.13).

With all of these, your program will subsequently carry on running until it reaches a goal that you wish to trace, given your new conditions. Depending on what version of Prolog you use, more local controls of tracing may be available. These help you to quickly get over bits of the program's execution that are of little interest, so that you can concentrate on where the bugs seem to be. Possible options here are:

□   ("creep") Carry on with the program, doing exhaustive tracing, until you are prompted again (at the next leashed port).

□   ("skip") Carry on with the program, and produce no trace messages at all until a port of the current goal is next arrived at.

□   ("leap") Carry on with the program, producing no trace messages until either a spy point is reached or a port of the current goal is arrived at.

The first of these is what you will want to use if you want to follow the program closely at this point. The second is for when you are not worried about how a certain goal is satisfied, and just want to move on quickly to what happens afterwards. The third is for when there may be a lot of uninteresting work going on in the satisfaction of a goal, but somewhere in the middle a goal that is of interest (which has a spy point) will occur. Hence you want to ignore everything until either that spy point is reached or (if the program is faulty) if the current goal succeeds or fails without ever reaching the spy point. Here is an example of the use of 'creep' and 'skip'. Let us assume that there is a bug in the naive sort program given in Section 7.7, but that we are confident that our program to generate permutations is all right. If you remember, the definition of **sort** started as follows:

```
sort(X,Y) :- permutation(X,Y), sorted(Y), !.
```

We can use the 'skip' option to avoid having to look at the gory details of how **permutation** works, and produce a trace that starts as follows:

```
CALL sort([3,6,2,9,20],_45) ? creep
CALL permutation([3,6,2,9,20],_45) ? skip
EXIT permutation([3,6,2,9,20],[3,6,2,9,20]) ? creep
CALL sorted([3,6,2,9,20]) ? creep
CALL sorted(0,[3,6,2,9,20]) ? creep
CALL 0<3 ?
       .
       .
       .
```

Altering the satisfaction of the goal

The following options enable you to alter how your program works. You can use these to repeat things that you want to look at in more detail, avoid choices which you know to be irrelevant and force the program to consider choices that it might not otherwise find. These can greatly speed up debugging, because they mean that you can subject the difficult parts of the program to repeated scrutiny without having to run the whole thing again.

☐ "retry". If you specify the option "retry" at a port of some goal, Prolog will go back to where it was when it originally came to the CALL port. Everything will be exactly as it was when the goal was first encountered (except for any additions to the database that may have been made). Hence you can look at what happens in the satisfaction of the goal once again. A common technique is to combine the use of the "retry" and "skip" options. If you are not sure whether a bug occurs in the satisfaction of some goal, you can "skip" over its satisfaction to start with. This means that you will not have to wade through lots of output about a goal that is satisfied completely correctly. If there is a bug, and the goal either fails or produces the wrong result, you can afterwards use the "retry" option to go back and look more closely.

☐ "or". If you are at the EXIT port of a goal, you can ask for alternatives (like when you type ';' to ask for alternative answers to a question). So if you know that the first answer found will not allow the rest of the program to succeed, you can immediately ask for another solution to be found. This means that you will be able to get quicker to the part of the program that has the bug. The alternative would be to have to watch the eventual failure after the first alternative was found.

☐ "fail". This is mainly to be used at the CALL port of a goal. If you know that the goal is going to fail eventually, and the goal is of no interest to you, you can cause it to fail immediately by using this option.

Here is an example of these options being used to alter the satisfaction of a question:

```
?- member(X,[a,b,c]), member(X,[b,d,e]).

CALL member(_44,[a,b,c]) ? creep
EXIT member(a,[a,b,c]) ? or
REDO member(a,[a,b,c]) ? creep
CALL member(_44,[b,c]) ? fail
FAIL member(_44,[b,c]) ? creep
FAIL member(_44,[a,b,c]) ? retry
CALL member(_44,[a,b,c]) ? creep
EXIT member(a,[a,b,c]) ? creep
CALL member(a,[d,c,e]) ? fail
FAIL member(a,[d,c,e]) ? creep
REDO member(a,[a,b,c]) ? creep
CALL member(_44,[b,c]) ? creep
```

```
EXIT member(b,[b,c]) ? or
REDO member(b,[b,c]) ? creep
CALL member(_44,[c]) ? fail
FAIL member(_44,[c]) ? retry
CALL member(_44,[c]) ? creep
EXIT member(c,[c]) ? creep
EXIT member(c,[b,c]) ? creep
EXIT member(c,[a,b,c]) ? creep
CALL member(c,[d,c,e]) ? creep
CALL member(c,[c,e]) ? creep
EXIT member(c,[c,e]) ? creep
EXIT member(c,[d,c,e]) ? or
REDO member(c,[d,c,e]) ? creep
REDO member(c,[c,e]) ? creep
CALL member(c,[e]) ? creep
CALL member(c,[]) ? creep
FAIL member(c,[]) ? creep
FAIL member(c,[e]) ? creep
FAIL member(c,[c,e]) ? retry
CALL member(c,[c,e]) ? creep
EXIT member(c,[c,e]) ? creep
EXIT member(c,[d,c,e]) ? creep
```

Other Options

Other options that may be open to you at a leashed port are:

☐   "break". This causes the current execution to be suspended and a new copy of the Prolog interpreter to be made available to you. You can use this to ask questions about what clauses you have, to set spy points, or anything else that you want. When you exit from the interpreter (by typing the end-of-file character), your previous program will be resumed.

☐   "abort". This causes all your current running programs to be abandoned, and you get "thrown back" to the Prolog interpreter, ready to give the next question.

☐   "halt". This causes you to leave Prolog completely. You might want to use this as soon as you discover a bug, because you want to edit a file that contains the bug-ridden program.

Summary

In conclusion, then, there are three things to think about when you start to look at your program as it runs:

1.   Which goals do you want to look at? If you look at everything (use exhaustive tracing with **trace**), you may become overwhelmed by the amount of information that appears

on your terminal. On the other hand, if you just look at what happens to a few predicates (setting spy points with **spy**), you may miss where the program is going wrong. The best solution is probably a compromise, with careful use of spy points to narrow down the search, and then exhaustive tracing at the end to isolate the bug.

2. How much do you want to control the program's progress from the terminal? If you have all ports unleashed, you will have no control at all over the program, which will rapidly run past the faulty bits before you can notice and look in more detail. On the other hand, if you have all ports leashed, you will get thoroughly fed up telling the program to keep going at each port.

3. Do you want to provide special output facilities for your goals? This will be useful if some of the goals will contain huge structures of little interest, which will only distract from the arguments that you are really interested in. In this case, you can provide a **portray** facility that suppresses this information.

8.5 Fixing Bugs

When you have watched your faulty program working and discovered something wrong with it, you will want to fix the bug and try the program again. Assuming that your program is of a reasonable size, you will already have it stored in disc files. At this point, you will need to use an editor program to change what is in those files. There are two possibilities now:

☐ Your Prolog system may allow you to use an editor and then return to Prolog with exactly the same database as before. You may be able to do this directly, by using an appropriate built-in predicate. Alternatively, Prolog may allow you to save the current state of the database in a special file and then restore it again later. You then save your current state, exit from Prolog, change your program, run Prolog again and restore the previous database state. Having returned to where you were before, but with one or more program files changed, all you need to do is **reconsult** these files to supersede the old definitions with new ones.

☐ If your Prolog system does not allow you to return to a previous state after using an editor, after changing your program files you will have to run Prolog and **consult** all your program files from scratch. You can make this process easier by having a single file containing commands to Prolog to **consult** all the files of your program. You can then read in the whole program by just asking Prolog to **consult** the first file. For instance, if you asked Prolog to **consult** a file containing:

```
?- [file1,file2,file3].
```

```
?- [file4,file5,file6].
```

then as a result each of **file1, ... file6** will be read in.

In some circumstances, the change to your program may seem so minimal that you can enter it from the terminal, by a **consult(user)** or **reconsult(user)**. However, you should beware of doing this too often. If you are not careful, you will forget all the little changes you have made this way and run across the same bugs when you run your program in a later session. Also, since you will want eventually to incorporate the changes into your program files, it is rather a waste to have to type them in at the terminal as well. So do not be tempted into entering clauses from the terminal by the prospect of getting the program to work quickly.

When you are making changes to a program, exercise the same care that you take when you write the first version of a program. Make sure that what you add is still compatible with your conventions about which variables should be instantiated when and what arguments are used for what purposes. Above all, take the opportunity to look over the program again -- there may after all be some other mistakes in it!

Chapter 9. Using Grammar Rules

9.1 The Parsing Problem

Sentences in a language like English are much more than just arbitrary sequences of words. We cannot string together any set of words and make a reasonable sentence. At the very least, the result must conform to what we consider to be grammatical.

A grammar for a language is a set of rules for specifying what sequences of words are acceptable as sentences of that language. It specifies how the words must group together into phrases and what orderings of these phrases are allowed. Given a grammar for a language, we can look at any sequence of words and see whether it meets the criteria for being an acceptable sentence. If the sequence is indeed acceptable, the process of verifying this will have established what the natural groups of words are and how they are put together -- that is, it will have established something of the underlying structure of the sentence.

A particularly simple kind of grammar is known as a "context free" grammar. Rather than give a formal definition of what such a thing is, we will illustrate it by means of a simple example. The following might be the start of a grammar of English sentences:

```
sentence --> noun_phrase, verb_phrase.

noun_phrase --> determiner, noun.

verb_phrase --> verb, noun_phrase.
verb_phrase --> verb.

determiner --> [the].

noun --> [apple].
noun --> [man].

verb --> [eats].
verb --> [sings].
```

The grammar consists of a set of rules, here shown one to a line. Each rule specifies a form that a certain kind of phrase can take. The first rule says that a sentence consists of a phrase called a 'noun_phrase' followed by a phrase called a 'verb_phrase'. These two phrases are what are commonly known as the 'subject' and 'predicate' of the sentence:

To see what a rule in a context free grammar means, read '-->' as saying "... can take the form: ..." and ',' as saying "... followed by ...". Thus the first rule can be read as:

> A 'sentence' can take the form:
> a 'noun_phrase' followed by a 'verb_phrase'

This is all very well, but what is a 'noun_phrase' and what is a 'verb_phrase'? How are we to recognise such things and to know what constitute grammatical forms for them? The second, third and fourth rules of the grammar go on to answer these questions. For instance,

> A 'noun_phrase' can take the form:
> a 'determiner' followed by a 'noun'

Informally, a noun phrase is a group of words that names a thing (or things). Such a phrase contains a word, the 'noun', which gives the main class that the thing belongs to. Thus "the man" names a man, "the program" names a program and so on. Also, according to this grammar, the noun is preceded by a phrase called a 'determiner':

Similarly, the internal structure for a 'verb_phrase' is described by the rules. Notice that there are two rules for what a 'verb_phrase' is – this is because there are two possible forms. A 'verb_phrase' can contain a 'noun_phrase', as in "the man eats the apple", or it need not, as in "the man sings".

What are the other rules in the grammar for? These say how some phrases can be made up in terms of actual words, rather than in terms of smaller phrases. The things inside square brackets name actual words of the language, so that the rule:

    determiner ⟶ [the].

can be read as:

  a 'determiner' can take the form:
  the word "the"

Now that we have got through the whole of the grammar, we can begin to see what sequences of words are actually grammatical sentences according to it. This is a very simple grammar and needs extending in many ways, especially as it will only accept sentences formed out of five different words. If we wish to investigate whether a given sequence of words is actually a sentence according to these criteria, we need to apply the first rule to ask,

  does the sequence decompose into two phrases, such that the first is an acceptable noun_phrase and the second is a valid verb_phrase?

Then order to test whether the first phrase is a noun phrase, we need to apply the second rule, asking,

  "does it decompose into a determiner followed by a noun?"

and so on. At the end, if we succeed, we will have looked at all the phrases and sub-phrases of the sentence, as specified by the grammar, and will have established a structure like, for instance:

This diagram showing the phrase structure of the sentence is called a *parse tree* for the sentence.

We have seen how having a grammar for a language means that we can construct parse trees to show the structure of sentences of the language. The problem of constructing a parse tree for a sentence, given a grammar, is what we call the *parsing problem*. A computer program that constructs parse trees for sentences of a language we shall call a *parser.*

This chapter will illustrate how the parsing problem can be formulated in Prolog, and will introduce the Prolog grammar rule formalism, which makes it rather more convenient to write parsers in Prolog. The ideas are not confined to applications concerned with the syntax of natural languages. Indeed, the same techniques apply to any problem where we are presented with an ordered sequence of items that seem to fall into natural groups and where the arrangement of these groups can be specified by a set of rules. However, for the sake of simplicity the rest of the chapter will concentrate on the problem of parsing English sentences and the generalisation to other fields will be left to you.

9.2 *Representing the Parsing Problem in Prolog*

The primary structure that we are talking about in discussing the parsing problem is the sequence of words whose structure is to be determined. We expect to be able to isolate subsequences of this structure as being various phrases accepted by the grammar, and to show in the end that the whole sequence is acceptable as a phrase of type 'sentence'. Since a standard way of representing a sequence is as a list, we will represent the input to the parser as a Prolog list. What about the representation of the words themselves? For the moment, there seems to be no point in giving the words internal structure -- all we want to do is compare words with one another. Hence is seems reasonable to represent them as Prolog atoms.

Let us develop a program to see if a given sequence of words is a sentence according to the grammar shown above. In order to do this, it will have to establish the underlying structure of the sentences it is given. We will later on consider how to develop a program that *remembers* this structure and displays it to us, but for now it will be easier if we ignore this extra complexity. Since the program involves testing to see if something is a sentence, let us define a predicate **sentence.** The predicate will only need one argument -- we will give it a meaning as follows:

> *sentence(X) means that:*
> *X is a sequence of words forming a grammatical sentence.*

So we anticipate asking questions like:

```
?- sentence([the,man,eats,the,apple]).
```

This will succeed if "the man eats the apple" is a sentence and fail otherwise.

It is rather unfortunate that we have to specify sentences artificially by giving lists of Prolog atoms. For a more serious application, we would probably want to be able to type

English sentences at the terminal in the normal way. In Chapter 5, we saw how a predicate **read_in** can be defined so that we can convert a sentence typed in to a list of Prolog atoms. We could obviously build this into our parser to allow a more natural means of communication with the program's user. However, we will ignore these "cosmetic" matters for now and concentrate on the real problem of parsing.

What is involved in testing to see whether a sequence of words is a sentence? Well, according to the first rule of the grammar, the task decomposes into finding a noun_phrase at the beginning of the sequence and then finding a verb_phrase in what is left. At the end of this, we should have used up exactly the words of the sequence, no more and no less. Let us introduce Let us introduce the predicates **noun_phrase** and **verb_phrase** to express the properties of being a noun_phrase or verb_phrase, so that:

> *noun_phrase (X) means that:*
> *sequence X is a noun_phrase.*

> *verb_phrase (X) means that:*
> *sequence X is a verb_phrase.*

The we can put together a definition of **sentence** in terms of these predicates. A sequence X is a sentence if it decomposes into two subsequences Y and Z, Y is a noun_phrase and Z is a verb_phrase. Since we are representing sequences as lists, we already have available the predicate **append** for dealing with one list decomposing into two others. So we can write:

```
sentence(X) :- append(Y,Z,X), noun_phrase(Y), verb_phrase(Z).
```

Similarly,

```
noun_phrase(X) :- append(Y,Z,X), determiner(Y), noun(Z).

verb_phrase(X) :- append(Y,Z,X), verb(Y), noun_phrase(Z).
verb_phrase(X) :- verb(X).
```

Notice that the two rules for **verb_phrase** give rise to two clauses for our predicate, corresponding to the two ways of verifying that a sequence is a verb_phrase.

Finally, we can easily deal with the rules that introduce words:

```
determiner([the]).

noun([apple]).
noun([man]).

verb([eats]).
verb([sings]).
```

So our program is complete. Indeed, this program will successfully tell us which sequences of words are sentences according to the grammar. However, before we consider the task complete, we should have a look at what actually happens when we ask questions about some example sequences. Consider just the **sentence** clause:

```
sentence(X) :- append(Y,Z,X), noun_phrase(Y), verb_phrase(Z).
```

and a question:

```
?- sentence([the,man,eats,the,apple]).
```

Variable X in the rule will be instantiated (to [the,man,eats,the,apple]), but Y and Z will be uninstantiated, so the goal will generate a possible pair of values for Y and Z such that when Z is appended to Y the result is X. On backtracking, it will generate all the possible pairs, one at a time. The **noun_phrase** goal will only succeed if the value for Y actually is an acceptable noun_phrase. Otherwise it will fail and **append** will have to propose another value. So the flow of control for the first part of the execution will be something like:

1. The goal is **sentence([the,man,eats,the,apple])**.

2. Decompose the list into two lists Y and Z. The following decompositions are possible:
   Y = [],   Z = [the,man,eats,the,apple]
   Y = [the],   Z = [man,eats,the,apple]
   Y = [the,man],   Z = [eats,the,apple]
   Y = [the,man,eats],   Z = [the,apple]
   Y = [the,man,eats,the],   Z = [apple]
   Y = [the,man,eats,the,apple],   Z = []

3. Choose a possibility for Y and Z from the above list of possibilities, and see if Y is a noun_phrase. That is, try and satisfy **noun_phrase(Y)**.

4. If Y is a noun_phrase, then succeed (and look for a verb_phrase). Otherwise, go back to Step 3 and try another possibility.

There seems to be a lot of unnecessary searching in this approach -- the goal **append(Y,Z,X)** ends up generating a large number of solutions, most of which are useless from the point of view of identifying noun phrases. There must be a more directed way of getting to the solution. As our grammar stands, a noun_phrase must have precisely two words in it, and so we might think of using this fact to avoid searching among possible decompositions of the sequence. The trouble is that this state of affairs may not stay true if we change the grammar. Even a small change in the rules for **determiner** could affect the possible lengths of noun_phrases and hence affect the way in which the presence of noun_phrases would be tested. In designing the program it would be nice to retain some modularity. If we wish to change one clause, it should not necessarily have ramifications for the whole program.

So, the heuristic about the length of noun phrases is too specific to be built into the program. Nevertheless, we can see it as a specific case of a general principle. If we wish to select a subsequence that is a noun_phrase, then we can look at the properties of noun_phrases to restrict what kinds of sequences are actually proposed. If the noun_phrase definition is liable to change, we cannot do this, unless we hand over the whole responsibility to the noun_phrase clauses. Since it is the noun_phrase clauses that express what the properties of noun_phrases are, why not expect them to decide how much of the sequence is to be looked at? Let us require the noun_phrase clauses to decide how much of the sequence is to be consumed, and what is to be left for the verb_phrase definition to work on.

This discussion leads us to consider a new definition for the noun_phrase predicate, this time involving two arguments:

noun_phrase(X,Y) is true if:
    there is a noun phrase at the beginning of sequence X and
    the part of the sequence left after the noun_phrase is Y.

So we might expect things like:

```
?- noun_phrase([the,man,eats,the,apple],[eats,the,apple]).
?- noun_phrase([the,apple,sings],[sings]).
```

to be questions that should succeed. We must now revise the definition of **noun_phrase** to reflect this change of meaning. In doing this, we must resolve how the sequence taken up by a noun_phrase decomposes into a sequence taken up by a determiner followed by a sequence taken up by a noun. We can again delegate the problem of how much of the sequence is taken up to the clauses for the embedded phrases, giving the following:

```
noun_phrase(X,Y) :- determiner(X,Z), noun(Z,Y).
```

So a noun_phrase exists at the beginning of sequence X if we can find a determiner at the front of X, leaving behind Z, and we can then find a noun at the front of Z. The amount of the sequence left behind by the whole noun_phrase is the same as that left behind after the noun. Expressed diagramatically:

```
[the,man,eats,the,apple]
 |_____X_____|
   |_____Z_____|
     |_____Y_____|
```

In order for this to work, we will have to adopt a similar convention with **determiner** and **noun** as we did with **noun_phrase**.

This clause tells us how the problem of finding a sequence that is a noun_phrase decomposes into finding subsequences that is a determiner followed by one which is a noun.

Similarly, the problem of finding a sentence decomposes into finding a noun_phrase followed by a verb_phrase. This is all very abstract. None of this tells us how many words are actually consumed in the determiner, noun_phrase or sentence. The information must be built up from our version of the rules that actually introduce English words. We can again express these as Prolog clauses, but this time we need to add an extra argument, to give for example:

```
determiner([the|X],X).
```

This rule expresses the fact that one can find a determiner at the front of a sequence beginning with the word "the". Moreover, the determiner only takes up the first word of the sequence, and leaves the rest behind.

In fact, we can add an extra argument to every predicate that recognises a kind of phrase, to express how that kind of phrase "uses up" some of the words of a sequence and leaves the rest. In particular, for consistency, it would be sensible to do this with the **sentence** predicate. How does the initial goal that we give to the program look now? We must decide on what two arguments to give to **sentence** in the question. The arguments indicate the sequence that it starts from and the sequence it is to leave behind. The first of these is obviously the same as the argument we gave to **sentence** before. Moreover, since we want to find a sentence that occupies the whole of the sequence, we want there to be nothing left after the sentence has been found. We want only the empty sequence to be left. Hence we must give the program a goal like:

```
?- sentence([the,man,eats,the,apple],[]).
```

Let us now see how the complete grammar looks after we have rewritten it with the above discussion in mind:

```
sentence(S0,S) :- noun_phrase(S0,S1), verb_phrase(S1,S).

noun_phrase(S0,S) :- determiner(S0,S1), noun(S1,S).

verb_phrase(S0,S) :- verb(S0,S).
verb_phrase(S0,S) :- verb(S0,S1), noun_phrase(S1,S).

determiner([the|S],S).

noun([man|S],S).
noun([apple|S],S).

verb([eats|S],S).
verb([sings|S],S).
```

So we now have a more efficient version of our program to recognise sentences accepted by the grammar. It is a pity, though, that the code looks more messy than that of the previous version. All the extra arguments seem to clutter it up unnecessarily. We will now see how to cope with this problem.

9.3 The Grammar Rule Notation

The Prolog grammar rule notation was developed as an aid to people writing parsers using the techniques we have just described. The notation makes the code easier to read, because it suppresses information that is not interesting. Because the notation is more concise than ordinary Prolog, there is also less chance of making silly typing mistakes if you use grammar rules for writing your parsers.

Although the grammar rule notation is self-contained, it is important to realise that it is only a shorthand for ordinary Prolog code. You can use grammar rules either because your Prolog system already knows about them, or because there is a library package that enables you to use a special form of `consult`. In either case, the way that the system handles grammar rules is to specifically recognise them when they are input and then translate them into ordinary Prolog. So your grammar rules end up as ordinary Prolog clauses, although naturally looking a bit different from what you typed in.

The actual notation is built around the notation for context-free grammars that we introduced at the beginning of this chapter. In fact, if the grammar as presented there (reproduced below) were given to Prolog, it would be translated into clauses exactly the same as what we ended up with as the final version of the parsing program:

```
sentence --> noun_phrase, verb_phrase.

noun_phrase --> determiner, noun.

verb_phrase --> verb.
verb_phrase --> verb, noun_phrase.

determiner --> [the].

noun --> [man].
noun --> [apple].

verb --> [eats].
verb --> [sings].
```

The actual grammar rules are Prolog structures, with main functor '-->', which is declared as an infix operator. All the Prolog system has to do is check whether a term read in (in a `consult` or similar) has this functor, and if so translate it into a proper clause.

What is involved in this translation? First of all, every atom that names a kind of phrase must be translated into a predicate with two arguments -- for the sequence provided and the sequence left behind, as in our program. Second, whenever a grammar rule mentions phrases coming one after another, it must be arranged that that the arguments reflect the

196

fact that what is left behind by one phrase forms the input to the next. Finally, whenever a grammar rule mentions that a phrase can be realised as a sequence of subphrases, the arguments must express the fact that the amount of words consumed by the whole phrase is the same as the total consumed by the subphrases mentioned on the right of the -->. These criteria ensure, for instance, that:

```
sentence --> noun_phrase, verb_phrase.
```

translates into:

```
sentence(S0,S) :- noun_phrase(S0,S1), verb_phrase(S1,S).
```

or, in English,

> There is a sentence between S0 and S if there is a noun phrase between S0 and S1, and if there is a verb phrase between S1 and S.

Finally, the system has to know how to translate those rules that introduce actual words. This involves inserting the words into the lists forming the arguments of the predicates, so that, for instance,

```
determiner --> [the].
```

translates into:

```
determiner([the|S],S).
```

Once we have expressed our parsing program as grammar rules, how do we specify the goals that we want it to work at? Since we now know how grammar rules translate into ordinary Prolog, we can express our goals in Prolog, adding the extra arguments ourselves. The first argument to add is the list of words that is to be looked at, and the second is the list that is going to be left, which is normally the empty list, []. So, we can specify goals like:

```
?- sentence([the,man,eats,the,apple],[]).
?- noun_phrase([the,man,sings],X).
```

As an alternative, some Prolog implementations provide an evaluable predicate **phrase** which simply adds the extra arguments for you. The predicate **phrase** is defined by:

> phrase(P,L) is true if:
> list L can be parsed as a phrase of type P.

So we could replace the first of the above goals by the alternative:

    ?- phrase(sentence,[the,man,eats,the,apple]).

Note that the definition of **phrase** involves the whole list being parsed, with the empty list being left. Therefore we could not replace the second goal above by a use of **phrase**.

If your Prolog implementation does not provide **phrase** already defined, you can easily provide a clause for it, as follows:

    phrase(P,L) :- Goal =.. [P,L,[]], call(Goal).

Note, however, that this definition will not be adequate when we consider more general grammar rules in the next section.

Exercise 9.1: You may wish to define in Prolog a procedure **translate,** such that **translate(X,Y)** is true if X is a grammar rule (of the kind we have encountered in this section) and Y is the term representing the corresponding Prolog clause. This is quite a hard exercise. Procedures that are much like **translate** are provided by the Prolog system, either built-in or as library programs, but it may help you to understand what translation process is involved if you actually write **translate**.

9.4 Adding Extra Arguments

The grammar rules we have come across so far are only of a fairly restricted kind. In this section we will consider one useful extension, which allows phrase types to have extra arguments. This "extension" is still part of the standard grammar rule facility that Prolog provides.

We have seen how an occurrence of a phrase type in a grammar rule translates to the use of a Prolog predicate with two extra arguments. So the rules we have seen so far give rise to a lot of two-argument predicates. Now Prolog predicates can have any number of arguments, and we may sometimes want to have extra arguments used in our parsers, apart from the ones dealing with the consumption of the input sequence. The grammar rule notation supports this.

Let us look at an example where extra arguments may be useful. Consider the problem of "number agreement" between the subject and verb of a sentence. Sequences like

    *The boys eats the apple.
    *The boy eat the apple.

are not grammatical English sentences, even though they might be allowed by a simple extension of our grammar. The reason they are not grammatical is that if the subject of a sentence is singular then the sentence must also use the singular form of the verb. Similarly, if the subject is plural, the plural form of the verb must be used. We could express this in grammar rules by saying that there are two kinds of sentences, singular_sentences and plural_sentences. A singular_sentence must start with a singular_noun_phrase, which must have a singular_noun, and so on. We would end up with a set of rules like the following:

```
sentence --> singular_sentence.
sentence --> plural_sentence.

noun_phrase --> singular_noun_phrase.
noun_phrase --> plural_noun_phrase.

singular_sentence --> singular_noun_phrase, singular_verb_phrase.

singular_noun_phrase --> singular_determiner, singular_noun.

singular_verb_phrase --> singular_verb, noun_phrase.
singular_verb_phrase --> singular_verb.

singular_determiner --> [the].

singular_noun --> [boy].

singular_verb --> [eats].
```

and also a whole lot of rules for plural phrases. This is not very elegant, and obscures the fact that singular and plural sentences have a lot of structure in common. A better way is to associate an extra argument with phrase types, according to whether they are singular or plural. Thus **sentence(singular)** names a phrase which is a singular sentence and, in general, **sentence(X)** a sentence of plurality X. The rules about number agreement then amount to consistency conditions on the values of these arguments. The plurality of the subject noun_phrase must be the same as that of the verb_phrase, and so on. Rewriting the grammar in this way, we get:

```
sentence --> sentence(X).

sentence(X) --> noun_phrase(X), verb_phrase(X).

noun_phrase(X) --> determiner(X), noun(X).

verb_phrase(X) --> verb(X).
verb_phrase(X) --> verb(X), noun_phrase(Y).

noun(singular) --> [boy].
noun(plural) --> [boys].

determiner(_) --> [the].

verb(singular) --> [eats].
verb(plural) --> [eat].
```

Note the way in which we can specify the plurality of "the". This word could introduce a singular or a plural phrase, and so its plurality is compatible with anything. Also note that in the second rule for verb_phrase the naming of the variables expresses the fact that the plurality of a verb_phrase (the thing that must agree with the subject) is taken from that of the verb, and not that of the object, if there is one.

We can introduce arguments to express other important information as well as number agreement. For instance, we can use them to keep a record of constituents that have appeared outside their "normal" position, and hence deal with the phenomena that linguists put under the heading "movement". Or we can use them to record items of *semantic* significance –– to say how the *meaning* of a phrase is composed of the meanings of the subphrases. We will not investigate these any more here, although Section 9.6 gives a simple example of incorporating semantics into the parser. However, one thing should be noted here. Linguists may be interested to know that once we introduce extra arguments into grammar rules, we cannot guarantee that the language defined by the grammar is still context-free, although it often will be.

An important use of extra arguments is to return a parse tree as a result of the analysis. In Chapter 3 we saw how trees can be represented as Prolog structures, and we will now make use of that in extending the parser to make a parse tree. Parse trees are helpful because they provide a structural representation of a sentence. It is more convenient to write programs that process this structural representation in a way analogous to processing the arithmetic formulae and lists in Chapter 7. The new program, given a grammatical sentence like:

>   *The man eats the apple.*

will generate a structure like:

```
sentence(
    noun_phrase(
                determiner(the),
                noun(man)
                ),
    verb_phrase(
                verb(eats),
                noun_phrase(
                            determiner(the),
                            noun(apple)
                            )
                )
    )
```

as a result. In order to make it do this, we only need to add an extra argument to each predicate, saying how the tree for a whole phrase is constructed from the trees of the various sub-phrases. Thus we can change the first rule to:

```
sentence(X,sentence(NP,VP)) --> noun_phrase(X,NP), verb_phrase(X,VP).
```

This says that if we can find a sequence constituting a noun_phrase, with parse tree NP, followed by a sequence constituting a verb_phrase, with parse tree VP, then we have found a sequence constituting a complete sentence, and the parse tree for that sentence is **sentence(NP,VP)**. Or, in more procedural terms, to parse a sentence one must find a noun_phrase followed by a verb_phrase, and then combine the parse trees of these two constituents, using the functor **sentence** to make the tree for the sentence. Note that the 'X' arguments are just the number agreement arguments used earlier, and that the decision to put the tree generating arguments after rather then before them was arbitrary. If you have any difficulty understanding this extension, it helps to see that this is all just a shorthand for an ordinary Prolog clause:

```
sentence(X,sentence(NP,VP),S0,S) :-
        noun_phrase(X,NP,S0,S1),
        verb_phrase(X,VP,S1,S).
```

where S0, S1 and S stand for parts of the input sequence. We can introduce tree-building arguments throughout the grammar in a routine way. Here is an excerpt from what is produced if we do this (number agreement arguments being left out for clarity):

```
sentence(sentence(NP,VP)) --> noun_phrase(NP), verb_phrase(VP).

verb_phrase(verb_phrase(V)) --> verb(V).

noun(noun(man)) --> [man].
verb(verb(eats)) --> [eats].
```

The translation mechanism needed to deal with grammar rules with extra arguments is a simple extension of the one described before. Previously a new predicate was created for each phrase type, with two arguments to express how the input sequence was consumed. Now it is necessary to create a predicate with two more arguments than are mentioned in the grammar rules. By convention, these two extra arguments are added as the last arguments of the predicate (although this may vary between Prolog systems). Thus the grammar rule:

```
sentence(X) --> noun_phrase(X), verb_phrase(X).
```

translates into:

```
sentence(X,S0,S) --> noun_phrase(X,S0,S1), verb_phrase(X,S1,S).
```

When we want to invoke goals involving grammar rules from the top level of the interpreter or from ordinary Prolog rules, we must explicitly add the extra arguments. Thus appropriate goals involving this definition of **sentence** would be:

```
?- sentence(X,[a,clergyman,eats,a,cake],[]).
?- sentence(X,[every,bird,sings,and,pigs,can,fly],L).
```

Exercise 9.2: Write a new version of **phrase** that allows grammar rules with extra arguments, so that one can provide goals like:

```
?- phrase(sentence(X),[the,man,sings]).
```

9.5 Adding Extra Tests

So far in our parser, everything mentioned in the grammar rules has had to do with how the input sequence is consumed. Every item in the rules has had something to do with those two extra argument positions that are added by the grammar rule translator. So every goal in the resulting Prolog clause has been involved with consuming some amount of the input. Sometimes we may want to specify Prolog goals that are not of this type, and the grammar rule formalism allows us to do this. The convention is that any goals enclosed inside curly brackets (....) are to be left unchanged by the translator.

Let us look at some examples of where it would be beneficial to use this facility -- in improving the "dictionary" of the parser, that is, the parser's knowledge about words of the language.

Firstly, consider the overhead involved in introducing a new word into the program with both sets of extra arguments. If we wished to add the new noun 'banana', for instance, we would have to add at least the rule:

```
noun(singular,noun(banana)) --> [banana].
```

which amounts to:

```
noun(singular,noun(banana),[banana|S],S).
```

in ordinary Prolog. This is a lot of information to specify for each noun, especially when we know that every noun will only occupy one word and will give rise to a small tree with the functor **noun**. A much more economical way would be to express the common information about all nouns in one place and the information about particular words somewhere else. We can do this by mixing grammar rules with ordinary Prolog. We express the general information about how nouns fit into larger phrases by a grammar rule, and then the information about what words are nouns in ordinary clauses. The solution that results looks like:

```
noun(S,noun(N)) --> [N], {is_noun(N,S)} .
```

where the normal predicate **is_noun** expresses which words are nouns and whether they are singular or plural:

```
is_noun(banana,singular).
is_noun(bananas,plural).
is_noun(man,singular).
   .
   .
   .
```

Let us look carefully at what this grammar rule means. It says that a phrase of type **noun** can take the form of any single word N (a variable is specified in the list) subject to a restriction. The restriction is that N must be in our **is_noun** collection, with some plurality S. In this case, the plurality of the phrase is also S, and the parse tree produced consists just of the word N underneath the node **noun**. Why does the goal **is_noun(N,S)** have to be put inside curly brackets? Because it expresses a relationship that has nothing to do with the input sequence. If we were to leave out the curly brackets, it would be translated to something like **is_noun(N,S,S1,S2)**, which would never match our clauses for is_noun. Putting it inside the curly brackets stops the translation mechanism from changing it, so that our rule will be correctly translated to:

```
noun(S,noun(N),[N|Seq],Seq) :- is_noun(N,S).
```

In spite of this change, our treatment of individual words is still not very elegant. The trouble with this technique is that we will have to have to write two **is_noun** clauses for every new noun that is introduced -- one for the singular form, and one for the plural form. This is unnecessary, because for most nouns the singular and plural forms are related by a simple rule:

If X is the singular form of a noun, then the word formed by adding an "s" on the end of X is the plural form of that noun.

We can use this rule about the form of nouns to revise our definition of **noun**. The revisions will give a new set of conditions that the word N must satisfy in order to be a noun. Because these conditions are about the internal structure of the word, and do not have anything to do with the consumption of the input sequence, they will appear within curly brackets. We are representing English words as Prolog atoms, and so considerations about how words decompose into letters translate into considerations about the characters that go to make up the appropriate atoms. So we will need to use the predicate **name** in our definition. The amended rule looks as follows:

```
noun(plural,noun(RootN)) --> [N],
   {(name(N,Plname), append(Singname,"s",Plname),
     name(RootN,Singname), is_noun(RootN,singular))} .
```

Of course, this expresses a general rule about plurals that is not always true (for instance, the plural of "fly" is not "flys"). We will still have to express the exceptions in an exhaustive way. Notice that the double-quote notation is used to represent the character 's' as a member of a list. We need now only specify **is_noun** clauses for the singular forms of regular nouns. Note that under the above definition the item inserted into the parse tree will be the "root" noun, rather than the inflected form. This may be useful for subsequent processing of the tree. Note also the syntax of curly brackets. This may differ slightly between different Prolog implementations, but the safest thing is to surround multiple goals inside curly brackets with an extra pair of round brackets and to leave a space between any curly bracket and the final '.'.

As well as knowing about curly brackets, most Prolog grammar rule translators will know about certain other goals that are not to be translated normally. Thus it is not normally necessary to enclose '!'s or disjunctions (';') of goals involving the input sequence inside curly brackets.

9.6 Summary

We will now summarise the syntax of grammar rules as described so far. We will then indicate some of the possible extensions to the basic system and some of the interesting ways that grammar rules can be used. The best way to describe the syntax of grammar rules is by grammar rules themselves. So here is an informal definition. Note that it is not completely rigorous, because it neglects the influence of operator precedences on the syntax.

```
grammar_rule --> grammar_head, ['-->'], grammar_body.

grammar_head --> non_terminal.
grammar_head --> non_terminal, [','], terminal.

grammar_body --> grammar_body, [','], grammar_body.
grammar_body --> grammar_body, [';'], grammar_body.
grammar_body --> grammar_body_item.

grammar_body_item --> ['!'].
grammar_body_item --> ['{'], prolog_goals, ['}'].
grammar_body_item --> non_terminal.
grammar_body_item --> terminal.
```

This leaves several items undefined. Here are definitions of them in English.

> A non_terminal indicates a kind of phrase that may occupy part of the input sequence. It takes the form of a Prolog structure, where the functor names the category of the phrase and the arguments give extra information, like the number class, the meaning, etc.

> A terminal indicates a number of words that may occupy part of the input sequence. It takes the form of a Prolog list (which may be [] or a list of any determinate length). The items of the list are Prolog items that are to match against the words as they appear in the order given.

Prolog_goals are any Prolog goals. They can be used to express extra tests and actions that constrain the possible analysis paths taken and indicate how complex results are built up from simpler ones.

When translated in Prolog, *prolog_goals* are left unchanged and *non_terminals* have two extra arguments inserted after the ones that appear explicitly, corresponding to the sequence provided to and the sequence left behind by the phrase. *Terminals* appear within the extra arguments of the *non_terminals*. When a predicate defined by grammar rules is invoked at the top level of the interpreter or by an ordinary Prolog rule, the two extra arguments must be provided explicitly.

The second rule for **grammar_head** in the above mentions a kind of grammar rule that we have not met before. Up to now, our terminals and non-terminals have only been defined in terms of how they consume the input sequence. Sometimes we might like to define things that insert items into the input sequence (for other rules to find). For instance, we might like to analyse an imperative sentence like:

Eat your supper.

as if there were an extra word "you" inserted:

You eat your supper.

It would then have a nice noun_phrase/verb_phrase structure, which conforms to our existing ideas about the structure of sentences. We can do this by having a grammar that looks in part like:

```
sentence --> imperative, noun_phrase, verb_phrase.

imperative, [you] --> [].
imperative --> [].
```

There is only one rule here that deserves mention. The first rule for **imperative** actually translates to:

```
imperative(L,[you|L]).
```

So this involves a sequence being returned that is longer than the one originally provided. In general, the left-hand side of a grammar rule can consist of a non-terminal separated from a list of words by a comma. The meaning of this is that in the parsing the words are inserted into the input sequence after the goals on the right-hand side have had their chance to consume words from it.

Exercise 9.3: The definition given for grammar rules, even if made complete, would not constitute a useful parser, given a sequence of tokens as its input.   Why?

Finally, we present an example (taken from Pereira and Warren's paper in the journal *Artificial Intelligence* Volume 13) of grammar rules used to obtain the meaning of sentences directly, without an intermediate parse tree.   The following rules translate from (a restricted number of) English sentences into a representation of their meaning in Predicate Calculus. For a description of Predicate Calculus and our notation for it, the reader is referred to Chapter 10.   As an example of the program at work, the meaning obtained for "every man loves a woman" is the structure:

```
all(X,(man(X) -> exists(Y,(woman(Y)&loves(X,Y))))))
```

Here are the grammar rules:

```
?- op(100,xfy,&).
?- op(150,xfy,->).

sentence(P) --> noun_phrase(X,P1,P), verb_phrase(X,P1).

noun_phrase(X,P1,P) -->
    determiner(X,P2,P1,P), noun(X,P3),
    rel_clause(X,P3,P2).
noun_phrase(X,P,P) --> proper_noun(X).

verb_phrase(X,P) --> trans_verb(X,Y,P1), noun_phrase(Y,P1,P).
verb_phrase(X,P) --> intrans_verb(X,P).

rel_clause(X,P1,(P1&P2)) --> [that], verb_phrase(X,P2).
rel_clause(_,P,P) --> [].

determiner(X,P1,P2, all(X,(P1->P2))) --> [every].
determiner(X,P1,P2, exists(X,(P1&P2))) --> [a].

noun(X,man(X)) --> [man].
noun(X,woman(X)) --> [woman].

proper_noun(john) --> [john].

trans_verb(X,Y,loves(X,Y)) --> [loves].

intrans_verb(X,lives(X)) --> [lives].
```

In this program, arguments are used to build up structures representing the meanings of phrases.   For each phrase, it is the last argument that actually specifies the meaning of that phrase.   However, the meaning of a a phrase may depend on several other factors, given in the other arguments.   For instance, the verb 'lives' gives rise to a proposition of the form 'lives(X)', where 'X' is something standing for the person who lives.   The meaning of 'lives' cannot specify in advance what 'X' will be -- the meaning has to be applied to some specific object in order to be useful.   The context in which the verb is used will determine what this object is.   So the definition just says that, for any X, when the verb is applied to X, the meaning is 'lives(X)'.   A word like 'every' is much more complicated.   In this case, the meaning has to be applied to a variable and two propositions containing that variable. The result is something that says that, if substituting an object for the variable in the first proposition yields something true then substituting that same object for the variable in the second proposition will also yield something true.

Exercise 9.4: Read and understand this program. Try running the program, giving it goals like

```
?- sentence(X,[every,man,loves,a,woman],[]).
```

What meaning does the program generate for the sentence "every man that lives loves a woman", "every man that loves a woman lives"? The sentence "Every man loves a woman" is actually ambiguous -- there could either be a single woman that every man loves, or there could be a (possibly) different woman that each man loves. Does the program produce the two possible meanings as alternative solutions? If not, why not? What simple assumption has been made about how the meanings of sentences are built up?

Chapter 10. The Relation of Prolog to Logic

The programming language Prolog was invented by Alain Colmerauer around about 1970. It was a first attempt at the design of a language that would enable a programmer to specify his tasks in logic, rather than in terms of conventional programming constructs about what the machine should do when. This motivation explains the name of the programming language, for "Prolog" stands for *Programming in logic*.

In this book, we have emphasised mainly how one can use Prolog as a tool for doing practical tasks, and we have not talked about the ways in which Prolog is a step towards the ultimate goal of a "logic programming" system. In this chapter, we intend to redress this imbalance somewhat by considering briefly how Prolog is related to logic and to what extent Prolog programming is really like "programming in logic".

10.1 Brief Introduction to Predicate Calculus

If we wish to discuss how Prolog is related to logic, we must first of all establish what we mean by "logic". Logic was originally devised as a way of representing the form of arguments, so that it would be possible to check in a formal way whether or not they were valid. Thus we can use logic to express propositions, the relations between propositions and how one can validly *infer* some propositions from others. The particular form of logic that we will be talking about here is called the *Predicate Calculus*. We will only be able to say a few words about it here. For a more detailed treatment, you can consult *Introduction to Mathematical Logic* by E. Mendelson, published in 1964 by Van Nostrand Reinhold, or any of the other books that deal with Symbolic Logic. Another text that may be of interest is *Symbolic Logic and Mechanical Theorem Proving*, by Chin Liang Chang and Richard Char-Tung Lee, published in 1973 by Academic Press.

If we wish to express propositions about the world, we must be able to describe the objects that are involved in them. In Predicate Calculus, we represent objects by *terms*. A term is of one of the following forms:

☐   A *constant symbol.* This is a symbol that stands for a single individual or concept. We can think of this as a Prolog atom, and we will use the Prolog syntax. So **apple1, agatha,** and **peace** are constant symbols.

☐   A *variable symbol.* This is a symbol that we may want to stand for different individuals at different times. Variables are really only introduced in conjunction with quantifiers, which are discussed below. We can think of them as Prolog variables and will use the Prolog syntax. Thus **X, Man,** and **Greek** are variable symbols.

☐   A *compound term.* A compound term consists of a *function symbol,* together with an ordered set of terms as its *arguments.* The idea is that the compound term represents some individual that depends on the individuals represented by the arguments. The function symbol represents how the first depends on the second. For instance, we could have a function symbol standing for the notion of "distance" and two arguments. In this case, the compound term stands for the distance between the objects represented by the arguments. We can think of a compound term as a Prolog structure with the function symbol as the functor. We will write Predicate Calculus compound terms using the Prolog syntax, so that, for instance, **wife(henry)** might mean Henry's wife, **distance(point1,X),** might mean the distance between some particular point and some other place to be specified, and **classes(mary,dayafter(W))** might mean the classes that Mary teaches on the day after some day W to be specified.

Thus in Predicate Calculus the ways of representing objects are just like the ways available in Prolog.

In order to express propositions about objects we must be able to express relationships between objects. We do this with *predicate symbols.* An *atomic proposition* consists of a predicate symbol, together with an ordered set of terms as its arguments. This is just like the kind of thing that can appear as a Prolog goal. So, for example, the following are atomic propositions: **human(mary), owns(X,donkey(X)), likes(Man,wine).** In Prolog, a structure can appear either as a goal or as an argument to another structure or both. This is not the case in Predicate Calculus, where a rigid separation is made between *function symbols,* which are functors that are used to construct arguments, and *predicate symbols,* which are functors that are used to construct propositions.

Out of atomic propositions, we can make compound propositions in various ways. It is here that we begin to find things that do not have direct analogues in Prolog. There are several ways in which we can make more complicated propositions out of simpler ones. First, we can use the *logical connectives.* These are ways of expressing the familiar notions "not", "and", "or", "implies" and "is equivalent to". The following summarises the connectives and their meanings. In this summary, α and β are meant to represent any propositions. We give both the traditional Predicate Calculus syntax and the syntax that will be used here.

Connective	PC Syntax	Our Syntax	Meaning
Negation	$\tilde{\ }\alpha$	$\tilde{\ }\alpha$	"not α"
Conjunction	$\alpha \wedge \beta$	α & β	"α and β"
Disjunction	$\alpha \vee \beta$	α # β	"α or β"
Implication	$\alpha \supset \beta$	α -> β	"α implies β"
Equivalence	$\alpha \equiv \beta$	α <-> β	"α is equivalent to β"

Thus, for example, man(fred) # woman(fred) could be used to represent the proposition that Fred is a man *or* Fred is a woman. man(john) -> human(john) might represent the proposition that John's being a man *implies* his being human (*if* John is a man *then* he is human). The notions of implication and equivalence are sometimes a little hard to grasp at first. We say that α implies β if, whenever α is true so is β. We say that α is equivalent to β if α is true in exactly those circumstances when β is true. In fact, these notions can be defined in terms of "and", "or" and "not", for:

α -> β means the same as $(\tilde{\ }\alpha)$ # β
α <-> β means the same as $(\alpha$ & $\beta)$ # $(\tilde{\ }\alpha$ & $\tilde{\ }\beta)$
                            (and also $(\alpha$ -> $\beta)$ & $(\beta$ -> $\alpha))$

So far, we have not made it clear what it means when variables appear inside a proposition. In fact, the meaning is only defined when such variables are introduced by *quantifiers.* Quantifiers provide a means of talking about sets of individuals and what is true of them. Predicate Calculus provides two quantifiers. If α represents any variable and Π any proposition, we can summarise them as follows:

PC Syntax	Our Syntax	Meaning
$\forall\alpha.\Pi$	all(α,Π)	"Π is true whatever α stands for"
$\exists\alpha.\Pi$	exists(α,Π)	"there is something that α can stand for, such that Π is true"

The first of these is called the *universal quantifier* because it talks about everything in the Universe (for all α, ...). The second is called the *existential quantifier* because it talks about the existence of some object(s) (there exists α such that ...). As examples of uses of the quantifiers, for instance, all(X, man(X) -> human(X)) means that, whatever X we choose, if X is a man then X is a human. We can read it as "for all X, if X is a man then X is a human" or, in English, simply "every man is human". Similarly, exists(Z, father(john,Z) & female(Z)) means that there is something that Z can stand for such that John is the father of Z and Z is female. We can read it as "there exists a Z such that John is the father of Z and Z is female" or, in English, simply "John has a daughter".

Here are some more complicated Predicate Calculus formulae for your amusement:

all(X, animal(X) -> exists(Y,motherof(X,Y)))

```
"every animal has a mother"

all(X, pcformula(X) <-> (atomicformula(X) # compoundformula(X)) )
```

"something is a Predicate Calculus formula if, and only if,
it is an atomic formula or a compound formula"

10.2 Clausal Form

As we saw in the last section, Predicate Calculus formulae expressed in terms of ->
(implication) and <-> (equivalence) can be rewritten in terms of & (conjunction), # (disjunction)
and ¨ (negation). In fact, there are many more identities of this form, and we would not
sacrifice any expressive power if we were to completely avoid using #, ->, <-> and
exists(X,P), for instance. As a result of the redundancy, there are many ways of writing
down the same proposition. If we wish to carry out formal manipulations on Predicate Calculus
formulae, this turns out to be very inconvenient. It would be much nicer if everything we
wanted to say could only be expressed in one way. So we will now consider how a Predicate
Calculus proposition can be translated into a special form, *clausal form*, where there are less
ways of saying the same thing. In fact, it will turn out that a Predicate Calculus proposition
in clausal form is very much like a set of Prolog clauses. So an investigation of clausal
form is essential for an understanding of the relation between Prolog and logic. In Appendix
B, we present briefly a Prolog program which will automatically translate a Predicate Calculus
formula into clausal form.

The conversion of a Predicate Calculus formula into normal form has six main stages.
We have based this particular formulation heavily on a description given by Martin Davis in
the *Proceedings of a Symposium in Applied Mathematics* (American Mathematical Society,
1963).

Stage 1 - Removing Implications

We start by replacing occurrences of -> and <-> in accordance with the definitions given
in Section 10.1. As a result of this definition, we would expect:

```
all(X,man(X)->human(X))
```

to be transformed to:

```
all(X, ¨man(X) # human(X))
```

Stage 2 - Moving negation inwards

This stage is involved with cases where ~ is applied to a formula that is not atomic. If such a case is detected, an appropriate rewrite is made. Thus, for instance,

    ~(human(caesar) & living(caesar))

is transformed to

    ~human(caesar) # ~living(caesar)

and

    ~all(Y,person(Y))

is transformed to:

    exists(Y,~person(Y))

The validity of this stage results from the following identities:

~(α & β)   means the same as   (~α) # (~β)
~(α # β)   means the same as   (~α) & (~β)
~exists(α,Π)   means the same as   all(α,~Π)
~all(α,Π)   means the same as   exists(α,~Π)

After Stage 2, negation will only appear in our formulae applied directly to atomic formulae. We call an atomic formula, or an atomic formula preceded by a ~ a *literal*. The next few stages will treat literals as single items, and the significance of which literals are negated will only be important at the end.

Stage 3 - Skolemising

The next stage involves removing the existential quantifiers. This is done by introducing new constant symbols, *Skolem constants*, in the place of the variables introduced by the existential quantifiers. Instead of saying that there exists an object with a certain set of properties, one can create a name for one such object and simply say that it has the properties. This is the motivation behind introducing Skolem constants. Skolemising does more damage to the logical properties of a formula than the other transformations we discuss. Nevertheless, it has the following important property. There is an interpretation for the symbols of a formula that makes the formula true if and only if there is an interpretation for the Skolemised version of the formula. For our purposes, this form of equivalence is enough. Thus, for example,

    exists(X, female(X) & motherof(X,eve))

is changed by Skolemisation to

    female(g1) & motherof(g1,eve)

where **g1** is some new constant not used elsewhere. g1 represents some female whose mother is Eve. It is important that we use a different symbol from any used previously, because the **exists(_,_)** proposition is not saying that some particular person is Eve's daughter, but only that there is such a person. It may turn out that **g1** will correspond to the same person as some other constant symbol, but that is extra information that is not conveyed by this proposition.

When there are universal quantifiers in a formula, Skolemisation is not quite so simple. For instance, if we Skolemised

```
all(X, human(X) -> exists(Y,motherof(X,Y)) )
```

("every human has a mother") to

```
all(X, human(X) -> motherof(X,g2) )
```

we would be saying that every human has the *same* mother -- the thing denoted by **g2**. When there are variables introduced by universal quantifiers, Skolemisation must instead introduce *function* symbols, to express how what exists *depends* on what the variables are chosen to stand for. Thus the above example should Skolemise to

```
all(X, human(X) -> motherof(X,g2(X)) )
```

In this case, the function symbol **g2** corresponds to the function in the world that, given any person, returns as its value the mother of that person. Here now is the Prolog definition of Skolemisation.

Stage 4 - Moving universal quantifiers outwards

This stage is very simple. We just move any universal quantifiers to the outside of the formula. This does not affect the meaning. As an example,

```
all(X, man(X) -> all(Y,woman(Y)->likes(X,Y)) )
```

is transformed to

```
all(X,all(Y, man(X) -> (woman(Y)->likes(X,Y)) ))
```

Since every variable in the formula is now introduced by a universal quantifier at the outside of the formula, the quantifiers themselves no longer provide any extra information. So we can abbreviate the formula by simply leaving the quantifiers out. We just need to remember that every variable is introduced by an implicit quantifier that we have left out. Thus we can now represent:

all(X,alive(X) # dead(X)) & all(Y,likes(mary,Y) # impure(Y))

as:

(alive(x) # dead(x)) & likes(mary,y) # impure(y)

The formula means that, whatever X and Y we choose, either X is alive or X is dead, and either Mary likes Y or Y is impure.

Stage 5 – Distributing '&' over '#'

At this stage, our original Predicate Calculus formula has changed a lot. We no longer have any explicit quantifiers, and the only connectives left are & and # (apart from where negation comes inside a literal). We now put this in a special normal form, *conjunctive normal form*, where conjunctions no longer appear inside disjunctions. Thus we can convert the whole formula into a bundle of &'s, where the things joined together are either literals or literals joined by #'s. To do this, we make use of the two identities:

    (A & B) # C   is equivalent to   (A # C) & (B # C)
    A # (B & C)   is equivalent to   (A # B) & (A # C)

As an example of what happens, the formula:

holiday(X) # (work(chris,X) & (angry(chris) # sad(chris)))

(For every X, either X is a holiday or both Chris works on X and Chris is angry or sad) is equivalent to:

(holiday(X) # work(chris,X)) & (holiday(X) # (angry(chris) # sad(chris)))

(For every X, first, X is a holiday or Chris works on X, and second, either X is a holiday or Chris is angry or sad).

Stage 6 – Putting into Clauses

The formula we have now is in general made up of a collection of &'s relating things which are either literals or composed of literals by #'s. Let us look first at the top level of this, not looking in detail at the #'s. We might have something like:

(A & B) & (C & (D & E))

where A, B, C, D, E perhaps represent complex propositions, but have no &'s in them. Now all this nesting of structure is unnecessary, because all the propositions

```
(A & B) & (C & (D & E))
A & ((B & C) & (D & E))
(A & B) & ((C & D) & E)
    .
    .
    .
```

mean the same thing. Although *structurally* the formulae are different, they have the same meaning. This is because, if I assert that some set of propositions are all true, then it does not matter how I group them together when I do so. It does not matter, for instance, whether I say "A is true, and so are B and C" or "A and B are true, and so is C". So the bracketing is unnecessary to the meaning. We can just say (informally):

```
A & B & C & D & E
```

Secondly, the order in which we write these formulae also does not matter. It does not matter whether I say "A is true and so is B" or "B is true and so is A" -- they both mean the same. Finally, we do not really need to specify the &'s between the formulae, because we know in advance that the top level of the formula is made up with &'s. So, really, we can be much more concise about the import of the formula we are given just by saying that it consists of the *collection* (A, B, C, D, E) (implicitly conjoined). By calling this a collection, we are saying that the order does not matter -- the collection {A, B, C, D, E} is exactly the same as {B, A, C, E, D}, {E, D, B, C, A}, and so on. The formulae that end up in this collection, when we convert a formula to Clausal form, are called *clauses*. So any Predicate Calculus formula is equivalent (in some sense) to a collection of clauses.

Let us now look in more detail at what these clauses are actually like. We said that they are made up of literals joined together by disjunctions. So in general a clause will be something like:

```
((V # W) # X) # (Y # Z)
```

where V, W, X, Y and Z are literals. Now we can do the same trick that we played with the top level of the formula. Once again the bracketing is irrelevant to the meaning, and the order is also unimportant. So we can simply say that the clause is the *collection* of literals {V, W, X, Y, Z} (implicitly disjoined).

Now our original formula has reached clausal form. Moreover the rules used for this have not altered whether there is an interpretation that makes it true or not. The clausal form consists of a collection of clauses, each of which is a collection of literals. A literal is either an atomic formula or a negated atomic formula. This form is quite concise, since we have left out things like implicit conjunctions, disjunctions and universal quantifiers. We must obviously remember the conventions about where these have been missed out when we look to see what something in clausal form means.

Let us look at some formulae (as they would be produced by stage 5) to see what they look like in clausal form.   First of all, the example used before:

    (holiday(X) # work(chris,X)) & (holiday(X) # (angry(chris) # sad(chris)))

This gives rise to two clauses.   The first contains the literals:

    holiday(X), work(chris,X)

and the second contains the literals:

    holiday(X), angry(chris), sad(chris)

As another example, the formula:

    (person(adam) & person(eve)) & ((person(X) # ~mother(X,Y)) # ~person(Y))

gives rise to three clauses.   Two of them contain one literal each.

    person(adam)

and

    person(eve)

The other one has three literals:

    person(X), ~mother(X,Y), ~person(Y)

To bring this section to a close, let us just consider one more example, and the various stages as it is translated into clausal form.   We start with the formula:

    all(X, all(Y,person(Y)->respect(Y,X)) -> king(X))

which says that, if everybody respects somebody then that person is a king (For every X, if every Y that is a person respects X, then X is a king).   When we remove implications (stage 1) we get:

    all(X, ~(all(Y,~person(Y)#respects(Y,X))) # king(X))

Moving negation inwards (stage 2) leads us to:

    all(X, exists(Y,person(Y) & ~respects(Y,X)) # king(X))

Next, Skolemising (stage 3) translates this to:

    all(X, (person(f1(X)) & ~respects(f1(X),X)) # king(X))

where **f1** is a Skolem function. Now comes the stage of removing universal quantifiers (stage 4), which leads to:

    (person(f1(X)) & ~respects(f1(X),X)) # king(X)

We now put this into conjunctive normal form (stage 5), where conjunctions do not appear within disjunctions, thus:

    (person(f1(X)) # king(X)) & (~respects(f1(X),X) # king(X))

This amounts (stage 6) to two clauses. The first has the two literals:

    person(f1(X))   king(X)

and the second has the literals:

    ~respects(f1(X),X)   king(X)

10.3 A Notation for Clauses

We clearly need a way of writing something down in clausal form, and this is what we will now present. First of all, something in clausal form is a collection of clauses. As good a convention as any is to write down the clauses one after the other, remembering that the order is actually irrelevant. Within a clause there is a collection of literals, some negated and some not negated. We will adopt the convention of writing the unnegated literals first and the negated ones second. The two groups will be separated by the sign ':-'. The unnegated literals will be written separated by ';'s (remembering, of course, that the order is not important), and the negated literals will be written without their ~'s and separated by ','s. Finally, a clause will be terminated by a full stop. In this notation, a clause with negated literals K, L, ... and unnegated literals A, B, ... would come out like:

    A; B; ... :- K, L, ...

Although we have introduced our convention for writing out clauses as something arbitrary, it actually has some mnemonic significance. If we write a clause including the disjunctions, with the negated literals separated from the unnegated ones, it will look something like:

    (A # B # ...) # (~K # ~L # ...)

which is equivalent to:

    (A # B # ...) # ~(K & L & ...)

which is equivalent to:

    (K & L & ...) -> (A # B # ...)

If we then write ',' for 'and', ';' for 'or' and ':-' for 'is implied by' (following the Prolog convention), the clause naturally comes out as:

    A; B; ... :- K, L, ...

Given these conventions, the formula about Adam and Eve:

    (person(adam) & person(eve)) &
    ((person(X) # ~mother(X,Y)) # ~person(Y))

comes out as:

    person(adam) :- .
    person(eve) :- .
    person(X) :- mother(X,Y), person(Y).

This is beginning to look rather familiar. This really looks just like a Prolog definition for what it is to be a person. However, other formulae give rise to more puzzling things. The example about holidays ends up as:

    holiday(X); work(chris,X) :- .
    holiday(X); angry(chris); sad(chris) :- .

which does not so obviously correspond to something in Prolog. We will see why this is in a later section.

In Appendix B, we present a Prolog program to print out clauses in this special notation. Written according to our convention, the clauses produced at the end of the last section come out as:

    person(f1(X)); king(X) :- .
    king(X) :- respects(f1(X),X).

10.4 Resolution and Proving Theorems

Now that we have got a way of putting our Predicate Calculus formulae into a nice tidy form, we should consider what we can do with them. An obvious thing to investigate, when we have a collection of propositions, is whether anything interesting *follows from* those propositions. That is, it is interesting to investigate what *consequences* they have. We shall call those propositions that we are taking as true for the sake of argument our *axioms* or *hypotheses*, and those propositions that we find to follow from them our *theorems*. This is consistent with the terminology used to describe one view of Mathematics -- a view which sees the work of a mathematician as involving the derivation of more and more interesting theorems from some exact axiomatisation of what sets and numbers are. In this section, we will look briefly at the activity of deriving interesting consequences from our given propositions, that is, we will look at the activity of *theorem proving*.

There was a great deal of activity in the 1960's as people began to investigate the possibility that digital computers could be programmed to automatically prove theorems. It was this area of scientific endeavour, which is still progressing healthily, that gave rise to the ideas behind Prolog. One of the fundamental breakthroughs made at this time was the discovery of the *resolution principle* by J. Alan Robinson, and its application to mechanical theorem proving. Resolution is a *rule of inference* -- that is, it tells us how one proposition can follow from others. Using the resolution principle, we can prove theorems in a purely mechanical way from our axioms. We only have to decide which propositions to apply it to, and valid conclusions will be produced automatically.

Resolution is designed to work with formulae in clausal form. Given two clauses related in an appropriate way, it will generate a new clause that is a consequence of them. The basic idea is that if the same atomic formula appears both on the left hand side of one clause and the right hand side of another, then the clause obtained by fitting together the two clauses, missing out the duplicated formula, follows from them. For example:

From:

    sad(chris); angry(chris) :- workday(today), raining(today).

and:

    unpleasant(chris) :- angry(chris), tired(chris).

follows:

    sad(chris); unpleasant(chris) :-
        workday(today), raining(today), tired(chris).

In English, if today is a workday and it is raining, then Chris is sad or angry. Also, if Chris is angry and tired, he is unpleasant. Therefore, if today is a workday, it is raining and Chris is tired, then Chris is sad or unpleasant.

In fact, we have over-simplified in two ways here. Firstly, things are actually more complicated when the clauses contain variables. Now the two atomic formulae do not have to be identical -- they only have to "match". Also, the clause that follows from the first two is obtained from the two fitted together (with the duplicated formula removed) by an extra operation. This operation involves "instantiating" the variables just enough so that the two matching formulae are identical. In Prolog terms, if we had the two clauses as structures and matched together the appropriate substructures, the result of fitting them together afterwards would be the representation of the new clause. Our second simplification is that in general resolution one is allowed to match *several* literals on a right hand side against several on a left hand side. Here, we will only consider examples where one literal is chosen from each clause.

Let us look at one example of resolution involving variables:

```
(1)  person(f1(X)); king(X) :- .
(2)  king(Y) :- respects(f1(Y),Y).

(3)  respects(Z,john) :- person(Z).
```

The first two of these are what we obtained as the clausal form of our formula saying "if every person respects somebody then that person is a king". We have renamed the variables for ease of explanation. The third expresses the proposition that every person likes John. Resolving (2) with (3) (matching the two **respects** literals), gives us:

```
(4)  king(john) :- person(f1(john)).
```

(Y in (2) matched with 'john' in (3) and Z in (3) matched with 'f1(Y)' in (2)). We can now resolve (1) with (4), to give:

```
(5)  king(john); king(john) :- .
```

This is equivalent to the fact that John is a king.

In the formal definition of resolution, the process of "matching" that we have referred to informally is called *unification*. Intuitively, a set of atomic formulae are *unifiable* if, as Prolog structures, they can be matched together. Actually, we will see in a later section that the matching in most Prolog implementations is not exactly the same as unification.

How can we use resolution to try and prove a specific thing? One possibility is that we can keep on applying resolution steps to our hypotheses and look to see if what we want appears. Unfortunately, we cannot guarantee that this will happen, even if the proposition

220

we are interested in really does follow from the hypotheses. In the above example, for instance, there is no way of deriving the simple clause **king(john)** from the clauses given, even though it is clearly a consequence. So must we conclude that resolution is not powerful enough for what we want? Fortunately, the answer is "no", for we can rephrase our aims in such a way that resolution is guaranteed to be able to solve our problem if it is possible.

The important formal property that Resolution has is that of being *refutation complete*. This means that, if a set of clauses are *inconsistent* then Resolution will be able to derive from them the *empty clause:*

        :-   .

Also, since Resolution is *correct*, it will only be able to derive the empty clause in this circumstance. A set of formulae is inconsistent if there is no possible interpretation for the predicates, constant symbols and function symbols that makes them simultaneously express true propositions. The empty clause is the logical expression of *falsity* -- it represents a proposition that cannot possibly be true. So Resolution can be guaranteed to tell us when our formulae are inconsistent by deriving this clear expression of contradiction.

How can these particular properties of resolution help us? Well, it is a fact that

If the formulae $(A_1, A_2, \ldots A_n)$ are consistent,

formula B is a consequence of formulae $(A_1, A_2, \ldots, A_n)$ exactly when the formulae $(A_1, A_2, \ldots A_n, \sim B)$ are inconsistent.

So, if our hypotheses are consistent, we just need to add to them the clauses for the negation of what we want to prove. Resolution will derive the empty clause exactly when the proposition follows from the hypotheses. We call the clauses that we add to the hypotheses the *goal statements*. Note that the goal statements do not look in any way different from the hypotheses -- all of them are just clauses. So, if we are presented with a set of clauses

$$A_1, A_2, \ldots A_n$$

and are told that the task is to show them to be inconsistent, we cannot actually tell whether this is in order to show that:

or $\sim A_1$ *follows from* $A_2, A_3, \ldots A_n$
or $\sim A_2$ *follows from* $A_1, A_3, \ldots A_n$
   $\sim A_3$ *follows from* $A_1, A_2, \ldots A_n$
etc.

It is a matter of emphasis which statements we actually consider to be the goal statements.

because in a Resolution system all these tasks are equivalent.

In our example about John being king, it is easy to see how we can obtain the empty clause if we add the goal statement:

(6) :- king(john).

(this is the clause for ˜king(john)). We saw before how the clause

(5) king(john); king(john) :- .

was derived from the hypotheses. Resolving (5) with (6) (matching either of the atomic formulae in (5)), we obtain:

(7) king(john) :- .

Finally, resolving (6) with (7) gives us:

:- .

So resolution has shown that as a consequence John is a king.

The completeness of Resolution is a nice mathematical property. It means that if some fact follows from our hypotheses, we should be able to prove its truth (by showing the inconsistency of its negation and the hypotheses) using Resolution. However, when we say that Resolution will be able to derive the empty clause, we mean that there is a sequence of Resolution steps, each involving axioms or clauses derived in previous steps, which ends in the production of a clause with no literals. The only trouble is to find the sequence of steps. For, although Resolution tells us how to derive a consequence from two clauses, it does not tell us either how to decide which clauses to look at next or which literals to "match". Usually, if we have a large number of hypotheses, there will be many possibilities for each. Moreover, each time we derive a new clause, it too becomes a candidate to take part in further resolutions. Most of the possibilities will be irrelevant for the task at hand, and if we are not careful we may spend so much time on irrelevances that we will never find the solution path.

Many refinements of the original resolution principle have been proposed, to address these issues. The next section considers some of these.

222

10.5   Horn Clauses

We will look now at refinements designed for resolution when all the clauses are of a certain kind -- when they are *Horn clauses.* A Horn clause is a clause with at most one unnegated literal. It turns out that, if we are using a clausal theorem prover to determine the values of computable functions, it is only strictly necessary to use Horn clauses. Because resolution with Horn clauses is also relatively simple, they are an obvious choice as the basis of a theorem prover which provides a practical programming system. Let us consider briefly what Resolution theorem proving looks like if we restrict ourselves to Horn Clauses.

Firstly, there are obviously two kinds of Horn Clauses -- those with one unnegated literal and those with none. Let us call these two types *headed* and *headless* Horn Clauses. The two types are exemplified by the following examples (remember that we write the unnegated literals on the left hand side of the ':-'):

    bachelor(X) :- male(X), unmarried(X).

       :- bachelor(X).

In fact, when we consider sets of Horn Clauses (including goal statements), we need only consider those sets where all but one of the clauses are headed. That is, any soluble problem (theorem-proving task) that can be expressed in Horn Clauses can be expressed in such a way that:

☐   There is one headless clause
☐   All the rest of the clauses are headed

Since it is arbitrary how we decide which clauses are actually the goals, we can decide to view the headless clause as the goal and the other clauses as the hypotheses. This has a certain naturalness.

Why do we only have to consider collections of Horn Clauses that conform to this pattern? First, it is easy to see that at least one headless clause must be present for a problem to be soluble. This is because the result of resolving two headed Horn Clauses is itself a headed Horn Clause. So, if all the clauses are headed, we will only be able to derive other headed clauses. Since the empty clause is not headed, we will not be able to derive it. The second claim -- that only one headless clause is needed -- is slightly more difficult to justify. However, it turns out that, if there are several headless clauses among our axioms, any Resolution proof of a new clause can be converted into a proof using at most one of them. Therefore, if the empty clause follows from the axioms the it follows from the headed ones together with at most one of the headless ones.

10.6   Prolog

Let us now summarise how Prolog fits into this scheme of things.   As we saw before, some of our formulae turned into clauses that looked remarkably like Prolog clauses, whereas others looked somewhat peculiar.   Those that turned into Prolog-like clauses were, in fact, those whose translation was into Horn clauses.   When we write a Horn clause according to our conventions, at most one atomic formula appears on the left of the ':-'.   In general, clauses may have several such formulae (these correspond to the literals which are unnegated atomic formulae).   In Prolog, we can express directly only the Horn clauses.   The clauses of a Prolog program correspond to headed Horn clauses in a certain kind of theorem prover. What in Prolog corresponds to the goal statement?   Quite simply, the Prolog question:

```
?- A1, A2, ... An.
```

corresponds exactly to the headless Horn Clause:

```
:- A1, A2, ... An.
```

We saw in the last section that, for any problem we want to solve with Horn Clauses, it suffices to have exactly one headless clause.   This corresponds to the situation in Prolog, where all the clauses of the "program" are headed and only one (headless) goal is considered at any one time.

A Prolog system is based on a resolution theorem prover for Horn clauses.   The particular strategy that it uses is a form of *linear input resolution*.   When this strategy is used, the choice of what to resolve with what at any time is restricted as follows.   We start with the goal statement and resolve it with one of the hypotheses to give a new clause.   Then we resolve that with one of the hypotheses to give another new clause.   Then we resolve that with one of the hypotheses, and so on.   At each stage, we resolve the clause last obtained with one of the original hypotheses.   At no point do we either use a clause that has been derived previously or resolve together two of the hypotheses.   In Prolog terms, we can see the latest derived clause as the conjunction of goals yet to be satisfied.   This starts off as the question, and hopefully ends up as the empty clause.   At each stage, we find a clause whose head matches one of the goals, instantiate variables as necessary, remove the goal that matched and then add the body of the instantiated clause to the goals to be satisfied. Thus, for instance, we can go from:

```
:- mother(john,X), mother(X,Y).
```

and

```
mother(U,V) :- parent(U,V), female(V).
```

to:

```
:- parent(john,X), female(X), mother(X,Y).
```

In fact, Prolog's proof strategy is even more restricted than general linear input resolution. In this example, we decided to match the first of the literals in the goal clause, but we could equally well have matched the second. In Prolog, the literal to be matched is always selected in the same way -- it is always the first one in the goal clause. This makes Prolog's strategy a kind of *SL resolution*. In addition, the new goals derived from the use of a clause are placed at the *front* of the goal clause -- this just means that Prolog finishes satisfying a subgoal before it goes on to try anything else.

So much for what happens when Prolog has decided what clause to match against the first goal. But how does it organise the investigation of alternative clauses to satisfy the same goal? Basically, Prolog adopts a *depth-first* strategy, rather than a *breadth-first* one. This means that it only considers one alternative at a time, following up the implications under the assumption that the choice is correct. For each goal, it chooses the clauses in a fixed order, and it only comes to consider the later ones if all the earlier ones have failed to lead to solutions. The alternative strategy would be one where the system kept track of alternative solution paths simultaneously. It would then move around from one alternative to another, following it up for a short time and then going on to something else. This latter, breadth-first, strategy has the advantage that, if a solution exists, it will be found. The Prolog depth-first strategy can get into "loops" and hence never follow up some of the alternatives. On the other hand, it is much simpler and less space-consuming to implement on a conventional computer.

Finally, a note about how Prolog matching sometimes differs from the unification used in Resolution. Most Prolog systems will allow you to satisfy goals like:

```
equal(X,X).

?- equal(foo(Y),Y).
```

that is, they will allow you to match a term against a subterm of itself. In this example, foo(Y) is matched against Y, which appears within it. As a result, Y will stand for foo(Y), which is foo(foo(Y)) (because of what Y stands for), which is foo(foo(foo(Y))), and so on. So Y ends up standing for some kind of infinite structure. Note that, whereas they may allow you to construct something like this, most Prolog systems will not be able to write it out at the end. According to the formal definition of Unification, this kind of "infinite term" should never come to exist. So Prolog does not act correctly as a Resolution theorem prover in this respect. In order to make it do so, we would have to add a check that a variable cannot be instantiated to something containing itself. Such a check, an *occur check*, would be straightforward to implement, but would slow down the execution of Prolog programs considerably. Since it would only affect very few programs, most implementors have simply left it out.

10.7 Prolog and Logic Programming

In the last few sections, we have seen how Prolog is based on the idea of a theorem prover. As a result of this, we can see that our programs are rather like our hypotheses about the world, and our questions are rather like theorems that we would like to have proved. So programming in Prolog is not so much like telling the computer what to do when, but rather like telling it what is true and asking it to try and draw conclusions. The idea that programming should be like this is an appealing one, and has led many people to investigate the notion of *logic programming*, that is, *programming in logic* as a practical possibility. This is supposed to contrast with using a conventional programming language like FORTRAN or LISP, where one specifies tasks much more clearly in terms of what the computer should do and when it should do it. The advantages of logic programming should be that computer programs are easier to read. For they will not be cluttered up with details about *how* things are to be done -- they will be more like specifications of *what* a solution will look like. Moreover, if a program is rather like a specification of what it is supposed to achieve, it should be relatively easy, just by looking at it (or, perhaps, by some automatic means) to check that it really does do what is required. In summary, the advantages of a logic programming language would result from programs having a *declarative* semantics as well as a *procedural* one. We would know *what* a program computes, rather than *how* it computes it. We will not be able to look at logic programming in general here. The interested reader is referred to R. Kowalski's book *Logic for Problem Solving* published by North Holland in 1979.

Let us briefly look at Prolog as a candidate logic programming language, and see how well it shapes up. First, it is clear that some Prolog programs do represent logical truths about the world. If we write:

```
mother(X,Y) :- parent(X,Y), female(Y).
```

we can see this as saying what it is to be a mother (it is to be a female parent). So this clause expresses a proposition that we are hypothesising to be true, as well as saying how to *show* that somebody is a mother. Similarly, the clauses:

```
append([],X,X).
append([A|B],C,[A|D]) :- append(B,C,D).
```

say what it is for one list to be appended at the front of another. If the empty list is put on the front of some list X, then the result is just X. On the other hand, if a non-empty list is appended on the front of a list, then the head of the result is the same as the head of the list being put on the front. Also, the tail of the result is the same list as would be obtained by appending the tail of the first list onto the front of the second. These clauses can definitely be seen as expressing what is true about the **append** relation, as well as (perhaps) how one should actually set about appending two lists together.

So much for some Prolog programs, but what possible logical meaning can we give to clauses like these?

```
member1(X,List) :- var(List), !, fail.
member1(X,[X|_]).
member1(X,[_|List]) :- member1(X,List).

print(0) :- !.
print(N) :- write(N), N1 is N-1, print(N1).

noun(N) :-
   name(N,Name1), append(Name2,[115],Name1),
   name(RootN,Name2), noun(RootN).

implies(Assum,Concl) :-
   asserta(Assum),
   call(Concl),
   retract(Concl).
```

The problem comes with all those "built-in" predicates that we use in our Prolog programs. Something like **var(List)** does not say anything about lists or membership, but refers to a state of affairs (some variable being uninstantiated) that may hold at some time during the proof. The "cut" similarly says something about the proof of a proposition (which choices may be ignored), rather than about the proposition itself. These two "predicates" can be regarded as ways of expressing *control information* about how the proof is to be carried out. Similarly, something like **write(N)** does not have any interesting logical properties, but presupposes that the proof will have reached a certain state (with **N** instantiated) and initiates a communication with the programmer at his terminal. **name(N,Name1)** is saying something about the internal structure of what, in Predicate Calculus, would be an indivisible symbol. In Prolog, we can convert symbols to character strings, convert structures to lists and convert structures to clauses. These operations violate the simple self-contained nature of Predicate Calculus propositions. In the last example, the use of **asserta,** means that the rule is talking about adding something to the set of axioms. In logic, each fact or rule states an independent truth, independent of what other facts and rules there may be. Here we have a rule that violates that principle. Also, if we use this rule, we will be in a position of having a different set of axioms at different times of the proof! Finally, the fact that the rule envisages **Concl** being used as a *goal* means that a logical variable is being allowed to stand for a proposition appearing in an axiom. This is not something that could be expressed in Predicate Calculus at all.

Given these examples, we can see that some Prolog programs can *only* be understood in terms of what happens when and how they tell the system what to do. As an extreme case, the program for **gensym** given in Chapter 7 can hardly be given any declarative interpretation at all.

So does it make sense to regard Prolog as a logic programming language at all? Can we really expect any of the advantages of logic programming to apply to our Prolog programs? The answer to both these questions is "yes", and the reason is that, by adopting an appropriate programming style, we can still get some advantages out of the relation of Prolog to logic. The key is to decompose our programs into parts, confining the use of the non-logical operations to within a small set of clauses. As an example, we saw in Chapter 4 how some uses of the "cut" could be replaced with uses of **not**. As a result of such replacements, a program containing a number of "cuts" can be reduced to one with the "cut" only used once (in the definition of **not**). Use of the predicate **not,** even though it does not capture exactly the logical '~', enables one to recapture part of the underlying logical meaning of a program. Similarly, confining the use of the predicates **asserta** and **retract** to within the definitions of a small number of predicates (such as **gensym** and **findall)** results in a program that is clearer overall than one where these predicates are used freely in all sorts of contexts.

The ultimate goal of a logic programming language has not, then, been achieved with Prolog. Nevertheless, Prolog provides a practical programming system that has some of the advantages of clarity and declarativeness that a logic programming language would offer. Meanwhile the work goes on to develop improved versions of Prolog that are truer to the logic than what we currently have available. Among the highest priorities of workers in this area is to develop a practical system that does not need the "cut" and has a version of **not** that exactly corresponds to the logical notion of negation.

Chapter 11. Projects in Prolog

This chapter contains a list of projects that you may wish to undertake in order to exercise your programming ability. Some of the projects are easy, but some may be appropriate as "term projects" as a part of a course in Prolog. The easier projects should be used to supplement the exercises in the previous chapters. The projects are in no particular order, although those in Section 11.2 are more open ended and ambitious, and will require some knowledge or background reading in various areas of artificial intelligence and computer science. A few of the projects assume knowledge about some particular field of study, so if you are not a mathematical physicist, do not feel discouraged if you cannot write a program to differentiate three dimensional vector fields.

A collection of Prolog programs is published in the report "How to solve it with Prolog", edited by H Coelho, J C Cotta, and L M Pereira. The report is distributed by the Laboratorio Nacional de Engenharia Civil, in Lisbon, Portugal. It contains over a hundred small examples, problems, and exercises in area such as deductive reasoning over databases, natural language, symbolic equation solving, and so forth. The report is not intended to be tutorial in nature, and so the Prolog programs in it are presented with limited explanatory accompaniment.

11.1 Easier Projects

1. Define a predicate to "flatten" a list by constructing a list containing no lists as elements, but containing all of the atoms of the original list. For example, the following goal would succeed:

   ```
   flatten([a,[b,c],[[d],[],e]], [a,b,c,d,e]).
   ```

2. Write a program to calculate the interval in days between two dates expressed in the form Day—Month, assuming they refer to the same year which is not a leap year.

Notice that '−' is simply an infix operator. For example, the following goal would succeed:

```
interval( 3-march, 7-april, 35 ).
```

3. In Chapter 7 sufficient information is given to construct programs to differentiate and simplify arithmetic expressions. Extend these programs so they will handle expressions containing trigonometric functions, and if you desire, differential geometry operators such as div, grad, and curl.

4. Write a program to produce the negation of a propositional expression. Propositional expressions are built up from atoms, the unary functor **not**, and binary functors **and, or,** and **implies.** Provide suitable operator declarations for the functors. The negated expression should be in simplest form, where **not** is only applied to atoms. For example, the negation of

```
p implies (q and not r)
```

should be

```
p and (not q or r).
```

5. A concordance is a listing of words that occur in a text, listed in alphabetical order together with the number of times each word appears in the text. Write a program to produce a concordance from a list of words represented as Prolog strings. Recall that strings are lists of ASCII codes.

6. Write a program that understands simple English sentences having the following forms:

```
_____ is a _____.
A _____ is a _____.
Is _____ a _____?
```

The program should give an appropriate response (yes, no, ok, unknown), on the basis of the sentences previously given. For example,

John is a man.
ok
A man is a person.
ok
Is John a person?
yes
Is Mary a person?
unknown

Each sentence should be translated into a Prolog clause, which is then asserted or executed as appropriate. Thus, the translations of the preceding examples are:

```
man( john ).
person( X ) :- man( X ).
?- person( john ).
?- person( mary ).
```

Use grammar rules if you find them appropriate. The top clause to control the dialogue might be:

```
talk :-
    repeat,
    read( Sentence ),
    parse( Sentence, Clause ),
    respond_to( Clause ),
    Clause = stop.
```

7. The alpha–beta (α–β) algorithm is a method for searching game trees that is mentioned in many books on artificial intelligence programming. Implement the α–β algorithm in Prolog.

8. The N-queens problem is also widely discussed in programming texts. Implement a program to find all the ways of placing 4 queens on a 4×4 chessboard so that no queen attacks another. One way is to write a permutation generator, which then checks each permutation to ensure that it places the queens correctly.

9. Write a program that rewrites propositional expressions (Problem 4), replacing all occurrences of **and, or, implies,** and **not** by the single operator **nand.** The functor **nand** is defined by the following equivalence:

α nand β ≡ not(α and β)

nand has the following truth table:

```
        0    1
    +---------
0 |  1    1
    |
1 |  1    0
```

10. One way of representing the positive whole numbers is as Prolog terms involving the integer 0 and the functor **s** with one argument. Thus, we represent 0 by itself, 1 by **s(0),** 2 by **s(s(0))** and so on (each number is represented by the functor **s** applied

to the representation of the number one less). Write definitions of the standard arithmetic operations addition, multiplication and subtraction, given this representation of numbers. For instance, you should define a predicate **plus** that exhibits the following behaviour:

```
?- plus(s(s(0)),s(s(s(0))),X).

X = s(s(s(s(s(0)))))
```

(2+3=5). For subtraction, you will have to introduce a convention for when the result of the operation is not a positive whole number. Also define the predicate "less than". What arguments need to be instantiated for your definitions to work? What happens in the other cases? How does this compare with the standard Prolog arithmetic operations? Try defining some more complicated arithmetic operations, like integer division and square root.

11.2 Advanced Projects

Although the projects in this section may seem open ended, all of them have been implemented in Prolog by various programmers around the world. Some of them are straightforward enhancements to programs discussed earlier, and some of them are completely new, and depend on knowledge of the artificial intelligence literature or computer science.

1. Given a map that describes roads that connect towns, write a progam that plans a route between two towns, giving a timetable of expected travel. The map data could include mileage, road conditions, gradients, availability of fuel along various roads.

2. Only integer arithmetic operations are built into current Prolog systems. Write a package of programs to support arithmetic over rational numbers, represented either as fractions or as mantissa and exponent.

3. Write procedures to invert and multiply matrices.

4. Compiling a high-level computer language into a low-level language can be viewed as the successive transformation of syntax trees. Write such a compiler, first compiling arithmetic expressions. Then add control syntax (like **if**...**then**...**else**). The syntax of the assembly output is not crucial for this purpose. For example, the arithmetic expression x+1 could be "simplified" into the assembly language statement **inc x,** where **inc** is declared as a unary operator. The problem of register allocation can be postponed by assuming that the code compiles into a form suitable for execution by

a stack machine (0-address machine).

5. Devise a representation for complex board games such as Chess or Go, and understand how the pattern matching capabilities of Prolog might be used to implement strategies for these games.

6. Devise a formalism for expressing sets of axioms, say from Group Theory, Euclidean Geometry, Denotational Semantics, and investigate the problem of writing a theorem prover for these domains.

7. An interpreter for Prolog clauses can be written in Prolog. Write an interpreter that implements different semantics for Prolog execution, such as more flexible execution order (instead of left-to-right), perhaps using an "agenda" or scheduling mechanism.

8. Consult the artificial intelligence literature on the area of generating plans to solve problems, and implement a plan generator.

9. Express in Prolog the problem of interpreting a line drawing in terms of some underlying scene. Features of the picture can be labelled with variables representing corresponding features of the scene. The picture then corresponds to a set of constraints these variables must satisfy.

10. Write a program, using Grammar Rules, to parse sentences of the form:

> Fred saw John.
> Mary was seen by John.
> Fred told Mary to see John.
> John was believed to have been seen by Fred
> Was John believed to have told Mary to see Fred?

11. A production system, used in artificial intelligence research, is a sequence of rules of the form "if *situation* then *action*". It has become fashionable within the artificial intelligence field to write "expert knowledge" in terms of production rules. For example, the following sentences are typical of those used in actual production systems that have been implemented:

> Pharmacology: If agent X is a quaternary ammonium salt and an anti-arhythmic, and agent Y is a salicylate, then X and Y will interact to produce increased absorption by ion pair formation.

> Playing chess: If the black king can move adjacent to the black knight and the distance from the white king to the knight is greater than one square, then the knight is safe.

> Medicine: If the site of the culture is blood, and the gram stain of the organism is negative, and the morphology of the organism is a rod, and the patient is a compromised host, then there is a 60% chance that the

organism is Pseudomonas aeruginosa.

Write a Prolog program to interpret a set of production rules. Consider some domain such as identifying plants or animals from identifying characteristics. For example, a rule from botany would read:

> *If a plant has a square stem, paired leaves, two-lipped hooded flowers, and fruit consisting of four tiny nuts enclosed in the calyx, then it belongs to the family Labiatae.*

So, if the program asked the question "Does the flower have a square stem?", then we would rule out the possibility that it belongs to the family *Labiatea* by answering "no".

12. Write a program to translate some corpus of English sentences into Predicate Calculus.

13. Write a program to prove theorems in Predicate Calculus.

14. Write a program to act as a simulated psychiatrist that makes a reply based on key words in the input, rather like the program in Chapter 3 that changed keywords in a sentence into other words. A typical dialogue might be (computer's responses in italics):

What is your problem?
This is too much work.
What else do you regard as too much work?
Writing letters.
I see. Please continue.
Also washing my mother's car.
Tell me more about your family.
Why should I?
Why should you what?

Here the appropriate key words were "this is", "mother", and "why". The lack of appropriate keyword evoked the response "I see. Please continue".

15. Write a program that parses sentences about happenings in an office building, such as "Smith will be in his office at 3 pm for a meeting". You might wish to use Grammar Rules to capture the "business English" language. The program should then print out a "summary" of the sentence telling who, what, where, and when; such as follows:

```
who: smith
where: office
```

234

```
when: 3 pm
what: meeting
```

The summary could be represented as assertions in the database, so that questions could be asked:

Where is Smith at 3 pm?

where: office
what: meeting

16. Write a natural language interface to the filing system of your computer to answer questions such as:

> *How many files does David own?*
> *Does Chris share PROG.MAC with David?*
> *When did Bill change the file VIDEO.C?*

The program must be able to interrogate various parts of the filing system such as ownership and dates.

We include here suggested answers to some of the exercises that appear in the text. With most programming exercises, there is rarely a single correct answer, and you may well have a good answer that looks different from what we suggest. In any case, you should always try out your program on your local Prolog system, to see whether it really works. Even if you have written a correct program that is different, it may still be instructive to spend some time looking at an alternative approach to the same problem.

Exercise 1.2

Here are possible definitions of the family relationships.

```
is_mother(Mum) :- mother(Mum,Child).

is_father(Dad) :- father(Dad,Child).

is_son(Son) :- parent(Par,Son), male(Son).

is_sister(Sis,Pers) :-
    parent(Par,Sis),
    parent(Par,Pers),
    female(Sis),
    diff(Sis,Pers).

granpa_of(Gpa,X) :- parent(Par,X), father(Gpa,Par).

sibling(S1,S2) :- parent(Par,S1), parent(Par,S2), diff(S1,S2).
```

Note that we must use the predicate **diff** in the definition of **is_sister** and **sibling**. This prevents the system thinking that somebody can be a sister or sibling of themselves. You will not be able to define **diff** at this stage.

Exercise 5.2

The following program reads in characters (from the current input file) indefinitely, printing them out again with 'a's changed to 'b's.

```
go :- repeat, get0(C), deal_with(C), fail.

deal_with(97) :- !, put(98).
```

`ut(X).`

`eal_with` rule is essential (why?). 97 and 98 are the ASCII codes for
`y`.

Why ... owing definition of **get** not work if we have a **get** goal with an instantiated
argument?

```
get(X) :- new_get(X), X>32.

new_get(X) :- repeat, get0(X).
```

Let's assume that we give Prolog the goal **get(97)** (is the next printing character an 'a'?)
when the very next character is in fact a 'b'. To satisfy **get(97)**, we try to satisfy **new_get(97)**.
The **repeat** goal succeeds, but then the goal **get0(97)** fails (the next character is not an
'a'). Now backtracking occurs. The **get0** goal cannot be resatisfied, but the **repeat** one
can be. So **repeat** succeeds again, and an attempt is made to satisfy **get0(97)** again.
This time, of course, the next character will be the one after the 'b'. If this is not an 'a',
the goal will fail and **repeat** will succeed again. Then the next character will be looked at.
And so on. What is actually happening is that the program is reading more and more
characters until it finally finds one that matches with the argument. This is not what **get**
was supposed to do. A good definition of **get**, which gets over this problem and also contains
a "cut" to remove the **repeat** choice, follows:

```
get(X) :- repeat, get0(Y), 32<Y, !, X=Y.
```

Exercise 7.10

Here is a program that generates "Pythagorean" triples:

```
pythag(X,Y,Z) :-
    intriple(X,Y,Z),
    Sumsq is X*X + Y*Y,
    Sumsq is Z*Z.

intriple(X,Y,Z) :-
    is_integer(Sum),
    minus(Sum,X,Sum1),
    minus(Sum1,Y,Z).

minus(Sum,Sum,0).
minus(Sum,D1,D2) :-
    Sum>0,
    Sum1 is Sum-1,
    minus(Sum1,D1,D3),
    D2 is D3+1.
```

```
is_integer(0).
is_integer(N) :-
    is_integer(N1),
    N is N1+1.
```

The program uses the predicate **intriple** to generate possible triples of integers (X, Y, Z). It then checks to see whether this triple really is a Pythagorean triple. The definition of intriple has to guarantee that *all* triples of integers will eventually be generated. It first of all generates an integer that is the sum of X, Y and Z. Then it uses a non-deterministic subtraction predicate, **minus**, to generate values of X, Y and Z from that.

Exercise 9.1

Here is the program for translating a simple grammar rule into Prolog. It is assumed here that the rule contains no phrase types with extra arguments, no goals inside curly brackets and no disjunctions or cuts.

```
?- op(255,xfx,-->).

translate((P1-->P2),(G1:-G2)) :-
    left_hand_side(P1,S0,S,G1),
    right_hand_side(P2,S0,S,G2).

left_hand_side(P0,S0,S,G) :-
    nonvar(P0),
    tag(P0,S0,S,G).

right_hand_side((P1,P2),S0,S,G) :- !,
    right_hand_side(P1,S0,S1,G1),
    right_hand_side(P2,S1,S,G2),
    and(G1,G2,G).
right_hand_side(P,S0,S,true) :-
    islist(P), !,
    append(P,S,S0).
right_hand_side(P,S0,S,G) :-
    tag(P,S0,S,G).

tag(P,S0,S,G) :-
    atom(P),
    G=..[P,S0,S].

and(true,G,G) :- !.
and(G,true,G) :- !.
and(G1,G2,(G1,G2)).

islist([]) :- !.
islist([_|_]).

append([A|B],C,[A|D]) :- append(B,C,D).
append([],X,X).
```

In this program, variables beginning with "P" stand for phrase descriptions (atoms, or lists of words) in grammar rules. Variables beginning with "G" stand for Prolog goals. Variables beginning with "S" stand for arguments of the Prolog goals (which represent sequences of words). In case you are interested, there follows a program that will handle the more general cases of grammar rule translation. One way in which a Prolog system can handle grammar rules is to have a modified version of **consult**, in which a clause of the form **A ⟶ B** is **translate** 'd before it is added to the database.

```
?- op( 251,fx,{ ).
?- op( 250,xf,} ).
?- op( 255,xfx,--> ).

translate((P0-->Q0),(P:-Q)) :-
    left_hand_side(P0,S0,S,P),
    right_hand_side(Q0,S0,S,Q1),
    flatten(Q1,Q).

left_hand_side((NT,Ts),S0,S,P) :- !,
    nonvar(NT),
    islist(Ts),
    tag(NT,S0,S1,P),
    append(Ts,S0,S1).
left_hand_side(NT,S0,S,P) :-
    nonvar(NT),
    tag(NT,S0,S,P).

right_hand_side((X1,X2),S0,S,P) :- !,
    right_hand_side(X1,S0,S1,P1),
    right_hand_side(X2,S1,S,P2),
    and(P1,P2,P).
right_hand_side((X1;X2),S0,S,(P1;P2)) :- !,
    or(X1,S0,S,P1),
    or(X2,S0,S,P2).
right_hand_side({P},S,S,P) :- !.
right_hand_side(!,S,S,!) :- !.
right_hand_side(Ts,S0,S,true) :-
    islist(Ts), !,
    append(Ts,S,S0).
right_hand_side(X,S0,S,P) :-
    tag(X,S0,S,P).

or(X,S0,S,P) :-
    right_hand_side(X,S0a,S,Pa),
  ( var(S0a), S0a == S, !, S0=S0a, P=Pa;
    P=(S0=S0a,Pa) ).

tag(X,S0,S,P) :-
    X=..[F|A],
    append(A,[S0,S],AX),
    P=..[F|AX].

and( true,P,P) :- !.
and(P,true,P) :- !.
and(P,Q,(P,Q)).

flatten(A,A) :- var(A), !.
flatten((A,B),C) :- !,
    flatten1(A,C,R),
    flatten(B,R).
flatten(A,A).

flatten1(A,(A,R),R) :- var(A), !.
flatten1((A,B),C,R) :- !,
```

```
        flatten1(A,C,R1),
        flatten1(B,R1,R).
flatten1(A,(A,R),R).

islist([]) :- !.
islist([_|_]).

append([A|B],C,[A|D]) :- append(B,C,D).
append([],X,X).
```

Exercise 9.2

The definition of the general version of **phrase is as follows**:

```
phrase(Ptype,Words) :-
    Ptype =.. [Pred|Args],
    append(Args,[Words,[]],Newargs),
    Goal =.. [Pred|Newargs],
    call(Goal).
```

where **append** is defined as in Section 3.6.

Appendix B

Clausal Form – Prolog Programs

As promised in Chapter 10, we will illustrate the process of converting a formula to clausal form by showing fragments of a Prolog program for doing this. The top level of the program is as follows:

```
translate(X) :-
    implout(X,X1),            /* Stage 1 */
    negin(X1,X2),             /* Stage 2 */
    skolem(X2,X3,[]),         /* Stage 3 */
    univout(X3,X4),           /* Stage 4 */
    conjn(X4,X5),             /* Stage 5 */
    clausify(X5,Clauses,[]),  /* Stage 6 */
    pclauses(Clauses).        /* Print out clauses */
```

This defines a predicate **translate,** such that if we give Prolog the goal **translate(X),** with X standing for a Predicate Calculus formula, the program will print out the formula's representation as clauses. In the program, we will represent Predicate Calculus formulae as Prolog structures, as we have indicated before. However, we will deviate from the previous descriptions in representing Predicate Calculus variables by Prolog atoms, as this makes certain manipulations easier. We can distinguish Predicate Calculus variables from constants by having some convention for their names. For instance, we could say that variable names always begin with one of the letters 'x', 'y', and 'z'. In fact, in the program we will not need to know about this convention because variables are always introduced by quantifiers and hence are easy to detect. Only in reading the program's output will it be important for the programmer to remember which names were Predicate Calculus variables and which were constants.

First, we will need the following operator declarations for the connectives:

```
?- op( 30,fx,~).
?- op( 100,xfy,#).
?- op( 100,xfy,&).
?- op( 150,xfy,->).
?- op( 150,xfy,<->).
```

It is important to note how we have defined these. In particular, ~ has a lower precedence than # and &. To start with, we must make an important assumption. The assumption is that the variables have been renamed as necessary, so that the same variable is never introduced by more than one quantifier in the formula at hand. This is to prevent accidental name clashes in what follows.

The actual programming technique we use to implement the conversion to clausal form is *tree transformation*, as discussed in Sections 7.11 and 7.12. By representing the logical connectives as functors, Predicate Calculus formulae become structures that can be depicted as trees. Each of the six main stages of conversion into clausal form is a tree transformation that maps an input tree onto an output tree.

Stage 1 - Removing Implications

We define a predicate **implout** such that **implout(X,Y)** means that Y is the formula derived from X by removing implications.

```
implout((P <-> Q),((P1 & Q1) # (~P1 & ~Q1))) :- !,
    implout(P,P1), implout(Q,Q1).
implout((P -> Q),(~P1 # Q1)) :- !,
    implout(P,P1), implout(Q,Q1).
implout(all(X,P),all(X,P1)) :- !,
    implout(P,P1).
implout(exists(X,P),exists(X,P1)) :- !,
    implout(P,P1).
implout((P & Q),(P1 & Q1)) :- !,
    implout(P,P1), implout(Q,Q1).
implout((P # Q),(P1 # Q1)) :- !,
    implout(P,P1), implout(Q,Q1).
implout((~P),(~P1)) :- !,
    implout(P,P1).
implout(P,P).
```

Stage 2 - Moving Negation Inwards

We need to define two predicates here -- **negin** and **neg**. **negin(X,Y)** means that Y is the formula derived by applying the "negation inwards" transformation to the whole of X. This is the main thing we will ask questions about. **neg(X,Y)** means that Y is the formula derived by applying the transformation to the formula ~X. With both of these, we assume that stage 1 has been carried out, and that we hence do not need to deal with -> and <->.

```
negin((~P),P1) :- !, neg(P,P1).
negin(all(X,P),all(X,P1)) :- !, negin(P,P1).
negin(exists(X,P),exists(X,P1)) :- !, negin(P,P1).
negin((P & Q),(P1 & Q1)) :- !, negin(P,P1), negin(Q,Q1).
negin((P # Q),(P1 # Q1)) :- !, negin(P,P1), negin(Q,Q1).
negin(P,P).

neg((~P),P1) :- !, negin(P,P1).
neg(all(X,P),exists(X,P1)) :- !, neg(P,P1).
neg(exists(X,P),all(X,P1)) :- !, neg(P,P1).
neg((P & Q),(P1 # Q1)) :- !, neg(P,P1), neg(Q,Q1).
neg((P # Q),(P1 & Q1)) :- !, neg(P,P1), neg(Q,Q1).
ned(P,(~P)).
```

Stage 3 – Skolemising

The predicate **skolem** has three arguments: corresponding to the original formula, the transformed formula and the list of variables that have been introduced so far by universal quantifiers.

```
skolem(all(X,P),all(X,P1),Vars) :- !, skolem(P,P1,[X|Vars]).
skolem(exists(X,P),P2,Vars) :- !,
    gensym(f,F), Sk=..[F|Vars],
    subst(X,Sk,P,P1),
    skolem(P1,P2,Vars).
skolem((P # Q),(P1 # Q1),Vars) :- !,
    skolem(P,P1,Vars), skolem(Q,Q1,Vars).
skolem((P & Q),(P1 & Q1),Vars) :- !,
    skolem(P,P1,Vars), skolem(Q,Q1,Vars).
skolem(P,P,_).
```

This definition makes use of two new predicates. **gensym** must be defined such that the goal **gensym(X,Y)** causes Y to be instantiated to a new atom built up from the atom X and a number. This is used to generate Skolem constants that have not been used before. As an example, we would expect the question

```
?- gensym(f,F).
```

to yield the answer **F = f1** the first time we ask it, **F = f2** the second time, and so on. The predicate **gensym** is defined in Section 7.8. The second new predicate that is mentioned is **subst**. We require **subst(V1,V2,F1,F2)** to be true if the result of substituting V2 for V1 every time it appears in the formula F1 is F2. The definition of this is left as an exercise for the reader, but it is similar to predicates defined in Sections 7.5 and 6.5.

Stage 4 – Moving Universal Quantifiers Outwards

After this point, of course, it will be necessary to be able to tell which Prolog atoms represent Predicate Calculus variables and which represent Predicate Calculus constants. We will no longer have the convenient rule that the variables are precisely those symbols introduced by quantifiers. Here is the program for moving out and removing the universal quantifiers:

```
univout(all(X,P),P1) :- !, univout(P,P1).
univout((P & Q),(P1 & Q1)) :- !,
    univout(P,P1), univout(Q,Q1).
univout((P # Q),(P1 # Q1)) :- !,
    univout(P,P1), univout(Q,Q1).
univout(P,P).
```

These rules define the predicate **univout** so that **univout(X,Y)** means that the version of

X with universal quantifiers moved out is Y.

It should be noted that our definition of **univout** assumes that this operation will only be applied after the first three stages are already complete. Hence it makes no allowance for implications or existential quantifiers in the formula.

Stage 5 – Distributing '&' over '#'

The actual program to put a formula into conjunctive normal form is rather more complicated than the last one. When it comes across something like **(P # Q)**, where P and Q are any formulae, it must first of all put P and Q into conjunctive normal forms, P1 and Q1 say, and only then look to see if the formula as a whole is suitable for translation by one of the equivalences. The process must happen in this order, because it may happen that neither of P and Q has & at the top level, but one of P1 and Q1 does. Here is the program:

```
conjn((P # Q),R) :- !,
    conjn(P,P1), conjn(Q,Q1),
    conjn1((P1 # Q1),R).
conjn((P & Q),(P1 & Q1)) :- !,
    conjn(P,P1), conjn(Q,Q1).
conjn(P,P).

    conjn1(((P & Q) # R),(P1 & Q1)) :- !,
        conjn((P # Q),P1), conjn((Q # R),Q1).
    conjn1((P # (Q & R)),(P1 & Q1)) :- !,
        conjn((P # Q),P1), conjn((P # R),Q1).
    conjn1(P,P).
```

Stage 6 – Putting into Clauses

Here, now, is the last part of our program to put a formula in clausal form. We define first of all the predicate **clausify**, which involves building up an internal representation of a collection of clauses. The collection is represented as a list, where each clause is represented as a structure **cl(A,B).** In such a structure, A is the list of literals that are not negated, and B is the list of literals that are negated (but without their ~'s). **clausify** has three arguments. The first is for the formula, as delivered by stage 5. The second and third are for defining the list of clauses. **clausify** builds a list terminating in a variable, instead of **[],** and returns this variable through the third argument. It is then possible for other rules to add things to the end of the list by instantiating the variable. One feature built into the program checks that the same atomic formula does not appear both negated and unnegated within the same clause. If this happens, the clause is not added to the list, because such a clause is trivially true and contributes nothing. Also, it is checked that the same literal does not appear twice within a clause.

```
clausify((P & Q),C1,C2) :- !,
   clausify(P,C1,C3), clausify(Q,C3,C2).
clausify(P,[cl(A,B)|Cs],Cs) :- inclause(P,A,[],B,[]), !.
clausify(_,C,C).

inclause((P # Q),A,A1,B,B1) :- !,
   inclause(P,A2,A1,B2,B1), inclause(Q,A,A2,B,B2).
inclause((~P),A,A,B1,B) :- !,
   notin(P,A), putin(P,B,B1).
inclause(P,A1,A,B,B) :-
   notin(P,B), putin(P,A,A1).

   notin(X,[X|_]) :- !, fail.
   notin(X,[_|L]) :- !, notin(X,L).
   notin(X,[]).

   putin(X,[],[X]) :- !.
   putin(X,[X|L],L) :- !.
   putin(X,[Y|L],[Y|L1]) :- putin(X,L,L1).
```

Printing out Clauses

In the previous section, we defined a predicate **clausify** which built up a representation for a Predicate Calculus formula in clausal form. We will now define a predicate **pclauses** which causes a formula represented in this way to be displayed according to our notation.

```
pclauses([]) :- !, nl, nl.
pclauses([cl(A,B)|Cs]) :- pclause(A,B), nl, pclauses(Cs).
pclause(L,[]) :- !, pdisj(L), write('.').
pclause([],L) :- !, write(':- '), pconj(L), write('.').
pclause(L1,L2) :- pdisj(L1), write(' :- '), pconj(L2), write('.').

   pdisj([L]) :- !, write(L).
   pdisj([L|Ls]) :- write(L), write('; '), pdisj(Ls).

   pconj([L]) :- !, write(L).
   pconj([L|Ls]) :- write(L), write(', '), pconj(Ls).
```

Appendix C

The ASCII Code

The following chart associates each printing character with the small integer that is used to represent the character in Prolog strings and for input/output predicates. For non-printing characters, only those characters that have an effect on the Prolog system are listed. Most non-printing characters are typed by holding down the CONTROL key and striking an appropriate key. The host operating system may assign special interpretations to some control characters for the purpose of editing input from computer terminals. For example, DEL is sometimes used to erase the last character typed, Control-u might be used to delete lines of input, and so forth. These are not listed here, as they depend on a particular computer installation.

Non-Printing Characters

A Prolog system may require two non-printing characters to be typed by the user. The interrupt character is used to cause a running program to be interrupted temporarily for debugging purposes. The end-of-file character is used to denote the end of the file **user** (Chapter 5). The normal assignments are shown below, although these may be changed to suit individual computer installations.

ASCII code	How Typed	Effect
3	Control c	Prolog temporarily stops the current program, and requests an action to be performed.
26	Control z	Marks the end of the 'user' file

246

Printing Characters

ASCII Code	Character	Description
33	!	exclamation mark: the "cut" symbol
34	"	double quote: delimits strings
35	#	sharp sign
36	$	currency symbol
37	%	percent
38	&	ampersand
39	'	single quote: delimits arbitrary atoms
40	(	round bracket: for grouping and structures
41	)	closing round bracket
42	*	asterisk: denotes multiplication in 'is' goals
43	+	plus: denotes addition in 'is' goals
44	,	comma: denotes conjunction of goals, and separates arguments
45	–	hyphen: denotes subtraction in 'is' goals
46	.	dot: ends clauses, denotes list constructor functor
47	/	stroke: denotes division in 'is' goals
48–57	0–9	digits 0 through 9
58	:	colon
59	;	semicolon: denotes disjunction of goals
60	<	less than: integer "less than" in 'is' goals
61	=	equals: denotes equality predicate
62	>	greater than: integer "greater than" in 'is' goals
63	?	question mark
64	@	'at' sign
65–90	A–Z	upper–case A through Z
91	[	square bracket: denotes list construction
92	\	backslash
93	]	closing square bracket
94	^	caret (or up–arrow)
95	_	underscore: denotes anonymous variable
96	`	accent
97–122	a–z	lower–case a through z
123	{	curly bracket: used in Grammar Rule notation
124	|	vertical bar: used in list notation
125	}	closing curly bracket
126	~	tilde

Appendix D

Different Versions of Prolog

Prolog is by now available in many different versions in many different places. The differences that exist are due partly to the different kinds of computers available at the various computer installations. No two kinds of computer make it equally easy to write all kinds of programs, and this is reflected in the facilities that the various Prolog implementors have got around to providing. Even if two installations have the same kind of computer, they may still run different operating systems on them. The operating system is the program in overall control of the computer, with tasks such as ensuring that the available resources are divided fairly between the different people who want to use the computer. Some operating systems allow the programmer to use a wide range of the facilities supported by the computer, whereas others are more restrictive. This leads again to differences between Prolog systems. Finally, the people who actually construct Prolog systems often have differing ideas about what features are aesthetically pleasing and what facilities are most needed. As a result, no two Prolog systems are completely alike. This situation is unlikely to change very quickly, because new ideas and improvements for Prolog implementation are constantly being thought up.

In this book, we have presented a version of Prolog that does not correspond exactly to any existing system. Rather, it is supposed to represent a "core" Prolog that will have a lot in common with any system you might encounter. If you have mastered the ideas of this book, you should not have too much difficulty adapting to any Prolog system that comes along. The syntax and some of the built-in predicates may be confusingly different, but underneath will be the same basic Prolog that has been described here.

The best way to get to know about your own Prolog system is to read the user's manual that is provided with it. This may well be somewhat terse and summary, but if you have a basic grounding in the language, it should not be too hard to work out how the system differs from what you know. This appendix mentions a few points that are worth looking out for, and also goes into more detail about two particular Prolog systems that are fairly widespread. However, we would like to emphasise the fact that many of the current Prolog systems are slowly changing, and there is really no substitute for looking at an up-to-date manual for your installation.

General Points to Look Out For

Here are some of the things that are most likely to differ between Prolog implementations.

1. Syntax. Everybody has his own idea about what forms of syntax are most natural and pleasing. Fortunately, the syntax of Prolog is quite simple, and so there is not much scope for variation. One matter of dispute is how one should distinguish variables from atoms. Here we have used names beginning with capital letters for variables and names beginning with small letters for atoms. In addition, we have allowed atoms consisting of sequences of symbols like '*', '.' and '='. Some Prolog systems have adopted the reverse convention as regards capital and small letters (variables begin with *small* letters). Others distinguish variable names by starting them with a special character, like '_PERSON' or '*PERSON'. This is convenient for a system that does not distinguish between capital and small letters. Another area where there is scope for variation is in the notation for clauses — how is the head separated from the body, and how are the goals in the body separated? Also, how are questions distinguished? It may just be a matter of some other symbols instead of ':-', ',' and '?-'. Or it may be more complicated. In one early system, the head and the goals of a clause were placed one after another, with a '+' in front of the head and a '−' in front of each of the goals. In summary, you may find clauses that look like any of the following, or are different again:

```
uncle(X,Z) :- parent(X,Y), brother(Y,Z).

Uncle(x,z) <- Parent(x,y) & Brother(y,z).

UNCLE(_X,_Z) :- PARENT(_X,_Y), BROTHER(_Y,_Z).

+UNCLE(*X,*Z) -PARENT(*X,*Y) -BROTHER(*Y,*Z).

((UNCLE X1 X3) (PARENT X1 X2) (BROTHER X2 X3))

uncle(X,Z): parent(X,Y); brother(Y,Z).
```

2. Arbitrary bounds on some numbers. Because of the way different computers organise their storage, it may be difficult for the Prolog implementor to allow certain things to grow to unlimited size. Some things that are liable to vary from computer to computer are the maximum size of Prolog integers, whether floating-point numbers are available, the maximum number of arguments that a functor can have, the maximum number of characters in an atom, the maximum number of clauses a predicate can have, and so on.

3. Environmental features. Because of the differences between different operating systems, some Prolog systems may allow you to interrupt your program while it is running, edit a disc file without losing the current state of your Prolog session, maintain several

simultaneously running Prolog programs, receive input from or send output to special devices. However, none of these can necessarily be provided in all systems, and so you can expect to find some variation here. As well as determining which of these facilities are available, the operating system of your computer will most likely attach special importance to certain characters that you type in. For instance, the character that you type to mark an "end of file" at the end of a consult(user) will vary between installations. Other characters may be interpreted as requests for information about the status of the machine or as requests to change characters already typed. Such features are not part of the Prolog system that you use, but are nevertheless important when you decide to actually use the system.

4. The option of compilation. Most Prolog systems work by storing your clauses in a form that is close to the original textual form. When a clause is used, such a system has to inspect the clause and decide what to do according to what form it has. Such a system is called an *interpreter*. Another possibility is for the system to translate from your clauses into instructions that can be directly executed by the machine. Such a system is called a *compiler*. Using a compiler, you have the advantage that your program is run directly, rather than having to go through an interpretation process. Hence you might expect your program to run quicker. On the other hand, since the textual form is normally no longer available with a compiler, you might expect not to have the same information available when you are debugging (for instance, you may not be able to ask for a listing of your clauses). In some systems, you may have the choice between compiling and interpreting your clauses. In this case, you must carefully weigh up what advantages each has to offer.

5. Particular built-in predicates. Whereas the basic flow of control may work just the same in most Prolog systems, the special built-in predicates will almost always differ. Sometimes it will simply be that extra predicates are provided for facilities that are easy to provide on a particular computer (as in point 3). Sometimes the same basic facilities may be provided by predicates that have slightly different effects. For instance, it would be sufficient for a Prolog system to provide either **functor** and **arg** or =... This is because the first two can be defined in terms of the last one and vice versa. You may have to work out how to use the facilities provided to mimic those that you are used to working with. Some Prolog systems may provide *libraries* of useful programs, providing optional facilities in addition to the built-in predicates. For instance, grammar rules may be provided as part of the basic system, or it may be possible to load in a Prolog program from a library that will provide these facilities.

6. Debugging facilities. It is still a matter for research to determine what debugging facilities are most suitable for Prolog. Meanwhile different systems present different conceptions of what features are needed. It is hoped that our general introduction of Chapter 8 will equip the reader to cope with whatever he finds.

Appendix E

The DECsystem-10 Prolog System

In this appendix, we describe briefly the Prolog system implemented for the DECsystem-10 machine by Warren, Pereira and Pereira. We will mention only the points where there are significant differences from the "core" Prolog we have presented. The version discussed is Version 3 -- other versions will, of course, differ in various ways. We first show what a session with DECsystem-10 Prolog looks like, and then go into more detail about how this system differs from our "core" Prolog.

Example Session

Here is what an example programming session with DECsystem-10 Prolog is like. In this example, we show exactly what appears on the terminal in the session. We also make various extra comments about what is happening. Here is the example session:

We start at the monitor level of the TOPS-10 operating system, and we ask it to run Prolog.

```
.r prolog

Prolog-10   version 3.3
Copyright (C) 1981 by D.  Warren, F.  Pereira and L.  Byrd

| ?- likes(X,Y).

no
```

The header information is, of course, liable to change slightly between different versions of the system. The characters "| ?- " were printed by Prolog as a "prompt". This tells us that it expects a question at this point. We have asked a question, and the answer was "no". Not surprising, since there are no facts in the database yet. Now we assume that there is a file 'test.pl', and we consult it:

```
| ?- ['test.pl'].

test.pl consulted   58 words     0.01 sec.

yes
```

To make Prolog read in clauses from a file, we give it a question consisting of the file name (as a Prolog atom) in list brackets.   Here we have a file of clauses about people liking one another.

```
| ?- likes(john,bertrand).

no
| ?- likes(john,albert).

no
```

Just asking a few questions about who likes whom.   Prolog cannot satisfy any of these.

```
| ?- listing(likes).

likes(john,alfred).
likes(alfred,john).
likes(bertrand,john).
likes(david,bertrand).
likes(john,_1) :-
    likes(_1,bertrand).

yes
```

To find out what clauses we have for a predicate, we ask a question about the special built-in predicate **listing**.   This particular question causes Prolog to print out all our clauses for **likes**.   Note that Prolog writes out uninstantiated variables as an underline followed by a number.   The clause at the end of the database was written in the file as: **likes(john,X) :- likes(X,bertrand).**

```
| ?- likes(john,X).

X = alfred ;

X = david ;

no
```

Here we have asked for alternative solutions to the question, by typing ';' and 'return'.   There were two possible solutions, and then Prolog could find no more.

```
| ?- likes(X,Y).

X = john,
Y = alfred ;

X = alfred,
Y = john ;

X = bertrand,
Y = john ;

X = david,
Y = bertrand ;

X = john,
```

```
Y = david ;

no
```

This time, each solution involves seeing what two variables are instantiated to. Again, we ask for alternatives by typing ';' and 'return' until there are no more solutions.

```
| ?- [user].
```

Now we ask Prolog to read in clauses from the special file **user**. This causes clauses to be read in from the terminal. These clauses will be added at the end of the database. When it is reading clauses (rather than questions), Prolog prompts with "| " rather than "| ?- ".

```
| likes(timothy,bertrand).
|
user consulted    10 words      0.03 sec.

yes
```

We told Prolog to stop reading clauses after the first one by typing ^Z (control-and-Z) at that point. We could have typed in several facts and rules before typing ^Z. Now Prolog has finished with that question and is expecting another question again.

```
| ?- likes(john,X).

X = alfred ;

X = david ;

X = timothy ;

no
```

Again, we ask for alternatives. Note that the new clause has lead to a new solution that was not present when we asked this question before.

```
| ?- likes(bertrand,Y).

Y = john

yes
```

This just illustrates the other way we can deal with alternatives. Here, we just typed 'return' after the first answer. This causes the question to succeed, and Prolog is now waiting for another question again.

```
| ?- core     36864  (7680 lo-seg + 29184 hi-seg)
heap       2560 =   1573 in use +    987 free
global     1177 =     16 in use +   1161 free
local      1024 =     16 in use +   1008 free
```

```
trail      511 =      0 in use +     511 free
    0.36 sec. runtime
```

In response to the last "! ?- ", we typed ^Z (control-and-Z), to indicate that we were finished. Prolog printed out some statistical information, and now we are back with the TOPS-10 monitor. A complete record of this session has been recorded on the file 'prolog.log' in your main directory.

Syntax

The syntax of DECsystem-10 Prolog is essentially as we have described. In fact, it is slightly less restrictive about valid atoms and variables than the rules we have given. Every example in this book should be valid according to DECsystem-10 Prolog syntax. One important point should be made about operators with high precedences. Because ',' is itself an operator, it is stipulated that to avoid ambiguity all terms written with operators with the same or higher precedence must be enclosed in brackets. This ensures that, for instance,

```
foo(a,b,c)
```

can only be interpreted as a structure with functor **foo** of three arguments, and not as, for instance, something equivalent to

```
foo(a,','(b,c))
```

or

```
foo(','(a,','(b,c)))
```

If we wanted to write this last term, we could do it with

```
foo((a,b,c))
```

The rule about operators of high precedence only affects a few operators like ':-' and ';'. It does mean that something like:

```
?- retract(parent(A,B) :- father(A,B)).
```

is *syntactically incorrect* in DECsystem-10 Prolog. We need to supply an extra pair of brackets to make it legal.

DECsystem-10 Prolog provides an alternative syntax, in case you are using a terminal or an operating system that does not provide small letters as well as capital letters. In this syntax, variables are distinguished from atoms by starting with the character '_'. A built-in predicate 'NOLC' is provided to cause Prolog to start using these alternative conventions.

The predicate 'LC' enables you to switch back to the normal rules.

Finally, a small point. The functor '.' (with two arguments) is not predefined as an operator in DECsystem-10 Prolog. You can define it yourself if you wish, but this is unnecessary if you always use the special list notation for lists.

Arbitrary Bounds

DECsystem-10 Prolog does not provide many arbitrary bounds that you are likely to encounter in practice. Operator precedences must be between 1 and 1200. Prolog integers must be in the range -131072 to 131071, although the evaluation of integer expressions is able to deal with intermediate results that are larger than this. Real numbers are not provided.

Environmental Features

DECsystem-10 Prolog provides the very useful facility of *logging*. In the normal case, during a Prolog session, the system makes a copy of (most of) what appears on your computer terminal in a disc file called 'prolog.log'. After you have finished, you can look at this file and see exactly what happened in the session. The 'prolog.log' file provides a useful record of what your program did when and what changes you made in the course of running it. Built-in predicates are provided for turning the logging facility on and off, in case you do not want it to operate all the time.

It is possible to interrupt a running program in DECsystem-10 Prolog by typing the character ^C (control-and-C). The system prompts you for an action to be performed. The options include 'break', 'continue' (carry on with the program), 'exit' (from Prolog), 'trace' and 'notrace'. The last two options involve continuing with the program after the amount of tracing has been altered. The 'break' option suspends the execution of your current program, and gives you a new "copy" of the Prolog system to interact with. When you exit the 'break', your program will continue running.

The Dec System-10 'end of file' character is ^Z (control-and-Z). Typing this causes an exit from Prolog, the end of a 'break' or the end of a 'consult', according to what situation you are in. The built-in predicate **read** matches its argument with the atom **end_of_file** if it encounters an end of file.

DECsystem-10 Prolog provides various facilities to help you save time reading in your programs again and again. It is possible to store the "state" of the Prolog system, including its current database, in a disc file in such a way that the state can be "restored" much faster than it would take to read in the program and get it to the same state. Also, DECsystem-10 Prolog will automatically read any input you may have in a file 'prolog.ini' at the beginning of a session before taking input from the terminal.

If an error occurs when you are running DECsystem-10 Prolog, the system prints out a message to tell you what has gone wrong. Most kinds of error will then cause a simple failure of the goals that caused them, and so your program will carry on running. Some errors are, however, more serious, and the system will abandon all currently running programs and ask you for the next question.

Compilation

DECsystem-10 Prolog provides the option of selectively compiling some of your clauses. This can increase space and time efficiency considerably. A built-in predicate provides a facility like **consult**, except that the clauses of the file are compiled, not interpreted. Efficiency of compiled clauses can be increased by the use of *mode declarations*, which allow you to specify how the clauses will be used (in terms of which arguments will be instantiated at which times). There are some restrictions on which clauses are suitable for compilation. It is also necessary to make certain other declarations to the system in order that it can properly function with a mixture of compiled and interpreted clauses.

Differences in built-in predicates

DECsystem-10 Prolog provides all the built-in predicates we have discussed, and will also deal correctly with grammar rules encountered inside a normal **consult**. Here are some of the differences from the descriptions we have given:

The predicate **display.** The effect of this predicate is always to print its argument on the terminal, not to the current output as we described.

In our description of arithmetic expressions, we stated that an arithmetic expression is only "evaluated" when it appears as the second argument of **is.** In all other circumstances, a structure like '2+3' just stands for itself. This is not the case in DECsystem-10 Prolog, where various other predicates also "evaluate" integer expressions appearing as arguments. Examples of this are the relational operators <, =<, etc. and the predicate **put.** Hence the following sequence will work in DECsystem-10 Prolog, but produce an error or a failure in our "core" Prolog:

```
?- 2+4 < 12*(2+8).

yes
```

As an extra twist, a structure which is a list consisting of a single number is considered to be an arithmetic expression with the same value as the number. Hence in

DECsystem-10 Prolog:

```
?- X is [25].

X = 25
yes
```

Because of this combination of features, the output of single characters can be specified in a mnemonic way, for instance:

```
?- put("a"), put("b").

ab
yes
```

(remember that "a" is the list consisting solely of the character code for the first letter of the alphabet in its lower case form).

Syntax of negation. There is no predicate named **not**, but the prefix operator \+ is used instead. There is no "not equals" predicate \= .

Variables as goals. This is really a matter of syntax, rather than anything else. We have seen how it is possible to invoke the goal corresponding to what a Prolog variable stands for by using the predicate **call**. DECsystem-10 Prolog provides an alternative way of doing the same thing. Instead of putting a goal like

```
..., call(X), ...
```

in a clause, it is possible to just put the variable on its own as a goal:

```
..., X, ...
```

It is still possible to use the **call** version, and indeed the system converts any goal **X** to a goal **call(X)** when it uses **asserta** or **assertz** on a clause.

Arguments to **retract**. In DECsystem-10 Prolog, because of difficulties associated with variables as goals, there are some differences about how bodies of clauses must be specified in goals for **retract**. The problem is that when we ask:

```
?- retract((mother(A,B) :- C)).
```

we might be asking Prolog to remove a clause specifically like:

```
mother(A,B) :- C.
```

with a variable as a goal in the body, or we might be asking it to remove a clause for **mother** with any body, like for instance:

```
mother(X,Y) :- parent(X,Y), female(Y).
```

To remove the possibility of ambiguity in these cases, DECsystem-10 Prolog always starts by replacing uninstantiated variables standing for single or multiple goals in **retract** arguments by structures using **call**. So the question:

```
?- retract((mother(A,B):-C)).
```

is actually treated like:

```
?- retract((mother(A,B):-call(C))).
```

If we wanted to remove the first clause for **mother** regardless of its body, we could specify instead:

```
?- clause(mother(A,B),C), retract((mother(A,B):-C)).
```

In this case, the previous **clause** goal results in C becoming sufficiently instantiated to escape the transformation.

Extra built-in predicates

As well as the built-in predicates we have described, DECsystem-10 Prolog provides a multitude of other facilities, including:

A "conditional" form. It is possible to provide goals that look like the following:

```
..., (likes(john,X) -> wooden(X); plastic(X)), ...
```

The idea of such a complex goal is that if the "condition" before the -> succeeds then the goal after the -> is invoked; otherwise the third goal is invoked. Any of the goals can themselves be Prolog goals. The conditional works exactly as if it were defined in DECsystem-10 Prolog as follows:

```
?- op(1050,xfy,->).
?- op(1100,xfy,';').

(X -> Y;  Z) :- call(X), !, call(Y).
(X -> Y;  Z) :- call(Z).
```


An "indexed" database. This allows you to "associate" information in the database with particular values, rather than having to use the standard Prolog retrieval mechanisms.

258

For instance, if you wanted to store information about the ages of hundreds of people, the standard technique would be to have hundreds of clauses for a predicate like **age**. But then when you wanted to find out a particular person's age, Prolog would have to search through all of these until it found the right one. The trouble is that information is normally associated with predicates, and so there can be a lot of search when a predicate has many clauses. The indexed database would allow you to associate information in a more direct way with particular names.

The ability to access ancestors. We discussed the notion of ancestor goals in the chapter on debugging. DECsystem-10 Prolog provides built-in predicates that allow you to access ancestors from within a Prolog program.

Statistical information. DECsystem-10 Prolog provides built-in predicates that enable you to find out how fast your program is running and how much space it occupies.

Debugging Facilities

DECsystem-10 Prolog provides debugging facilities along the lines we have described. In addition to the built-in predicates mentioned, there is a predicate that enables you to affect which ports are leashed during tracing.

References

User's Guide to DECsystem-10 Prolog, by L M Pereira, F Pereira, and D Warren, 1979. Laboratorio Nacional de Engenharia Civil, Lisbon, Portugal.
Also available as *DAI Occasional Paper 15*, Department of Artificial Intelligence, University of Edinburgh, Edinburgh, Scotland.

A Guide to Version 3 of DEC-10 Prolog and Prolog Debugging Facilities, by L Byrd, F Pereira, and D Warren, 1980. *DAI Occasional Paper 19*, Department of Artificial Intelligence, University of Edinburgh, Edinburgh, Scotland.

Appendix F

The PDP-11 UNIX Prolog System

We will now describe some of the features of the Prolog system developed for the DEC PDP-11 machine (running under the UNIX operating system) by C. Mellish. Our description applies to version NU7. We first of all show what a session with UNIX Prolog looks like, before going into details about how the system differs from our "core" Prolog.

Example Session

Here is what an example programming session with UNIX Prolog is like. In this example, we show exactly what appears on the terminal in the session. We start by typing to the "Shell". We ask the system to run Prolog.

```
% prolog
PROLOG Version NU7.1

?- likes(X,Y).

no
```

The characters "?- " were printed by Prolog as a "prompt". This tells us that it expects a question at this point. We have asked a question, and the answer was "no". Not surprising, since there are no facts in the database yet. We assume that the file '/us/qris/test' appears in the filesystem, and we consult it:

```
?- ['/us/qris/test'].

/us/qris/test consulted

yes
```

To make Prolog read in clauses from a file, we give it a question consisting of the file name (as a Prolog atom) in list brackets. Here we have a file of clauses about people liking one another.

```
?- likes(john,bertrand).

no
```

```
?- likes(john,albert).
```

```
no
```

Just asking a few questions about who likes whom.   Prolog cannot satisfy any of these.

```
?- listing(likes).
```

```
likes(john,alfred).
```

```
likes(alfred,john).
```

```
likes(bertrand,john).
```

```
likes(david,bertrand).
```

```
likes(john,_45)
    :- likes(_45,bertrand).
```

```
yes
```

To find out what clauses we have for a predicate, we ask a question about the special built-in predicate **listing**.   This particular question causes Prolog to print out all our clauses for **likes**.   Note that Prolog writes out uninstantiated variables as an underline followed by a number.   The clause at the end of the database was written in the file as: **likes(john,X)** :- **likes(X,bertrand)**.

```
?- likes(john,X).
```

```
** (top) PROVED : likes(john,alfred) ? ;
```

```
** (top) PROVED : likes(john,david) ? ;
```

```
no
```

Here we have asked for alternative solutions to the question, by typing ';' and 'return'.   There were two possible solutions, and then Prolog could find no more.

```
?- likes(X,Y).
```

```
** (top) PROVED : likes(john,alfred) ? ;
```

```
** (top) PROVED : likes(alfred,john) ? ;
```

```
** (top) PROVED : likes(bertrand,john) ? ;
```

```
** (top) PROVED : likes(david,bertrand) ? ;
```

```
** (top) PROVED : likes(john,david) ? ;
```

```
no
```

This time, each solution involves seeing what two variables are instantiated to. Again, we ask for alternatives by typing ';' and 'return' until there are no more solutions.

    ?- [user].

Now we ask Prolog to read in clauses from the special file **user**. This causes clauses to be read in from the terminal. These clauses will be added at the end of the database. When it is reading clauses (rather than questions), Prolog dispenses with the "?- " prompt.

    likes(timothy,bertrand).

    user consulted

    yes

We told Prolog to stop reading clauses after the first one by typing the UNIX end-of-file character, which is ^Z (control-and-Z) for most UNIX versions. We could have typed in several facts and rules before typing the end-of-file character. Now Prolog has finished with that question and is expecting another question again.

    ?- likes(john,X).

    ** (top) PROVED : likes(john,alfred) ? ;

    ** (top) PROVED : likes(john,david) ? ;

    ** (top) PROVED : likes(john,timothy) ? ;

    no

Again, we ask for alternatives. Note that the new clause has lead to a new solution that was not present when we asked this question before.

    ?- likes(bertrand,Y).

    ** (top) PROVED : likes(bertrand,john) ?

    yes

This just illustrates the other way we can deal with alternatives. Here, we just typed 'return' after the first answer. This causes the question to succeed, and Prolog is now waiting for another question again.

    ?-

    End of PROLOG execution

    %

In response to the last "?- ", we typed the end-of-file character (^Z for most UNIXes) to indicate that we were finished. Now we are back with the "shell" again.

Syntax

As in Dec10 Prolog, the PDP-11 UNIX system is slightly more flexible than the rules we have given about what are valid atoms and variables.

Operator declarations in UNIX Prolog are somewhat restricted. Firstly, any atom can only be declared as an operator in one way. If multiple declarations are made, only the latest one has any effect. Secondly, the only permissible operator types are:

    fx, xf, yfx, xfy

The rule for using these is simple - use **fx** for a prefix operator, **xf** for a postfix operator, and either **xfy** or **yfx** for an infix operator, according to whether it is right or left associative. This Prolog system will actually allow certain syntactic forms that are theoretically illegal, if they are unambiguous. For instance, if **not** are **fx** operators, then

    not not a.

is unambiguously read as

    not(not(a)).

even though in theory it is not possible for the argument of **not** to be a term with the same precedence.

Arbitrary Bounds

The PDP-11 machine is relatively restricted as regards the amount of memory that a program can access. As a result, the UNIX Prolog system has had to be very careful about how information is stored. There are many arbitrary bounds that arise because of this.

The number of distinct atoms that a Prolog program can use is restricted to 1024 in the UNIX system. Of these, some are already taken up by the system before your program is read in. In practice, this limit seems to only affect programs that maintain large databases of facts. An atom can also have no more than 253 characters. A functor cannot have an arity greater than 15. Prolog integers are restricted to the range 0 to 16383. Arithmetic on these takes place *modulo* 16384. Operator precedences must be between 0 and 255.

Finally, the system will only **write** terms to a "depth" of 20. Subterms of the **write** argument that are deeper than this are simply written out as "**~**". This helps you to avoid getting unmanageable amounts of information if you accidentally ask Prolog to print out a rather large structure. The "depth" of a subterm of the **write** argument is computed as follows.

The "top level" of the argument -- either the argument itself (if it is atomic) or the argument excluding its components (if it is a structure) -- has depth 0. If the **write** argument is a structure, then the "top levels" of its components have depth 1. The "top levels" of their components have depth 2, and so on. The only exception is that the "top levels" of all the elements of a list have the same depth as the first one.

Environmental

The UNIX Prolog system allows you to interrupt a Prolog program while it is running. The appropriate character to type is the UNIX "interrupt" character, which is ^C (control-and-C) in most versions. When you interrupt a program, you are offered the possibilities of 'abort', 'break', 'continue' (carry on with the program), 'exit' (from Prolog), 'notrace' and 'trace'. These last two options involve continuing with the program after the tracing has been suitably altered. The 'abort' option involves abandoning all running programs and going back to ask for the next question. The 'break' involves suspending the current program and giving you a new "copy" of the Prolog interpreter to interact with. When the 'break' is exited, your program continues running.

The UNIX Prolog allows you to use various facilities provided by that operating system. These include the ability to set up several programs (not necessarily all Prolog programs) that run simultaneously and communicate through devices called "pipes". Also UNIX Prolog allows you to leave Prolog temporarily, interact with the operating system (to perhaps edit a disc file) and then resume exactly where you left off. If you have several Prolog programs running at once, the effect of the "interrupt" character will changed for all the programs except the one that you started with. When you type this character, all the programs except the first will immediately abandon running any programs and revert to asking for the next question. The first one will prompt you for an option, as usual. An extra facility is that if you type the UNIX "quit" character (possibly ^\ -- control-and-\) all your Prolog programs will immediately finish and you will find yourself talking to the operating system "shell" again.

The character to type to indicate "end of file" is the UNIX end-of-file character, which is ^Z (control-and-Z) for most versions of UNIX. This is the character you type to finish a **consult(user)**, to exit from a **break** or to leave Prolog. However, whatever character marks an "end of file" as far as the operating system is concerned, Prolog will always convert it to ASCII code 26 (^Z). This means that your Prolog programs that need to detect "end of file" should look for ^Z in any case. The system is also set up so that **read** finds the structure:

```
?- end
```

if an end of file is encountered.

There is a slight complication in UNIX Prolog that arises from the fact that UNIX allows you to run programs that receive their primary input from and send their primary output to

things apart from your terminal. Thus, for instance, you can run Prolog with clauses and
questions already prepared in a disc file, or you can send all the output to a disc file.
In UNIX Prolog, a distinction is made between the special file **user,** which refers to the UNIX
standard input and output files, whatever they are, and the special file **tty,** which always refers
to your terminal. The "top level interpreter" can tell whether **user** is using your terminal for
both input and output. If not, it is slightly less "chatty" than it would otherwise be.

When an error is encountered in the UNIX Prolog system, first of all a message is printed
on your terminal to tell you what has happened. After that, one of three possible things
can happen. If it is a syntax error (the predicate **read** could not interpret the input properly),
Prolog prints out the best it could make of the input and then causes a **fail** of the **read**
goal. If this happens during a **consult,** or at the top level, Prolog just goes on to read
what comes next. Most other errors cause a **break** to occur. If you exit from the break
normally (by typing "end of file"), your program will behave as if the goal with the error just
failed. As another option, you can, of course cause an **abort.** The final possibility, which
only happens with a few kinds of errors, is that an **abort** takes place immediately.

Compilation

The PDP-11 UNIX Prolog system does not offer the possibility of compilation. It provides
only a Prolog *interpreter.*

Particular Built-In Predicates

The UNIX Prolog system does not provide grammar rules automatically. However, it allows
you to load programs from a "Prolog library", which includes a grammar rule package. Here
are some other bits and pieces that are worth looking out for:

The list notation for **consult** and **reconsult.** In this notation, you must precede a file
name with '$' (*not* '−') if you want to **reconsult** it. Thus, for instance, the following
two goals are equivalent:

```
?- [myfile,$fred,'a/foo'].

?- consult(myfile), reconsult(fred), consult('a/foo').
```

A "backtrace" facility. This facility enables you to look at the ancestors of the current
goal. You can also use it when inside a **break** after an error. It is quite useful
in such a situation, because it gives you some idea of the context in which the error
occurred. This facility is provided by the built-in predicate : **backtrace.**

Debugging Facilities

The UNIX Prolog system is not as elegant at answering questions as we have suggested Prolog systems usually are. Instead of printing out the values of variables in a format as in:

```
?- likes(X,Y).

X = _251, Y = apples
```

it prints out instead the whole of the successful goal:

```
?- likes(X,Y).

** (top) PROVED : likes(_251,apples)
```

and then asks is you are interested in alternative solutions (in the normal way).

What about other debugging facilities? In the UNIX Prolog system, there is an exhaustive unleashed tracing facility and also the possibility of setting spypoints. These two facilities are essentially independent. Because the exhaustive tracing is unleashed, you are recommended to use spypoints extensively. In this way, you can avoid getting overwhelmed by the exhaustive tracing (by turning it on only at carefully selected places). You can also make better use of the options like 'retry' and 'skip' if you have lots of spypoints (because you can *only* use them at spypoints.

References

The Unix Prolog System, by W Clocksin and C Mellish, 1979. *Software Report 5*, Department of Artificial Intelligence, University of Edinburgh, Edinburgh, Scotland.

Appendix G

The LSI-11 RT-11 Prolog System

We will now describe some of the features of the Prolog system developed for the DEC LSI-11 machine (running the RT-11 operating system) by R. Fisher. The system runs on the LSI-11/23 and any other LSI-11 with the EIS option installed. Because this system was translated from the PDP-11 system of the last appendix, the two systems are very similar in most places. Our description applies to version NR7. We first of all show what a session with LSI-11 Prolog looks like, before going into details about how the system differs from our "core" Prolog.

<u>Example Session</u>

Here is what an example programming session with LSI-11 Prolog is like. In this example, we show exactly what appears on the terminal in the session. We start by typing to the RT-11 monitor. We ask the system to run Prolog.

```
.RU PROLOG
PROLOG Version NR7.1


?- likes(X,Y).


no
```

The characters "?- " were printed by Prolog as a "prompt". This tells us that it expects a question at this point. We have asked a question, and the answer was "no". Not surprising, since there are no facts in the database yet. We assume that the file TEST.TXT appears on the QX1: directory, and we consult it:

```
?- ['QX1:TEST'].

DK1:TEST consulted

yes
```

To make Prolog read in clauses from a file, we give it a question consisting of the file name (as a Prolog atom) in list brackets. The system assumes an extension .TXT for the file.

Here we have a file of clauses about people liking one another.

```
?- likes(john,bertrand).


no
?- likes(john,albert).


no
```

Just asking a few questions about who likes whom. Prolog cannot satisfy any of these.

```
?- listing(likes).

likes(john,alfred).

likes(alfred,john).

likes(bertrand,john).

likes(david,bertrand).

likes(john,_45)
       :- likes(_45,bertrand).


yes
```

To find out what clauses we have for a predicate, we ask a question about the special built-in predicate listing. This particular question causes Prolog to print out all our clauses for **likes**. Note that Prolog writes out uninstantiated variables as an underline followed by a number. The clause at the end of the database was written in the file as: **likes(john,X) :- likes(X,bertrand)**.

```
?- likes(john,X).

** (top) PROVED : likes(john,alfred) ? ;

** (top) PROVED : likes(john,david) ? ;

no
```

Here we have asked for alternative solutions to the question, by typing ';' and 'return'. There were two possible solutions, and then Prolog could find no more.

```
?- likes(X,Y).

** (top) PROVED : likes(john,alfred) ? ;

** (top) PROVED : likes(alfred,john) ? ;

** (top) PROVED : likes(bertrand,john) ? ;
```

```
** (top) PROVED : likes(david,bertrand) ? ;

** (top) PROVED : likes(john,david) ? ;

no
```

This time, each solution involves seeing what two variables are instantiated to. Again, we ask for alternatives by typing ':' and 'return' until there are no more solutions.

```
?- [user].
```

Now we ask Prolog to read in clauses from the special file **user**. This causes clauses to be read in from the terminal. These clauses will be added at the end of the database. When it is reading clauses (rather than questions), Prolog does not make the "?- " prompt.

```
likes(timothy,bertrand).

user consulted

yes
```

We told Prolog to stop reading clauses after the first one by typing ^Z (control-and-Z) at that point. We could have typed in several facts and rules before typing ^Z. Now Prolog has finished with that question and is expecting another question again.

```
?- likes(john,X).

** (top) PROVED : likes(john,alfred) ? ;

** (top) PROVED : likes(john,david) ? ;

** (top) PROVED : likes(john,timothy) ? ;

no
```

Again, we ask for alternatives. Note that the new clause has lead to a new solution that was not present when we asked this question before.

```
?- likes(bertrand,Y).

** (top) PROVED : likes(bertrand,john) ?

yes
```

This just illustrates the other way we can deal with alternatives. Here, we just typed 'return' after the first answer. This causes the question to succeed, and Prolog is now waiting for another question again.

```
?-

End of PROLOG execution
```

In response to the last "?- ", we typed ^Z (control-and-Z), to indicate that we were finished. Now we are back with the RT-11 monitor again.

Syntax

As in Dec10 Prolog, the RT-11 system is slightly more flexible than the rules we have given about what are valid atoms and variables.

Operator declarations in RT-11 Prolog are somewhat restricted. Firstly, any atom can only be declared as an operator in one way. If multiple declarations are made, only the latest one has any effect. Secondly, the only permissible operator types are:

fx, xf, yfx, xfy

The rule for using these is simple – use **fx** for a prefix operator, **xf** for a postfix operator, and either **xfy** or **yfx** for an infix operator, according to whether it is right or left associative. This Prolog system will actually allow certain syntactic forms that are theoretically illegal, if they are unambiguous. For instance, if **not** are **fx** operators, then

not not a.

is unambiguously read as

not(not(a)).

even though in theory it is not possible for the argument of **not** to be a term with the same precedence.

Arbitrary Bounds

The LSI-11 machine is relatively restricted as regards the amount of memory that a program can access. As a result, the RT-11 Prolog system has had to be very careful about how information is stored. There are many arbitrary bounds that arise because of this.

The number of distinct atoms that a Prolog program can use is restricted to 1024 in the RT-11 system. Of these, some are already taken up by the system before your program is read in. In practice, this limit seems to only affect programs that maintain large databases of facts. An atom can also have no more than 253 characters. A functor cannot have an arity greater than 15. Prolog integers are restricted to the range 0 to 16383. Arithmetic on these takes place *modulo* 16384. Operator precedences must be between 0 and 255.

Finally, the system will only **write** terms to a "depth" of 20. Subterms of the **write**

270

argument that are deeper than this are simply written out as "~". This helps you to avoid getting unmanageable amounts of information if you accidentally ask Prolog to print out a rather large structure. The "depth" of a subterm of the **write** argument is computed as follows. The "top level" of the argument -- either the argument itself (if it is atomic) or the argument excluding its components (if it is a structure) -- has depth 0. If the **write** argument is a structure, then the "top levels" of its components have depth 1. The "top levels" of their components have depth 2, and so on. The only exception is that the "top levels" of all the elements of a list have the same depth as the first one.

Environmental

The RT-11 Prolog system allows you to interrupt a Prolog program while it is running. The appropriate character to type is ^C (control-and-C), and it must be typed twice in quick succession in accordance with RT-11 conventions. When you interrupt a program, you are offered the possibilities of 'abort', 'break', 'continue' (carry on with the program), 'exit' (from Prolog), 'notrace' and 'trace'. These last two options involve continuing with the program after the tracing has been suitably altered. The 'abort' option involves abandoning all running programs and reverting to asking you for the next question. The 'break' option suspends the current program and gives you a new "copy" of the Prolog interpreter to interact with. When you exit the 'break', your program will continue running.

The RT-11 Prolog system provides optional facilities for drawing pictures on the display screen of the Terak 8510 personal computer. These include facilities for drawing points, lines, and regions, moving the cursor and activating the available display.

The character to type to indicate "end of file" is ^Z (control-and-Z) for RT-11 Prolog. This is the character you type to finish a **consult(user)**, to exit from a **break** or to leave Prolog. If an end-of-file is encountered by **read**, it finds the structure:

```
?- end.
```

When an error is encountered in the RT-11 Prolog system, first of all a message is printed on your terminal to tell you what has happened. After that, one of three possible things can happen. If it is a syntax error (the predicate **read** could not interpret the input properly), Prolog prints out the best it could make of the input and then causes a **fail** of the **read** goal. If this happens during a **consult**, or at the top level, Prolog just goes on to read what comes next. Most other errors cause a **break** to occur. If you exit from the break normally (by typing "end of file"), your program will behave as if the goal with the error just failed. As another option, you can, of course cause an **abort**. The final possibility, which only happens with a few kinds of errors, is that an **abort** takes place immediately.

Compilation

The RT-11 system does not offer the possibility of compilation. It provides only a Prolog *interpreter.*

Particular Built-in Predicates

The RT-11 Prolog system does not provide grammar rules automatically. However, the system should be distributed together with a Prolog program that you can run to get access to grammar rules. Here are some other bits and pieces that are worth looking out for:

The list notation for **consult** and **reconsult.** In this notation, you must precede a file name with '**$**' (*not* '-') if you want to **reconsult** it. Thus, for instance, the following two goals are equivalent:

```
?- [myfile,$fred,'dkl:foo'].

?- consult(myfile), reconsult(fred), consult('dkl:foo').
```

A "backtrace" facility. This facility enables you to look at the ancestors of the current goal. You can also use it when inside a **break** after an error. It is quite useful in such a situation, because it gives you some idea of the context in which the error occurred. This facility is provided through the built-in predicate **ans** (standing for "ancestors").

Debugging Facilities

The RT-11 Prolog system is not as elegant at answering questions as we have suggested Prolog systems usually are. Instead of printing out the values of variables in a format as in:

```
?- likes(X,Y).

X = _251, Y = apples
```

it prints out instead the whole of the successful goal:

```
?- likes(X,Y).

** (top) PROVED : likes(_251,apples)
```

and then asks is you are interested in alternative solutions (in the normal way).

What about other debugging facilities? In the RT-11 Prolog system, there is an exhaustive unleashed tracing facility and also the possibility of setting spypoints. These two facilities are essentially independent. Because the exhaustive tracing is unleashed, you are recommended to use spypoints extensively. In this way, you can avoid getting overwhelmed by the exhaustive tracing (by turning it on only at carefully selected places). You can also make better use of the options like 'retry' and 'skip' if you have lots of spypoints (because you can *only* use them at spypoints.

Reference

The RT-11 Prolog System, by W Clocksin, C Mellish, and R Fisher, 1980. *Software Report 5a (revised)*, Department of Artificial Intelligence, University of Edinburgh, Edinburgh, Scotland.

Appendix H

The 2980 EMAS Prolog System

A version of Prolog has been implemented by Luis Damas for the Edinburgh Regional Computing Centre's ICL 2980 machine, running under the EMAS operating system. Unfortunately, at the time of going to press we do not have detailed information about this Prolog system. However, we understand that it provides facilities very close to the "core" Prolog presented in this book. The EMAS Prolog system is modelled on DECsystem-10 Prolog, but provides no facilities for compilation. We suggest that you consult Appendix E to see approximately what a session with EMAS Prolog looks like.

Appendix I

Other Prolog Systems

There are many other Prolog systems available around the world. It is impossible to list them all here. Some Prolog systems available have been derived from the Edinburgh systems described in previous appendices, and most Prolog systems in the world owe their parentage to the original Marseille interpreter. In the other appendices we have concentrated on those systems conforming most closely to the "core" Prolog described in this book. In this appendix, we have listed a representative sample of Prolog systems drawn from around the world. We apologise to other Prolog implementors if we have not given their systems the attention they deserve.

References

PROLOG -- Manuel de Reference et d'Utilisation, by P Roussel, 1975. Groupe d'Intelligence Artificielle, UER de Luminy, Universite d'Aix-Marseille II

An Implementation of Prolog, by G M Roberts, 1977. Department of Computer Science, University of Waterloo, Canada

PROLOG Reference Manual, P Szeredi and I Futo, 1977 (in Hungarian). *Szamologep* **VIII** (5-130)

An Interpreter for Predicate Logic Programs, by M Bruynooghe, 1976. Afdeling Toegepaste Wiskunde en Programmatie, Katholieke Univ., Belgium.

Control Facilities of IC-PROLOG, by K L Clark and F G McCabe, 1979. in *Expert Systems in the Microelectronic Age* (ed D Michie), Edinburgh University Press.

A micro-PROLOG Primer by K. L. Clark, J.R Ennals, F.G. McCabe, 1981

Micro-PROLOG, Programmer's Reference Manual, by F.G. McCabe, 1980

Index

Note:

In this index, where there are multiple entries for an item, we have asterisked the page numbers for the major entries. For built-in predicates, these are the entries in Chapter 6.

276

278

W. E. Riddle, R. E. Fairley

Software Development Tools

1980. 26 figures. VIII, 280 pages
ISBN 3-540-10326-0

Contents: Introduction. – Needs. – Experiences. – Development Support Systems. – Procedural Description Techniques. – Non-Procedural Description Techniques. – Analysis Tools. – Summary. – Bibliography and References. – List of Attendees.

This book contains the papers presented at the "Software Development Tools" workshop held at Pingree Park, Colorado, in May, 1979. Also included are reports on the discussions generated by presentation of the papers. Among the topics covered are: the need for tools, experiences with tools, integration of tools to form homogeneous environments, procedural and non-procedural notations, and testing and verification tools.
The papers and discussions describe: problems facing toolsmiths; the need for experimental evaluation of tools; the general problems of fitting tools together to provide development support systems, and the general applicability of analysis tools in the preimplementation phases of software development. The text provides a well-rounded picture of the current state of software development tools. Numerous short term and long term research topics are suggested.

Springer-Verlag
Berlin
Heidelberg
New York

High Level
Programming Languages

H. Ledgard
Ada
An Introduction
Ada Reference Manual (July 1980)
1981. XXXII, 358 pages. ISBN 3-540-90568-5

The Programming Language Ada
Reference Manual
Proposed Standard Document
United States Department of Defense
1981. X, 243 pages. (Lecture Notes in Computer Science, Volume 105). ISBN 3-540-10693-6

Towards a Formal Description of Ada
Editors: D. Bjørner, O. N. Oest
1980. With numerous figures. XIV, 630 pages. (Lecture Notes in Computer Science, Volume 98)
ISBN 3-540-10283-3

Studies in Ada Style
By P. Hibbard, A. Hisgen, J. Rosenberg, M. Shaw, M. Sherman
1981. VII, 104 pages. ISBN 3-540-90628-2

Alphard
Form and Content
Editor: M. Shaw
1981. VIII, 321 pages. ISBN 3-540-90663-0

F. J. Anscombe
Computing in Statistical Science through APL
1981. 70 figures. XV, 426 pages. (Springer Series in Statistics). ISBN 3-540-90549-9

CLU Reference Manual
By B. Liskov, R. Atkinson, T. Bloom, E. Moss, J. C. Schaffert, R. Scheifler, A. Snyder
1981. VIII, 190 pages. (Lecture Notes in Computer Science, Volume 114). ISBN 3-540-10836-X

W. R. Fuller
FORTRAN Programming
A Supplement for Calculus Courses
Universitext
1977. 23 figures. XII, 145 pages
ISBN 3-540-90283-X

S. Alagić, M. A. Arbib
The Design of Well-Structured and Correct Programs
1978. 68 figures. X, 292 pages. (Texts and Monographs in Computer Science)
ISBN 3-540-90299-6

K. L. Bowles
Microcomputer
Problem Solving Using PASCAL
Springer Study Edition
1977. 110 figures. IX, 563 pages
ISBN 3-540-90286-4

S. Eisenbach, C. Sadler
PASCAL for Programmers
1981. 78 figures. IX, 201 pages
ISBN 3-540-10473-9

A. C. Hartmann
A Concurrent Pascal Compiler for Minicomputers
1977. VI, 119 pages. (Lecture Notes in Computer Science, Volume 50). ISBN 3-540-08240-9

K. Jensen, N. E. Wirth
PASCAL User Manual and Report
Springer Study Edition
2nd corrected reprint of the 2nd edition. 1978.
VIII, 167 pages. ISBN 3-540-90144-2

Springer-Verlag
Berlin
Heidelberg
New York